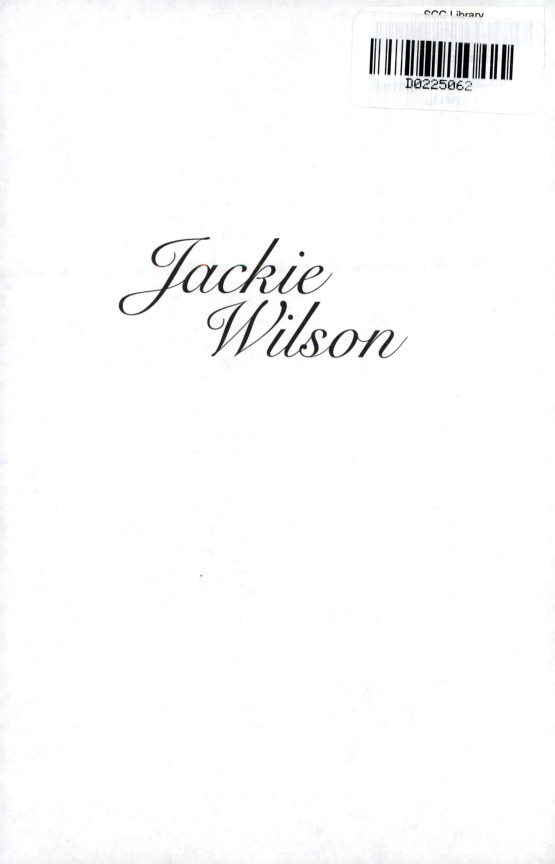

Jackie
Wilson

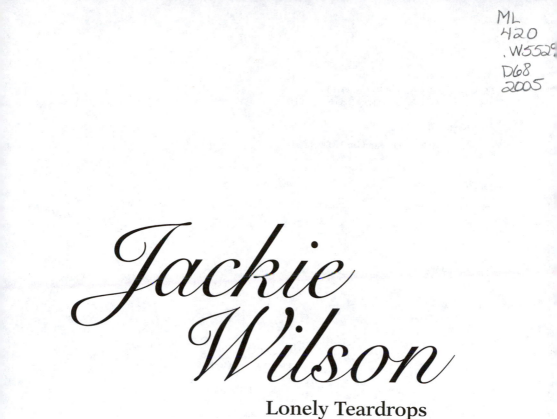

Jackie Wilson

Lonely Teardrops

Tony Douglas

Routledge
Taylor & Francis Group
NEW YORK AND LONDON

OCM 58647937

First published in Great Britain in 2001 by
Mainstream Publishing Company (Edinburgh) LTD
7 Albany Street
Edinburgh EH1 3UG

Typeset in Dustine, Gill Condensed, and Perpetua

Published in 2005 by
Routledge
Taylor & Francis Group
270 Madison Avenue
New York, NY 10016

Published in Great Britain by
Routledge
Taylor & Francis Group
2 Park Square
Milton Park, Abingdon
Oxon OX14 4RN

© 2001 and 2005 by Tony Douglas
Routledge is an imprint of Taylor & Francis Group

Printed in the United States of America on acid-free paper
10 9 8 7 6 5 4 3 2 1

International Standard Book Number-10: 0-415-97430-5 (Softcover)
International Standard Book Number-13: 978-0-415-97430-1 (Softcover)

Library of Congress Cataloging-in-Publication Data

Catalog record is available from the Library of Congress

Taylor & Francis Group
is the Academic Division of T&F Informa plc.

Visit the Taylor & Francis Web site at
http://www.taylorandfrancis.com

and the Routledge Web site at
http://www.routledge-ny.com

Why a Book on Jackie Wilson 7

Acknowledgements 9

Introduction 13

Chapter One: Danny Boy 14

Chapter Two: You Can't Keep a Good Man Down 34

Chapter Three: Reet Petite 50

Chapter Four: You'd Better Know It... 80

Chapter Five: A Woman, a Lover, a Friend 84

Chapter Six: I'm Wanderin', ... 94

Chapter Seven: Higher and Higher 114

Chapter Eight: A Kiss, a Thrill and Goodbye................................. 139

Chapter Nine: Soul Galore 150

Chapter Ten: I Don't Need You Around 165

Chapter Eleven: Those Heartaches 177

Chapter Twelve: This Love Is Real 183

Chapter Thirteen: Beautiful Day 197

Chapter Fourteen: It's All Over... 214

Chapter Fifteen: Your Loss, My Gain... 241

Chapter Sixteen: The Greatest Hurt 247

Chapter Seventeen: Postscript 252

Bibliography 256

Discography 258

WHY A BOOK ON JACKIE WILSON

BETWEEN 1957 AND 1968 Jackie Wilson had 55 Top 100 and 24 Top 40 hits. Compare this achievement to the nine and six Top 40 hits of Little Richard and Jerry Lee Lewis respectively. More importantly, Jackie was one of the most remarkable vocalists in contemporary music and could quite easily could have become an opera singer. His vocal range and unique, rapturous presentation ensured he would never be confused with anyone else. As a stage performer, he was untouchable. Impeccably dressed, he appeared to glide, and his entrances sometimes involved sliding on his knees to the edge of the stage. Audiences were under his spell the moment he stepped out. Other times he would dive into the audience, where his clothing would be shredded by hysterical female fans. He loved every minute of it, and it was a brave artist that would go on after him. When Jackie was finished, both he and the audience were drained; the show was over!

Jackie pushed everything he did to the extreme. He married three times and had untold extra-marital affairs, fathering numerous offspring throughout the nation. His generosity was like his alcohol consumption; unbounded. He developed a chronic addiction to amphetamines and cocaine, yet recorded around 400 songs ranging from gospel and blues, where his roots were, to standard evergreens like 'Stardust' and light operatic classics, like 'Night' and 'Alone At Last'. Not content there, he could just as effortlessly do raunchy rock 'n' roll or emotional soul tunes. His hallmark was to have his voice soar from its normal rich tenor range to notes in the high female range, with perfect control and pitch. He was said to have 'invented notes'.

Like many artists of the period, Jackie was owned outright by the Mafia. Frankly, as a black artist of the 1950s and 1960s, he needed them to gain

JACKIE WILSON

entry to Las Vegas and the plush cabaret night spots. Record promotion and distribution also required their ' expertise'. Early in his career he was shot and critically wounded by a female admirer. Despite losing a kidney, with the bullet remaining lodged next to his spine for the rest of his life, he recovered fully.

The public weren't Jackie's only fans. He was greatly admired by his peers, among them Elvis Presley, who saw Jackie perform in 1956 in Las Vegas while lead singer with The Dominoes, when Elvis was just starting out. Elvis was in awe of Jackie and remained one of his biggest fans and, later, his friend. Likewise, the young Michael Jackson would study Jackie and emulate his stage moves. In every way, Jackie was a pioneer for the 'crossover' of black artists into the broader appeal of the more lucrative white audience market – the Pop charts.

Jackie's earnings were unheard of at the time for all but a few black performers, yet he was constantly dogged by the tax man and the courts for outstanding family maintenance payments. He eventually suffered the indignity of having his family home seized by the IRS, in lieu of unpaid tax, and sold at auction. Throughout his career Jackie was dogged by legal hassles, some of which involved associations with white women that a still-segregated southern United States did not tolerate. He had the indignity of having to perform to fully segregated audiences and, despite being a worldwide star, was unable to stay in some of the major hotels of his own country.

In September 1975, Jackie suffered a heart attack on stage in New Jersey. For the next eight-and-a-quarter years he survived in a state between life and death, unable to communicate for the entire period. He died in January 1984 and was buried in an unmarked grave outside his home city of Detroit.

Jackie's charisma was so huge that he would instantly be the focus of attention when he entered a room and today, 25 years after he collapsed on stage in New Jersey and 16 years since his death, he remains firmly focused in the minds of all those who knew and loved him.

The main purpose of *Jackie Wilson: The Inside Story Of 'Mr Excitement' And The Mob* is to ensure that this great man will never be forgotten and that those who have not heard of him will take the trouble to listen to and discover the fabulous talent that he was. Indeed, had his time come just a decade later, he would have been one of popular music's true superstars.

Melbourne, Australia,
September 2001.

ACKNOWLEDGEMENTS

IN 1994, when I embarked on my search for Jackie Wilson, the fact that I'd never seen or met either him or anyone who had any association with him presented me with special difficulties. Not only did I live in Australia, half a planet away, but I needed to locate those who had known him and persuade them to divulge details that were not always flattering. My first break came through Rhino Records in California, who had released a three-CD boxed set of Jackie's recordings. The 72 songs in the set had been selected by Simon Rutberg, who'd known Jackie for 13 years as a fan and a friend. Rhino generously put me in touch with Simon, who was a mine of information. My sincere thanks go to him. Next I came to know a young Detroiter, David Yellen, a record collector and major fan of Jackie and Motown artists. Resourceful and helpful, David assisted me in Detroit and over the next couple of years we were in regular contact. It would have been much harder without him. Former Brunswick producer, Carl Davis in Chicago, was unstinting in his knowledgeable contribution and clearly held Jackie in the highest regard.

Possibly reluctantly in the beginning, Jackie's first wife, Freda, welcomed me into her home. From her I learned the most intimate details of life with Jackie, from his teenage years to the height of his fame. To me, Freda was an heroic figure who has suffered much more than most and yet speaks with no bitterness. To my mind she always had a special place in Jackie's life.

Through a remarkable chance meeting I met with guitarist Roquel 'Billy' Davis in his home in Highland Park, Michigan. Billy grew up with Jackie, later becoming a guitarist in his touring band, and loves him, considering him the world's greatest singer. He was there when Jackie was in an emotionally low state and contributed towards his overcoming it. Without doubt he was one of Jackie's true friends and is now one of mine as well.

Few are more knowledgeable about the music industry than Billy, who co-wrote most of Jackie's earliest hit songs. I will always be indebted to him for inviting me into his home and giving me so much vital information concerning the industry and Jackie's early career.

It was through Jackie's third wife, Lynn Guidry, that I made contact with Lynn Ciccone, who had known and loved Jackie over many years, largely unknown to all but a few insiders. Lynn had researched and started a book of her own concerning her relationship with Jackie, the father of her only child. In a most unselfish gesture she handed over all her considerable notes and recorded interviews, with no thought of reward. Over the next few years we were in constant touch and she seemed never to lose faith that I would eventually come up with a book about the man she still loves. My very special thanks to Lynn.

On a more personal level, my mother encouraged my efforts and maintained a keen interest in my progress. Sadly, she died in July 1996 before my work was complete. My wife, Seda, put up with the most. The long hours and my heavy drawing upon family savings must have given her serious cause for concern, yet she didn't complain. Indeed, she provided the sounding board that such an enterprise requires. Likewise my young son, Dion, who often had to take second place to Jackie. He would often ask me when it would all be finished, and every time he did I was racked with guilt.

On a more personal level I am thankful to my good friends Trevor Baverstock and Vince Peach, who were ever willing to lend an ear or give of their wonderful knowledge of the genre. With their encouragement, giving up was never an option. One friendship I formed through my search was that of former music arranger with Motown, Gil Askey, who fortunately had become domiciled not far from my home in Melbourne, Australia. Gil had worked with Jackie in his touring band before, doing arrangements for him on his dance hit 'Baby Workout' and the 'Something Else' album. Our conversations probably totalled weeks. To Gil I am eternally thankful, besides holding him in the highest regard. When I 'dropped' his name to those in the music industry, doors opened.

Many wonderful photographs were supplied by numerous people for which I am indebted. Sadly, few film clips of Jackie in concert or on tour could be found. It seems extraordinary that it was only rarely that anybody bothered to film these marvellous events. There are, however, video clips from his numerous TV appearances, especially *The Ed Sullivan Show*, *Shindig*, *American Bandstand* and *The Jerry Lee Lewis Show*. One rare bit of footage that has been preserved is a 1975 performance in Michigan, at the Club

Paradise. While the band doesn't suit and the audience is small, glimpses of the great performer shine through.

I make no apology for the large number of quotes in this book. This is the story of the colourful life of Jackie Wilson, whom I never even saw in concert. Jackie's friends, family and acquaintances tell the story in their own words, as best they recall.

Listed below are the many people who co-operated, to varying degrees, with my search for 'the real Jackie'. Some had only an incident or two, while others divulged intimate and fascinating details. To all of them, my sincere thanks.

Abrams, Al; Abrams, Reginald Jnr, Jackie's grandson; Abrams, Reginald; Acklin, Barbara; Adourian, Edward 'Ted' New Jersey attorney and Jackie's court-appointed guardian; Askey, Gil; Atkins, Cholly; Ballard, Hank; Barge, Gene; Barksdale, Chuck; Bass, Ralph; Bateman, Robert; Bennett, Irma 'Mary'; Billingslea, Joe; Blavat, Jerry 'The Geator'; Bolden, Sheila; Bonner, Joel 'Joey'; Bowen, Ruth; Bowles, Thomas 'Beans'; Bradford, Janie; Byndon, Molly; Byndon, Sabrina; Cannon, LindaJ; Ciccone, Lynn; Clark, Dick; Collins, Johnny; Crochet, Lennie 'Lynn'; Davis, Billy; Davis, Carl; Davis, Roquel 'Billy'; Day, Jacqui; De Loach, Loretta; De Venne, Walter; Drake, Tony; Dunn, Ron; Edwards, Esther; Fox, John 'Peanut'; Fuqua, Harvey; Gaines, Grady;

Gaines, Roy; Gallimore, Jonathan; Gibson, Jack 'The Rapper'; Goodman, Gene; Green, Cal; Harris, Jenny; Holland, Eddie; Hopkins, Linda; Hunt, Tommy; Hunter, Joe; Jackson, Chuck; Jerome, Henry; John, Mabel; Johnson, Trina 'Cookie'; Kirschner, Leah; Lavette, Betty; Lee, Nate; Lewis, Barbara; Lewis, Pat; Maslon, Jimmy; Maxwell, Larry; McCoy, Rosemary; McRae, Joyce; Mirow, Harriet; Mitchell, Billy; Moore, Melvin; Nahan, Irv; Odneal, Linda; Odneal, Virginia 'Babe'; Overstreet, Dion 'Little Dion'; Parks, Gino; Payton, Lawrence; Perry, Jeffrey; Pitt, Rebecca 'Hot'; Potts, Sylvester; Pride, Alice; Pride, Eddie; Pride, Michael; Record, Eugene; Respess, Harry; Rice, 'Sir' Mack; Robinson, Claudette; Rutberg, Simon; Ryan, Jack; Sanders, William 'Sonny'; Schiffman, Bobby; Sherborne, Audrey 'Lee Angel'; Silverman, Isidore; Singleton, Eddie; Smith, Ernestine; Smith, Jimmy; Spain, Horace; Stubbs, Levi; Sutton, Charles; Tarnopol, Paul; Tate, Marlene; Taylor, Zola; Terry, Mike; Thiele, Bob; Thompson, Dick 'Dickie'; Toledo, Launa; Trudell, Johnny; Van de Pitte, David; Ward, 'Singin'' Sammy; Ward, Billy; Weatherspoon, William; Weiss, Hy; West, Sonny; Williams, Paul; Wilson, Brenda; Wilson, Freda; .Wilson, Mary; Wyne.

The music business is a cruel and shallow money trench, a long plastic hallway where thieves and pimps run free, and good men die like dogs. There's also a negative side.

Hunter S. Thompson

This book is dedicated to my lovely wife, Seda, who was so patient throughout the long period of writing it.

'If I am dead, as I well may be,
you come and find the place where I am lying
and kneel and say an Ave there for me.'
Danny Boy

THESE FITTING LYRICS, written in the last century, accompany the traditional Irish tune 'Londonderry Air', which is centuries older. Known now as 'Danny Boy', it was Jackie Wilson's favourite song. At 11 a.m. on Saturday, 21 January 1984, the heart of one of the world's great entertainers stopped beating. Fourteen minutes later he was pronounced dead. This remarkable man had sung his heart out and the world was a sadder place. Jackie Wilson was just 49 years old.

Singing is a practice common to every culture and particularly strong vocal traditions have developed in the Afro-American community. Having been transported from Africa in the most degrading and inhuman conditions and then subjected to generations of slavery, the emigrants had few ways of alleviating their life of toil and trouble except through religious faith and singing. Two vocal styles resulted from this; gospel and the blues.

Jackie Wilson didn't experience slavery; he experienced its offspring – bigotry, prejudice and the humiliation that stems from it. He also had an advantage in having a loving mother, but quite possibly he sang for the same reason as the slaves – to hide the pain in his heart for all the injustices he and his community suffered purely as a consequence of their race.

Jackie Wilson was far more than a good singer, he was a complete entertainer. He was, as songwriter Jeffrey Perry, who knew him well said, 'a singers' singer'. As fellow Detroit singer Betty Lavette related, 'Many singers achieved stardom through pure good luck, perhaps a timely hit or a pretty face. However, some people seem to be on earth for one purpose only; to express human emotion through song.' Jackie was one of these people.

JACKIE WILSON, as Jack Leroy Wilson became known, was born at 5.30 a.m. on Saturday, 9 June 1934 at the Herman Kiefer Hospital in Highland Park, Michigan. Jackie was the only surviving son of his black American parents: Jack Wilson, then aged 38, and Eliza Mae Wilson, aged 30. Eliza Mae was born on 22 April 1904, to Bill and Rebecca (nee Cobb) Ranson of Columbus, Mississippi. The Ransons lived on a fair-sized farm on what is known as 'Cobbs' Hill', Motley, just outside Columbus. They were Methodists and gospel singing was a large part of family life – Eliza Mae was a powerful singer, with a large, smiling mouth – and the house shook with foot stomping and singing when the family got together. Jack Wilson Snr, a farmer, was born in 1896, just across the border in Alabama. His mother Anna lived in the nearby town of Starksville, Mississippi. After he married Eliza Mae in 1922, Jack Snr worked for the railroad. They lived for about three years in Columbus before heading to Detroit prior to the Great Depression. Other relatives also made the move 'up north' to Michigan, where they settled in Kalamazoo, Muskegon, Pontiac and Detroit. They were helped to find work in the enormous car plants by Jackie's cousin, Tom Odneal. Many Wilson relatives still live there and carry the names of Taylor, Brown, Gray and Odneal.

Following the move to Detroit came children. Eliza Mae and Jack Snr had had two children previously, but they didn't survive. Jackie's birth certificate lists his father as 'unemployed' and his mother as a 'housewife'. While in Detroit, no one can recall Jackie's father holding down a job. He is best remembered for his drinking: he was a chronic alcoholic who sought the company of similar men. Being the only child of the marriage to survive, Jackie became the apple of Eliza Mae's eye.

JACKIE WILSON

They lived at 1533 Lyman Street, in north-eastern Detroit, a black neighbourhood known as Northend, close to the former Ford foundry plant and the former Chrysler headquarters and assembly plant. The modest little weatherboard house still stands, albeit in a dilapidated state. Jackie was baptised in the nearby Russell Street Baptist church, where he would sing as a child – and where his funeral service would be conducted. To family and close friends Jackie quickly became known as 'Sonny'.

When Jackie was born in 1934, the world was emerging from the Depression and many people, especially blacks, had headed north to the cities of Chicago, New York, Pittsburgh, Philadelphia and Detroit. All sought to better their situation in life through work in the factories and, in the case of Detroit, this generally involved automobile manufacture. Detroit was a meltingpot of social groups and, although not as segregated as in the south, racial barriers prevailed. Blacks and whites mostly lived a separate existence: blacks mainly lived on the east side of Woodward Avenue, rarely the west, and for a member of the black community to become successful by white standards he or she had to have exceptional abilities.

Between the ages of three and ten, Jackie lived with his family on Kenilworth Street in northern Detroit and the first school he attended was Alger Elementary, on Alger Street. His cousin, Virginia Odneal, recalls that Jackie could sing from the age of six: 'He always said he was going to become a star, and when he became a star and made 25 cents he'd give his mother 15 and keep ten.' Jackie's aunt, Rebecca 'Hot' Smith, said: 'Jack was beautiful – he had a God-given voice. He got it from his mother and grandmother; both could sing real good.'

Eliza Mae divorced in 1940, when Jackie was six, and began a common-law relationship with John Lee, a hard worker at the Ford auto plant. John Lee, who was younger than Eliza Mae, was 'a big, quiet man' who enjoyed his root cigars and usually owned an impressive car such as a Cadillac. They were, however, never formally married.

Around 1943 Jackie and his family moved a short distance to 248 Cottage Grove, off Woodward Avenue, in Highland Park, an area of three square miles entirely surrounded by the city of Detroit. It was the site of Chrysler Corporation's international automotive headquarters and the original site of Henry Ford's first mass-production car plant. Highland Park was a tree-lined working-class neighbourhood of around 35,000 people, with two-storey family homes surrounded by well tended lawns and gardens. To the east was the black neighbourhood, known as the Bowery; to the west the white. The segregation was not clear cut, however. Quite a few black families lived to the west of Woodward without any problems. There were also numerous Arabs, Jews and Italians in the area.

During the same period Jackie befriended Don Hudson and was a constant visitor to his house on Delmar Avenue. Hudson would die at the age of 29 after serving in the Korean War as a 15-year-old and winning the Bronze Star and Purple Heart. He was severely injured, with shrapnel in his head, and was repatriated. He died of a brain seizure around 1963. His sister, Freda, an attractive girl with long hair, was just one year older than Jackie. They soon became sweethearts. 'He was nine when he told me he was going to marry me,' said Freda. 'He told my mother at ten. He'd stay with my brother so he could see me. When he got to ten years old – I thought he was older – he said, "Can I kiss you?" He was like my shining knight, my everything.'

Freda had moved to Detroit with her family from Georgia. Her mother Leathia remarried and the family name became Hood.

> When he was little, Jack told me he didn't want to do nothing else but sing,

recalled Freda.

> He said he was going to be an entertainer. That was it; he was not going to do no hard work. We didn't have no record player, and I don't think he had no record player at home; he probably listened to the radio. His mother could sing, his father could sing. He'd sing . . . my goodness. Even in church; he did that on Russell Street, Holbrook, Oakland, all that. They all knew him.
>
> He knew a lot of people who sang – he also used to sing on the corner. In the neighbourhood on the Northend, he'd stand up there in front of the store from about ten or twelve-years-old; he'd say, 'Hey mama, what you wanna hear, some church songs or some blues?', or 'Mama, I'm going to sing you a song, you wanna hear it?' They'd be giving him money for singing for them. He was just born to sing.

Jackie was always older than his years, in part as a result of his mother's very liberal upbringing. Freda explained:

> When I first knew him, he was ten, singing on the street corner.

He'd get this wine; his mother would buy him this Cadillac Club Sweet Red or corn whisky. That's why I thought he was so old. After you got to know him, he was really very soft – he always acted different. Jack started doing things early [sexually], before most kids even think about it. He was way ahead of himself mentally.

Jackie's stepfather John ('Johnny') Lee worked at the Ford plant for 40 years. By all accounts he and Jackie got along well, although Eliza Mae always put her son's well-being ahead of John's. In Freda's words, 'She could do anything with his [Johnny's] money; she liked to play cards. Jack could have anything he wanted.' A childhood friend of Jackie's, Eddie Pride, knew his stepfather and mother well.' He was a very decent, nice man. His mother was a beautiful lady. I couldn't think of nothing but nice things about her. She was a big help to him – an inspiration.' Freda remembers that Jackie always had a sense of parental respect, even if deep down he resented an instruction: 'I don't care how drunk he got or whatever; he never said nothing to his mother or Johnny. His daddy [Johnny] could be drunk and if his daddy said, "The sky is purple,'then it was purple!"'

On 15 June 1945, when Jackie was 11, Eliza Mae had her second and only other surviving child, Joyce Ann. Her birthday, six days from Jackie's, caused some to speculate that their both being Geminis was the reason the relationship later became strained. Nevertheless, Jackie always loved her and would do whatever he could to assist her.

The Lee home didn't have a record player, but it did have a radio. The singers that Jackie listened to and whom he most admired were Al Jolson, Mario Lanza, the rhythm and blues (R&B) singer Roy Brown, big band baritone Al Hibbler and the gospel great Mahalia Jackson. A common pastime of black families was group singing, especially families who had moved up from the south. Before the days of television, group singing was one of the main forms of home entertainment.

In 1945, Jackie transferred to Thomson Elementary School on Brush Street in Highland Park. (The school has since been torn down and the area has become part of the Chrysler complex.) Jonathan Gallimore, who was two years older than Jackie, captained the Highland Park High School track team. It was the role of the older children to look out for the grade children from the nearby Thomson Elementary School, and Gallimore introduced Jackie to track sports. He remembered Jackie as a fast runner with plenty of track potential: 'He was a very active little kid, always in trouble,' he recalls.

No doubt Jackie had gained plenty of running practice eluding the school authorities, for he was an incorrigible truant. The truant officers took their jobs very seriously; they knew Jackie and his close friend, Freddy Pride, by name and these two, along with a few others who had also decided early on that their futures lay in careers as singers, regarded attendance at school as a waste of time. The authorities' solution to truancy was the Lansing Correctional Institute and, at about the age of 12, Jackie served the first of two detentions there. Despite this, in 1947 Jackie, then aged 13, was enrolled at the respected Highland Park High School; reputed to be one of the best in the nation. At Highland Park High the majority of students were white: of the 400 students who graduated in 1949, 12 were black. Jackie remained uninterested in school.

The Pride family lived in west Highland Park, a predominantly white section. Eddie Pride, who also attended Jackie's school, comments: 'Highland Park was an excellent school; I was really proud. Highland Park at that time went up to the fourteenth grade. That way they got to give the kids a chance to do two years of college – free.' Regarding racism, Eddie says, 'You know, I didn't know nothing about no race shit until I got in the army. Everybody in the class was white. We used to have to go through the whole school looking for somebody black. We didn't get too involved in that race thing. My neighbours were white, and all the people on my paper route were white. I just happened to be black.'

Freddy Pride, twin brother of Eddie and now deceased, was one of Jackie's closest friends as well as being a fine singer. Freddy, who was two years older than Jack, became one of the original Midnighters group. Jackie was a regular and welcome visitor to the Pride home, where they met to practise their singing. Eddie said:

> I knew Jack since high school. He lived fast; even at 15 he was singing at clubs. He was quite fabulous, even then, as a youngster. Way ahead of himself. Jack sang 'Danny Boy' when he was in high school. I said, 'Man, that'd be a hell of a recording.' He could sing opera. At that time Mario Lanza was out and Jack imitated him a lot. Jack didn't hardly go to school at all, but he would come down for music and excelled at music. His mother had him in church; had him in the choir. She had a voice, too. She taught Jack all the things, falsetto, and all that stuff he could do. He was doing that at 13, 14, 15 years old.

The school Glee Club also met at the Pride house and was under the tutelage of an elderly woman, Mrs Kent. Eddie Pride's sister, Alice, a year younger than Jackie, was also a member of the Glee Club, which she recalls had about 15 members. 'She'd always tell him he was going to make it,' said Alice. 'The song she liked was "Silent Night" and she told everybody, "Everybody be quiet! Jack! Come up here. I want you to sing. Jack, you're going to be good." She praised him so. We would be laughing. He was about 15 then. She discovered him. She'd say, "You're going to make it, you have the voice." He could hit those high notes, even back then.'

Jackie spent much of his time at Northern High, Freda's school. 'He would go into Highland Park High School and straight out the back door,' stated Freda. 'He spent more time over at my school than he did at his. We'd be looking out the window at him; he'd be standing outside messing with the girls. I'd know to go to that window in the study hall and wait . . .' Jackie was a womaniser from an early age, and was usually to be found wherever there were girls.

Martha Scott, who was at school with Jackie and became Highland Park's mayor, always knew he was going to be a star. Once a month a student would sing at school assembly. She remembers how nobody would miss morning assembly on the days Jackie sang. In 1949, Jackie's teacher prophetically remarked on his report card: 'Jack's story is a sad one. He has a voice out of this world, but can't get to school on time to do anything about it. He has talent without ambition and charm without responsibility. I have doubts as to his future in 9-B or in life.' Jackie went only as far as the ninth grade, dropping out in 1950 when he was 16. His ambitions lay outside anything he could learn in school and he loathed discipline. Ernestine Smith, a few years older and a near neighbour, stated, 'I think he dropped out early and did all the things my dad said he was going to do; drink and get girls pregnant.' Martha Scott recalls, amazingly, that Jackie had impregnated around 15 girls before he left school. Freda also confirmed this.

Another Highland Park student, Loretta Deloach, was a friend of Jackie's and the Pride family, living in their apartment building. 'He always had this lovely voice. He would always sing when somebody asked him to sing for church or school; or if the kids wanted to raise some money for a program we'd have these talent shows and we'd ask him to sing, and he always would sing for us. A delightful young man; not conceited like some.

'We had this Sanders candy store and bakery [nearby] and the guys would go there and kinda get this candy without paying for it. We girls would try to make ourselves look attractive so the guys would give us some candy. Jack he always held out, but he'd give you more than the other guys. He'd give you a pound of candy. He was outgoing and everyone accepted him. As a youngster he was still good looking. The women were after him.' Loretta recalls that after Jackie became famous he was still the same warm person, 'He didn't forget his friends. He'd always come back to Highland Park. When he came back, it was a big deal.'

Detroit during that period was a boom town. Roquel 'Billy' Davis was a close friend and neighbour of Jackie's and became one of his songwriters, co-writing most of his major hits. He recalls: 'In Highland Park in those days there was a sense of community. Everyone looked out for one another; it was like a big family. We played together, we entertained together, we ate together, we shared everything together. Poor little rich kids; that's what I called us.'

At around the age of 12, Jackie formed a small group he called 'The Ever Ready Gospel Singers'. Naturally, he sang lead. Jackie's best friend throughout most of his life was a lanky fellow with a big jaw and a friendly smile, Johnny Jones. 'JJ', as he was generally known, was three years Jackie's senior and lived nearby. They often spent the night at each other's homes and attended the same Russell Street Baptist Church. JJ was part of the gospel group and sang bass. Two brothers, Emmanuel and Lorenzo, made up the quartet.

Jack was the group,

according to Freda.

> They performed at all kinds of churches throughout the day. A collection would be taken for them – a quarter at least. They could tear up a church! In the evening, after church, they'd shoot craps and he'd win all their money. Those people believed they were giving to God; these were children of God. They didn't know Jack was shooting craps. Jack was just smart from the street. He always knew what notes he could reach. He did his own stuff; nobody trained him, they didn't have to.' They sang the church circuit around the Northend area of Detroit, remaining active until he was 15 or 16.

Jonathan Gallimore recalls, 'They formed a group and used to sing on all

the corners: the corner of Oakland and Connecticut, then they was around
the west side and on the playground at the Highland Park High School and
at Northern High School and the Community Centre.'
Ernestine Smith lived on Russell Street, close to where Jackie lived.
Ernestine's father was strict, religious and hardworking. He discouraged
Ernestine from any involvement with Jackie or his friends. The back porch
of the Smith house looked out on the alley where Jackie and his group often
hung out. It was also the place where his father gathered with his 'wino'
cronies.

Jack was basically a good young man,

said Ernestine.

> He liked to drink that wine, though. My dad picked who I mixed
> with. For some reason he didn't like me to mix too much with
> Jack. He was good looking; I always admired him and liked him,
> but had a little fear in my heart because he could be a little
> demanding: 'Come here!', like that. The way he'd talk to you!
> 'When I tell you to come over here, I mean it!' He said, 'I like
> you. Do you wanna be my girl' I said, 'No, no.' I figured he was
> younger than me. One night he was with the fellas and he called
> me. I ran, I beat O.J. [Simpson] running.
>
> My daddy said, 'He's out there in the world, he's rough.' That's
> the way he grew up and survived. In winter they'd put on a heavy
> coat and gloves. Some had holes in the gloves, mittens. If it was
> cold, that wine would heat them up. There was a Standard gas
> station in the alley. He liked to shoot dice with the guys. Jack
> would come up the alley to be with his dad and those men. There
> was a store nearby where they'd buy their liquor. They'd drink and
> solve the world's problems. There'd be six, seven or eight men.
> But if the minister came down the street, they had respect for him.
>
> They'd buy the wine and pass the bottle; they'd be laughing. If
> Jack would come up, they'd sing. They seemed always to be having
> fun. My dad resented that; he worked hard and thought they should.
> He'd say, 'Get away from my porch.' They would get carried away
> and be cussing. Jack did have a split life. I had seen him in church
> and saw him sing, but he could cuss! My dad was a churchgoer and
> didn't like the cussing. They'd say, 'Here comes that man, he's

going to give us a sermon.' They used to enjoy taunting him. They'd tell my dad, 'You don't own this street!' If it was too cold you wouldn't see 'em.

Eddie Pride also has stories of Jackie's drinking: 'Jack drank, too, you know; I was with him. Cadillac Club and Mr Boston – cheap wine – about 89 cents. We'd put our quarters together and sing on that wine, instead of being in school. Mostly we hung out on Fourth and Hamilton [streets] – there was a liquor store up there. We'd get the older guys to buy the wine and let them have the first drink: 'take the poison off the top', as we'd say. Then we'd have a ball.' They generally sang blues-style numbers and often composed their own songs.

Freda recalls that it was through his group that Jackie first met popular singer Sam Cooke. She explained, 'Back then Jack's group hung around the radio station. That's how he met Sam Cooke. They went on the radio because Sam asked them to give them a break. WJLB or WJBK, I believe it was.' Cooke, who was from Chicago, was seven months Jackie's junior, but had been in a family gospel group since the age of nine. Later he became lead singer with the Soul Stirrers. With his exceptionally good looks, charisma and unique, mellow vocal skills he quickly became a singing sensation; loved equally by black and white audiences, especially the female fans.

In the tough Detroit environment in which Jackie grew up, where the racial divide was wide and deep, blacks were generally the last to be hired. While in his teens Jackie became a member of the Shaker Gang, known as 'the baddest gang around' and 'a pretty tough bunch, always in trouble'. The Shakers' territory was around Woodward Avenue. Gang leaders were Maurice Munson, Calvin 'Clem' or 'Bo Bo' Thomas, and Donald Penniman; other members included JJ, Charles Hardaway, Nelson Small, the four Pashae brothers (Fred, Jim, Mack, Robin), Leroy Munson, 'Red' (whose real name could not be established) and Harry 'Dale' Respess.

Otis Williams of The Temptations, in his book *Temptations*, describes gang leader Munson as 'truly frightening', with a big ugly scar above his lip and long hair parted down the middle and tied in a 'doo rag' (a kerchief-like cloth bound around the head and fashionable amongst certain black youths at the time). Maurice Munson was feared, while Calvin Thomas was described as 'bad news'. Mack Pashae became a professional fighter and served time in jail. Later on he was murdered.

Roquel 'Billy' Davis knew the Shakers well: 'They were feared by the whole of Detroit, but Jack wasn't a running part of the gang. No more than a dozen guys made up the most prominent part; the meanest and most vicious.' Former Shakers' member Respess said that although only a dozen or so strong, the group was 'the scourge of the city. Everyone was scared to death of us. We were little thugs. We'd look for fights and punch people out. Jack was pretty tough. Johnny Jones was there, of course. JJ was almost his alter ego, his shadow.' Respess fondly remembers they'd sit in an alley off Oakland Avenue, drinking muscatel wine and listening to Jackie sing 'Danny Boy' for them, 'just as though we'd paid 20 dollars for a ticket. Man, we really got off on that after drinking that wine. We always said one day he's going to make it, if he kept trying. That was our idol and we were his faithful followers.'

The girls were known as Shaker Rats. Not surprisingly, Freda Hood became a Shaker Rat: 'I wanted to be a Shaker Rat. I didn't know what it was all about. They'd go over to Hamtramck and beat up this Polish gang, and they would go to the Northend and beat up this other gang that was supposed to be bad. We'd have these long skirts on and felt we were looking sharp.'

Around five' seven" Jackie was reasonably small, but 'he was a street fighter', remembers Freda. 'All we did was hot-wire cars and fight for territory. But Jack did that with his fists – he was really something. He never got his face hurt because the other guys would step in if he looked like getting his face hurt, and they'd catch the blows themselves.' Freda rationalises his macho behaviour thus: 'He would fight, but I don't think he really liked fighting all that much. He knew he had a lot of people to cover for him. He could go in and do his thing and somebody was going to interfere. I think Jack liked to'scrap to show he was a man. 'I've got it,'he'd say. He didn't have a bad temper. He could smile at you and his eyes would be saying "get the heck away from me".'

Loretta Deloach knew the Shakers: 'They were dangerous, but not into killing like today. They were into claiming their territory and their women and proving they were tough. They could smack you around a little bit. Jackie wasn't a dumb kid – he had skills. He could run fast – he had to!' Mack Rice, one of the original Falcons R&B group, was also from the neighbourhood. He recalls, 'Jack was adopted. He didn't have nothing to do with that stuff. They were mean, but not like today. When you were a star like Jack you were an honorary member; they looked out for him. They would boost him up there, boy.' Ernestine Smith also remembers Jackie's gang involvement: 'He got into his little mysteries – stealing and things. Jack had a temper too. The Shakers sort of ruled; I was afraid of the gang. They'd intimidate people. They used fists, maybe a chain. They'd "woop" your ass real good. I'd stay clear of them and I would walk fast coming home from school. My daddy said, "That boy is a hoodlum." Jack wasn't all that well dressed, but he dressed decent. I've seen him with holey pants on. Blue jeans wasn't that fashionable back then. His shoes might be a bit run over.'

According to Freda, Jackie was returned to the Lansing Correctional Institute when he was 16. Freda remembers:

> 'I didn't want him to go to jail – he'd been to jail when he was a juvenile. That was a lark to him anyway; he acted like he was going on a vacation.' It's possible that this period of incarceration had more to do with juvenile delinquency than truancy, but Freda wasn't prepared to elaborate. She went on: 'He told his mother to bring me down. I said to him, 'Why haven't you got shoelaces?' He said, 'They don't let us have shoelaces.' He had blue jeans, T-shirt – that's it. Gym shoes, no shoelaces. I said, 'Well, that's silly.' The guard says, 'Jack, I know that's not your sister, I met your sister Joyce – so go ahead and kiss her.' So he kissed me through the bars. He told his mother to go buy him some wine sometime, 'cause he was sick – and she did. She did everything he said to.

At Lansing he took to boxing and may have considered this as a career option. Detroit was the home town of 'the Brown Bomber', world heavyweight champion Joe Louis. Louis was home town hero to Detroit's black youth. On his release Jackie became a regular at Brewster's Gym, where he worked out and trained to become a professional boxer. In 1961, when he'd become a star, Jackie was interviewed by Mary Akon for New York's Sunday News [22 October, 1961]: 'My ma took me along regularly when she went to choir practice in church, but I wanted to be a prize fighter when I grew up. When I was sixteen I said I was eighteen so I could compete in the Detroit Golden Gloves. I won the welterweight championship and turned pro; which was a terrible mistake. I won only two fights out of ten. One time I got flattened in the fourth round. I was seventeen when I began thinking about another way to make a living, especially since I had married Freda who'd been my girl in Highland Park High School.'

Jackie's reminiscences were not always accurate; the Golden Gloves title was a later fiction he perpetuated. His claim to have only thought of another career path at seventeen also seems unlikely, as Freda and many others believe he'd been planning a singing career since early childhood. But this wasn't the last time he embellished a story.

In the early 1970s Jackie did a radio interview with New York DJ Norman N Nite (on WCBS—FM). 'Boxing, actually I didn't want to leave,' he said. 'My mother just grabbed me by the hair one day and told me, 'No more.' I was getting real good and she walked into the arena one night, and I was boxing. I always looked for her in a certain seat and she wasn't there. All of a sudden she walked in. My nickname is Sonny and she hollers out real loud, 'Hey, Sonny.' And I turn around, and wop, wop, wop. She finally saw me beat to bits. So she told me, 'No more!''

His mother never went to see him boxing being strongly opposed to it. Freda said Jackie's mother didn't know he'd been boxing and was furious on finding out. She forbade him from boxing again. 'He liked boxing; that's the one thing I could never understand,' says Freda. 'I'm glad he gave it up, because of his face. His mother was very concerned, and he did everything she told him.'

At the time an important arena for aspiring black singers was the amateur nights at the Paradise Theatre (also called The Orchestra Hall): Detroit's equivalent of Harlem's Apollo Theatre. As well as the Paradise, Jackie participated at amateur nights at the Park, State, Gold Coast, Grant, Booker T and Warfield theatres. These were movie theatres that charged only twenty-five cents entry and would feature fifteen to twenty acts. The competition was fierce and the enthusiastic black audiences took the outcome very seriously, so it was useful to have your own cheer squad.

Jackie was regularly up against the vocal talents of Little Willie John, 'Singin'' Sammy Ward, Della Reese, his friends, Ralph Peterson and Freddy Pride, and Levi Stubbs, who went on to become lead singer of The Four Tops. More often than not, the talented Little Willie John would win over Jackie.

As he did on the street corners, Jackie liked to perform 'Danny Boy' at these evenings, which he sang with the emotional passion that was to become his hallmark. Freda recalls, 'He'd always win amateur nights doing 'Danny Boy', and when he recorded it he did [sang] it the same way.' Music writer Don Waller later wrote of hearing him do 'Danny Boy': 'By the time Wilson hit the final cadenza in which he wrings 23 – count 'em – notes out of the word "there for", I was convinced there wasn't a pop singer alive who could stretch such a thin piece of material into the aural equivalent of an Armani suit.'

The contests provided the opportunity for young artists to be noticed by talent scouts from recording companies and tour promoters. Alice Pride remembers that Jackie was already developing the footwork and falling-down splits that would later become part of his stage act.

Ernestine Smith saw Jackie perform at the Grant Theatre: 'On Fridays and Saturdays neighbourhood people could come and perform. Jack had on nice pants, nice shoes, nice shirt. I thought he'd have been 16 or 17. He won singing "Danny Boy", and after that he became famous. He had that charisma, and he could always dance; great body movements. He brought the house down, and those kids could be cruel, too. They were cheering and stood up and clapped.'

His hair would have to look right as well. 'He used to "conk",his hair,' she recounts. 'He would process his hair.' This was the style favoured by blacks at that time, which involved the quite painful practice of treating their hair with lye in order to straighten it. Jackie would then use Brylcream to ensure his hair remained in place.

Singer Johnny Otis, born in 1921 to Greek parents, was from California but travelled all over the USA seeking out R&B talent. Otis, who discovered many artists during the 1950s, recalls one time that Jackie came in third to Little Willie John and The Royals at an amateur night at the Paradise Theatre, and credits himself with 'discovering' the singer. Otis apparently tried to sign Jackie to Syd Nathan's King/Federal record label in Cincinnati, but they weren't interested. Instead, they signed up The Royals and Little Willie John. Jackie, Little Willie John and Levi Stubbs (later of The Four Tops) would often get together at each other's homes to rehearse. 'Little Willie John, [sister] Mabel John and Jack would always be over at Mrs Stubbs'house, or they would be over at Jack's mother's singing and carrying on,' says Freda. Stubbs admits modestly, 'I used to perform at amateur nights at the Paradise and the Warfield Theatre on Hastings Street. Little Willie John and Jackie would perform at the same time. It's not a question of trying to outperform each other; it's a matter of doing what you do. I personally never put myself on the same level as Jack and Little Willie John.'

Freda was a regular at the Paradise: 'They had an amateur show on Tuesday night. They had a lot of amateur shows and shows with Sonny Til And The Orioles and Lionel Hampton. Jack, Ralph [Peterson] and Johnny [JJ] would win sometimes, then they would let Levi Stubbs and his people win the next time. Jack and Ralph were on it every week. They had it all worked out. They had it all set up. Jack said, "You win tonight, I'll win next night."' He was as confident of success in the professional world: 'He kept saying – I was working in the kitchen at that time – "Don't worry, it'll be all right."'

Levi Stubbs recalls: 'Jack had a terrific voice. Jack had an influence on me. When you won the amateur night you got either 25 or 50 dollars. That's the world to them [the winners], and you had the chance to work with professional shows that they brought in. All the big black acts were there.' The black audiences were very boisterous, very vocal. You could get booed off the stage. It was a good training ground, but it was useful to have supporters in the audience.

The amateur night contests sometimes took Jackie over to Holbrook and Delmar Streets, the Herokies Gang's territory. He needed Shaker Gang muscle to ensure his safety and to give him some vocal and moral support. 'Jack would mostly win the shows there,' remembers former Shaker gang member Respess. 'Not only because he had the audience stacked or packed, but because he was the best singer.' 'Singin'' Sammy Ward, who often competed against Jackie, remembers the enjoyment his opponent took from performing: 'He was the kind of guy who would like to sing anytime, anywhere – for money or no money. Mostly for no money.'

Eddie Pride formed his own group, Eddie Pride And The Nightcaps. 'I used to call myself a singer, but after listening to Jackie I gave up,' says Eddie. 'He could go high C and above – and do bass. I couldn't understand how he could do that.' Brother Freddy Pride was so close to Jackie that many considered them brothers. Freddy went on to become part of the original Midnighters group, only to die of a drug overdose before he was 30.

Apart from singing in church or contests, the other outlet for black singers was the street corner. It was extremely commonplace for small groups of youths to sing vocal harmonies. These became known as 'doo wop' groups, because they couldn't afford to buy instruments and had to vocally improvise them. Around 1950 a doo wop group called The Royals was formed, which included Levi Stubbs, Lawson Smith, Sonny Woods, Henry Booth and Charles Sutton, with Alonzo Tucker or Arthur Porter on guitar.

Besides playing guitar, Tucker also wrote many of their songs, despite his inability to read music. He later became Jackie's most prolific songwriter, co-writing numerous tunes with him. Twenty-five years older than Jackie and referred to as 'the old man', he passed on a great deal of his musical expertise and was loved by one and all. He is described as 'a songwriter from the old school' by fellow songwriter Roquel 'Billy' Davis. 'Tucker taught us a lot about R&B. To write a song, you come up with a concept. You create a phrase that becomes a title. Tucker's spirit was young and he always had a smile. He was missing a tooth or two in the front, so that every time he laughed or smiled, which he did a lot, he would hold his hand over his mouth. He was a wonderful guy.' Similarly, Cal Green, who later became The Midnighters' lead guitarist, also fondly recalls Alonzo Tucker: 'Alonzo would have all the youngsters out on the corner singing. He'd help people to put a song together and end up doing it and then teaching them how to sing it . . . the whole nine yards. He was a good guy, a nice guy.'

One of the original Royals, Charles Sutton, lived in downtown Detroit, where many of the rehearsals took place. Sutton recalls Tucker, singer Hank Ballard, Jackie and his group visiting his home in 1952. 'They came to our rehearsals. My wife and I had a couple of kids, but she'd tolerate it; all the singing and stuff,' says Sutton. 'Alonzo and I were friends a long time before all this. He only lived three doors from me.'

The Royals went on to have limited success on Syd Nathan's King label in Cincinnati but, because of ongoing confusion with The Five Royales, they changed their name to The Midnighters. R&B singer Johnny Otis wrote the classic ballad 'Every Beat Of My Heart' for Jackie, but The Royals recorded it instead, in 1952, with Sutton doing the lead. However, the song only became a hit when Gladys Knight recorded it many years later. Levi Stubbs was with The Royals for a time, although he never recorded with them.

As The Midnighters, with Hank Ballard as their lead, they became the first black group from Detroit to achieve national success. With Ballard's emotional style of delivery success soon followed, starting with the 1953 R&B Top 10 hit 'Get It'. In 1954 they reached the big time with three hits, 'Work With Me Annie', 'Sexy Ways' and 'Annie Had A Baby'. Singing with a group taught Jackie the importance of harmonising: singing without musical backing emphasised the primacy of his voice as a musical instrument. But Jackie wasn't alone in benefiting from the style of the era, as Roquel 'Billy' Davis explains: 'The 1950s gave birth to a lot of black 'bird' groups [eg Ravens, Orioles, Flamingos, Robins, Penguins], which gave birth to doo wop groups. Every kid on the corner thought, "I can sing."' Doo wop was the ideal way to sing harmoniously and spawned some incredible talents.

Davis formed a group called The Thrillers, but after achieving only local success they disbanded. Davis, who had singing aspirations of his own, formed another group called The Aims. He quickly realised that to be a singer he needed original songs. According to him, he had 'always loved poetry, but only had elementary music training at school – trumpet and drums. The poetry helped with the singing; it came easy. To song-write you have to be inspired. You'd have to have an idea.' Davis had many ideas, co-writing songs with Charles Sutton and Alonzo Tucker, and a friend of Tucker's, William Weatherspoon. An early success was the hit 'Seesaw', co-written with Sutton. Davis, through his songwriting skills, would become instrumental in Jackie's career success.

All the while the romance between Jackie and Freda was blossoming. 'He used to spend the night with my brother, Don,' says Freda. 'My mother found out he was saying those things [about Freda being cute] and said, "You can't stay here no more; I don't know about you." I didn't know how to speak to a boy. I liked Jack because he could sing and he was handsome. All the girls liked him; all my friends tried to take him from me. He liked someone soft, someone he could control.'

He had a vain streak. Freda elaborated, 'My mother had this big mirror over the buffet – he didn't say nothing to me; he'd walk straight past, look in the mirror, lick his lips, and come back and say, "Hey, baby." Jack always knew how to dress. He was handsome and he knew it. He just knew how to put nothing together and look real good. He never wore blue jeans, he always wore suits then, even when he was 15 or 16. He also wore Stacey Adams shoes – alligator shoes – and all that. His hat would be "couched" over one eye.'

Freda, whom Jackie always referred to by the pet name of 'Pee Wee' on account of her initially being slim and taller than himself, soon became pregnant and a marriage was arranged at her home on 22 February 1951. As the time for the wedding drew near, the groom disappeared.

> Jack was already drunk when he went. The minister was there, I was there; everybody was sitting there looking stupid. I said, 'I know where he is.' It was amateur night at the Paradise Theatre. My stepfather finally took me down there. He said, 'I know. I'm going down there to get him.' I said, 'I'll have to go there with you.'
>
> We got there; it was [a contest] between Ralph Peterson, Levi Stubbs and Jack. Ralph and Jack were so drunk on stage. Ralph was jerking the microphone from Jack when he was trying to sing. Jack was jerking the microphone from him. Jack was just hollering, it was nothing – people were just booing. So we went backstage. He said, 'Baby, I was coming. I was getting my nerves up.' So we just picked him up and took him to our house and that's where we got married.

All of Jack's buddies were at the wedding, including JJ and Ralph Peterson. My mother was there with her boyfriend, and my grandparents. We went back and got married and we had a party. They already had some liquor and they got some more. Jack was 16 and I was 17. He used the name Richards; a friend Elija Richards loaned him the ID, as he was underage at the time. Jack used the same ID so he could perform at Lee's Club Sensation, a black club on nearby Owen Street.

Amazingly, Jackie's mother wasn't present.

His mother knew about it,

says Freda,

and that was the first time he did something his mother told him not to. He didn't hide anything from her. She just accepted it [the marriage] and she liked me after; we got along very well. The minister across the road from us performed the ceremony. Jack had some money because he had won some at an amateur night a few weeks before. He gave it to pay the minister.

After the wedding they lived together at Freda's family home on Delmar Street, on Detroit's northside. Later on they moved about a mile away to 248 Cottage Grove, off Woodward Avenue, living with his mother and John Lee. Freda says: 'Johnny was good to us and helped raise us. Even though I couldn't cook. They didn't have no phone. Johnny was a nice man. He used to let Jack have his kind of [Cadillac] limo to take me to my little society things. We were the only ones who had a big car.'

The big car wasn't the extent of Freda's aspirations, though. She had ambitions of her own: 'I didn't want to get married in the first place, I wanted to be a doctor.' She was a trainee nurse and none of her colleagues knew she was married, let alone pregnant. 'In 1951 they were already throwing girls out of school that was pregnant. I felt if I didn't tell anybody, Denise would just appear. I graduated in January, got married in February and had Denise in March. And nobody at the college knew. My counsellor kept coming over and asking why I hadn't gone on to college, because I had won a scholarship. He said, "If it's money, I can arrange something." I said, "No." He said, "Whose cute little baby's sitting on the couch?" I said,

"Mine." He answered, "That Jack Wilson, I told you to stay away from him; I told you I knew he was bad."'

When their first child, Jacqueline Denise, was born on 24 March, the Wilson family's future looked uncertain. Jackie had dropped out of school and was unemployed, and his wife was suffering: 'The delivery room was the worst place I've ever seen, it was like a torture chamber. They put me on this table, my feet in this thing; I kept sliding back. I said, "What is this? This is like hell." Anyway, I had her. I don't know if Jack called the hospital or what, but he found out I had that baby. He'd been singing at Lee's Club Sensation to make a little money. Anyhow, he came in the hospital about three or four o'clock in the morning. How he got in, I'll never know. "You had a girl, eh? What's her name?" he said. I said, "I ain't named her yet." Jack said, "Her name's Jacqui." I said, "You get away from me. All you want to do is do that thing; that's horrible and it hurts and I can't stand it." Jack said, "Be quiet, I ain't supposed to be in here."'But his late-night presence was discovered. 'They were trying to put him out. He said, "Just do me a favour; just let me see my little baby one time and I'll go and come back tomorrow, or whatever." Then he left.'

Freda became wary of Jackie's excessive sexual demands. 'When he came to bed, I got up,' she admits. 'I was pregnant 15 times before I was 30. I was a baby factory! When Jack came near me I said, "No, no, don't! Go away! Please go away." For a long time I couldn't stand to see sausages, hot dogs, none of those things. Each time I became pregnant I'd say, "Please don't let this one look like him." I wanted girls.'

All their children would carry the last name 'Richards', in accordance with the marriage certificate. But regardless of surname, Jackie was proud of his new daughter and took her to where his father 'hung out' with the other winos on Holbrook Street. He loved his father, despite his shortcomings; so did Freda, but that wasn't what she had in mind for her child. 'I liked Mr Jack too, but I didn't want Denise up there,' she explains. 'His father drank wine in the alley and pushed a push-cart. I figured there'd be germs and everything. So Jack told me he was taking her to the doctor; she had a cold. I said, "I'll come, too." He said, "No, I can take her." He knew I wouldn't want him taking her.

'He was gone so very long that day. I finally said, "I wonder where he could be?" I said, "I know, I'm going up to Holbrook." It was off Russell Street. I walked down there, and sure enough, there was my baby in the garage. Jack was singing, drinking wine. Mr Wilson was holding the baby and talking about his granddaughter. That's the only one [of their four children] he saw before he died [in 1953]. He carried Denise around and held her out in front of him. I didn't like for him to hold her when he'd been drinking, 'cause I was scared he might drop her. Jack said, "Leave him alone – he ain't going to drop her. he knows what he's doing.'''

Jackie's championing of his father didn't just upset Freda. John Lee was a quiet and tolerant man, but his tolerance was tested to the limit when Jackie would bring his father back home to Cottage Grove. Although John Lee never openly objected to this, he wasn't pleased, either. In Freda's words, 'That [Jack Snr] was Eliza's husband until he died. She didn't care how many husbands you had, the first husband was your husband. Until one of them died, that's it. So he'd bring his daddy over there to get him cleaned up. She'd put in the tub, get him all cleaned up; wash his hair, take him and give him a haircut, or someone in the house would cut it. She'd put him in some of Johnny's clothes. Johnny would be walking around slamming doors; boom, boom, boom. But he didn't say nothing! After, Mr Wilson had a guitar and he'd be playing; he could sing, too. Then Jack and he would sing together. Jack loved Johnny too, but that was his daddy, and they was real tight. Your mom and your dad was family, that's it.'

Freda, both attractive and intelligent, was a good anchor for Jackie. Whenever she was able Freda worked as a trainee nurse at the hospital, but times were tough. Jackie was never known for his reliability or ability to take care of details, so it was not an easy time for them. 'Eliza Mae kept Jack in clothes after we got married,' said Freda. 'Every time I had a baby he'd pawn his good suit to get the milk and stuff. He'd go to the pawn shop and get what he needed – he always stayed neat and everything. He could chew a pawn shop down; he could get what he wanted for less than they wanted to sell it.'

But everyone who knew Jackie then believed his success was just a matter of time and a little luck. Freda says, 'Jack had a sort of driving personality. He was determined to succeed. He could do anything he wanted – and he could sing. Everyone knew he could sing.' Quite naturally, though, Freda was concerned about their prospects. 'He said, "Don't worry, everything's going to be okay." All my friends would say, "If the man makes it you can forget him, because he don't want to die with his shoes on," and all this stuff. I wasn't worried about it 'cause I said, "I think he loves me." My mother told me, "He's never going to be anything, I don't know why you went and got yourself pregnant by him. He ain't going to be nothing." Guess who was down there [when he became successful] counting his money from the Greystone Ballroom? My mother!'

JACKIE WILSON

In 1952, aged 17, Jackie had his first opportunity to record some songs. Not surprisingly, 'Danny Boy' was his first recording and a regular blues number, 'Rainy Day Blues', the next. Both recordings were done at Joe Syracuse's United Sound Studios in Detroit, where many of the great Motown recordings would be cut in later years. They were released under the name of Sonny Wilson as two 78s on the Dee Gee (Dizzy Gillespie) label. The flip sides were mainly instrumentals with some male group vocals, which included Jackie.

Detroit sax player and band leader, Billy Mitchell, who'd performed with Count Basie's and Dizzy Gillespie's bands, arranged the recording and his band was used as back-up. Mitchell remembers that Dave Usher, Dizzy Gillespie's partner on the small label, spotted Jackie performing around town and suggested the session. Mitchell says he put Jackie on a recording contract, but fortunately didn't hold him to it when, next year, he was given the opportunity to join Billy Ward And The Dominoes.

Although Jackie's uniquely marvellous voice comes through on the 1952 recording of 'Danny Boy', he tries too hard to make it unique and the result is rather unremarkable. 'Rainy Day Blues' had a lot more promise as an R&B number, but the two singles didn't sell well once they were released, although there is an inkling of the incredible voice that was recorded the following year with The Dominoes.

Jack Snr died in January 1953, just before Jackie achieved real success. He was 57. Like many father-son relationships Jackie and his father had sometimes clashed, but the love between them was always there. 'While he was living in Highland Park, they had some knock-down, drag-out fights when his dad got soused,' explains Harry Respess. 'They had a love-hate relationship.' But as Freda says, her husband lost one of his biggest fans: 'Jack Snr thought his son was the greatest, anyhow.'

They learned of Jack Snr's death in a typically convoluted fashion. 'Jack's mother had put him in the hospital,' says Freda. 'It rained that night. The doorbell rang; it hadn't never rang before. We were sitting in the kitchen at 248 Cottage Grove. At the time he died we didn't have a phone, so they had sent a telegram to my mother-in-law.' The telegram had been sent by the hospital to inform them that Jack Snr's prospects were not good. 'That doorbell rang at the exact time he had died at the hospital. She [Eliza Mae] got up and went in the room.'

After his father died, Jackie locked himself in his bedroom for a few days. His half-sister, Joyce, told Susan Morse of the *Detroit Free Press* (11 January 1976), 'He [Jackie] was a spiritual fanatic up to the time his father

33

died. When his father died, he took every spiritual record in the house and broke them. He knew his father was weak and an alcoholic, but Jackie loved him.' Jackie didn't attend the funeral and instead had someone take pictures of his father in the casket. In the 1960s he still carried around a photo of his father who looked a lot like him, but with a little pencil moustache. Jackie never came to terms with his death. His friend Harry Respess recalls that time: 'I went to his funeral. Jack didn't go. He went to see his body. He was mortified by his father's death, but he also had a guilt complex about it. He loved Mama more, believe you me.'

Jack Snr was buried at Lincoln Memorial Park Cemetery on Fourteen Mile Road, north of Detroit. 'Big Jack' would push his cart around Russell and Holbrook Streets no longer. Eliza Mae had loved the man dearly and now that he was buried, she could focus her love on John Lee and her beloved son, Jackie.

At the end of the month of Jack Snr's death, Freda gave birth to their second child, Sandra Kay. Their prospects were grim, with money in short supply. Jackie had an underground following among the seedy bars of northern Detroit, but, at 19, had his eyes set on far bigger things. He was convinced that he could hold his own in the fiercely contested talent shows and of his own performing talent. All Jackie needed was a lucky break; he didn't have long to wait.

Writer Jeff Beckman, in the music periodical *Big Town Review* (February–March 1972), wrote a detailed piece on musician Billy Ward, uncovering much about his life and career: 'Ward was born in Los Angeles of a preacher father and a choir-singing mother ... From the age of six Billy sang soprano as a member of the church choir and later became the church organist. Sometime during this period, Billy began what was to be a long and illustrious career as a composer ... But Billy was talented in these areas as well, for at the age of 14 he won a New York City-wide contest for a classical piece he had composed.'

WARD WAS BORN IN 1921, making him 13 years' Jackie's senior. Like Jackie, he was interested in boxing. He spent the Second World War years in the army, where his musical training came to the fore in the choir, which had a gospel leaning. After returning to civilian life, he attended various schools including the Chicago Arts Institute and the famous Julliard School of Music in New York. Ward settled in New York and worked for Carnegie Hall as a voice coach for white males. He met Bobby Schiffman, the owner of the famous Apollo Theatre, and it was arranged for Schiffman to recommend Amateur Night singers with potential to Ward, for regular vocal training.

Ward was a strict disciplinarian, who believed in rehearsing until the act was perfected. From the ranks of his vocal students he formed a group he initially named The Ques and later changed to The Dominoes, which he decided to enter in the hugely popular Wednesday Amateur Night contest at the Apollo. One night, early in 1950, The Ques won. As a result they were given the opportunity to appear on the Arthur Godfrey Talent Scouts Show, where amateur acts competed. Broadcast out of Dallas, this radio show (later becoming a TV show) had a huge, nationwide audience.

At that time, Arthur Godfrey had a quartet called The Mariners. Ward admired them, but believed his quintet sang even better and decided to perform his own arrangement of the Leadbelly song 'Goodnight Irene', which eventually became a standard. Ward's group won on the night.

During the day, Ward worked as a graphic artist for a businesswoman, Mrs Rose Marks, in her New York advertising agency, while doing his vocal training after hours. She recognised the remarkable talent Billy Ward and his group possessed and recommended that they should consider a professional career. So, in 1950, that's what happened: Ward did the arrangements himself and played piano, but rarely sang lead.

Syd Nathan's King Record Company offered Ward the opportunity to record. Ralph Bass had recently joined the King group with his Federal label, and Ward was one of the first to record for this subsidiary.

The Dominoes first single record release, 'Do Something For Me', was recorded in December 1950 and followed early in 1951 with the popular ballad 'Harbour Lights', later a hit for The Platters. Both achieved moderate success on the R&B charts. The lead tenor was Clyde McPhatter. Born in 1932, McPhatter was raised in New York City and sang gospel as a 14-year-old with the Mount Lebanon Singers. Jackie was in awe of McPhatter's magnificent and impassioned voice. Their hit '60 Minute Man', complete with suggestive lyrics by Ward, was arguably the forerunner to rock 'n' roll. The song's success led to concert appearances all over the northern States, including a return to Harlem's Apollo Theatre.

JACKIE WILSON

In 1952, around the time Billy Ward And The Dominoes were having their remarkable success, Jackie was still performing in Detroit's black clubs, especially Lee's Club Sensation. Freda says that for some reason Jackie suggested that he and his close friend JJ should enlist in the US Army, which they did. But when the time came for them to enter, however, Jackie thought better of it. Freda explained: 'So when it come time to go JJ went on down there, Jack didn't go. So JJ was in the army. The MPs came and got Jack.' He was now in a serious predicament, having signed up to join but failed to report. There were serious penalties for the offence. They were both instructed to appear before the Military Board: 'I was pregnant with Sandy and already had Jacqueline,' Freda says. 'There was one lady on that board, too. I don't know what Jack said . . . why he joined the army. Anyway, they believed his story and the fact they weren't at war, and that I already had a child, was expecting and needed him at home to take care of the children helped. I was the one that was taking care of the children. He was trying to make it [as a singer] and I was working. So they let him out of there. JJ was mad that Jack didn't come. He had to do two years, mandatory; he couldn't get out of there. Jack felt he owed him something for those years. JJ would never have gone if Jack hadn't suggested it.'

At 18 Jackie had built up a big local following as a nightclub act. This nearly came to an end when he was stabbed by a prostitute. Freda recalls:

> A white girl, she stabbed him. Rebecca [Pitt, his cousin] and my mother-in-law saw Jack come home with stab wounds to his stomach. My mother-in-law grabbed a knife and said, 'Are you coming?' I said, 'No, ma'am, I'm staying right here in the house.' I had to take care of the children.
>
> They went walking down to Hastings Street. My mother-in-law was going to stab her, but the police got involved somehow. They came down and got Jack; they grabbed him and my mother-in-law. She dropped the knife. I guess the girl must have called them or something.

Both Jackie and his mother were held by the police, and it was to Freda that they turned to for help.

> Jack didn't call; my mother-in-law called, and I went down to get 'em. Eliza said, 'Don't tell Sonny, there's some money in my bed;

find it.' I go down there to her and the police said, 'How many wives has he got? There's so many women coming down here.' My mother-in-law said, 'I'm his mother, and I know this is his wife!' So they brought Jack out for us to see him. They brought him out without his shirt on. He said, 'Wait a minute; show respect, that's my wife and mother. They're not street people. Let me put my shirt on; you can have it back when I go back.' The police came and hit him in the head. He said, 'I'll be out some time today, because I didn't do nothing. They are just trying to check me out to see if they can prove some kind of scandal.' Anyway, he got out of this one.

In 1953 Billy Ward sought a new singer for his Dominoes group. Dominoes member William Lamont was leaving to do military service, while fellow member David McNeil would soon follow. Jackie did not audition for the role of lead tenor and it is quite likely that at this stage McPhatter had no intention of leaving the group.

There are different versions of how Jackie came to be signed up with The Dominoes. They had an engagement at the Michigan State Fair in Detroit. According to Ward, he was in his room at the Gotham Hotel and about to retire for the night. The hotel manager called and said there were some people downstairs who wanted to see him. Ward invited them up. It was Jackie, with his mother, wanting to audition. Ward says he always travelled with a portable piano and had Jackie sing for him. Although he can't remember what was sung, he was impressed. In his words, Jackie was: 'A diamond in the rough; he had to be polished.' To create a diamond from coal requires time and pressure. Jackie had put in the time from his early childhood. Ward would be the pressure that was needed to create the gem.

As usual, Jackie, had his own version of events. One was that he went to meet Ward with a girl on each arm. Another was that he told Ward, 'I'm the baddest thing to happen to Detroit.' Certainly he could be quite brash, even cocky. Ward says that after the audition, Jackie's mother called him aside and, with tears streaming down her face, begged him to give Jackie a chance. She was in fear of his being killed on the streets.

The young singer had made a powerful impression, but he would have to compete in a public audition, after which Ward would make his choice.

The big night was at the Paradise Theatre, a second home to Jackie. When he arrived at the audition he bragged, 'I can sing much better than Clyde McPhatter.' Alice Pride recalls the event vividly: 'It was talent night.

He won singing "Danny Boy".' In an interview with *Melody Maker* in October 1972, Jackie gave his version of how it all happened: 'I'd liked all their [Dominoes] records, particularly for their lead singer, so I went up to Ward and I told him I could outsing Clyde. Billy sent one of his fellows to listen to me at an amateur night at the Paradise Theatre in Detroit, and he said he'd try to help me. Four or five months [more likely weeks] later, when Clyde was leaving to form The Drifters, I got a call. I didn't dare tell my mother, though – I just packed up and left.' In the same interview, Jackie gave great credit to his mentor, Billy Ward: 'I learned just about everything I know from him. Breath control . . . and how to dance during one number and then come back and sing a ballad. That's hard, and they don't move too much on stage these days.'

Freda wasn't able to go to the formal audition at the Paradise Theatre because she had just given birth to their second child, Sandra Kay (born 29 January 1953). She recalls Jackie's colourful version of the event: 'Jack went down to audition and, even though he didn't know the song, he said that he could sing better than Clyde. He sang in front of Clyde and he made up the words, so Billy told him that since he had so much nerve, doing what he did, he could use him.'

Although Jackie won that night, Ward did not inform him immediately that he had a place in the group. Freda told me: 'Billy Ward told him he "may have something" for him. Then a few weeks later he sent him a telegram telling him to call collect. So we went to a phone booth, his mother and I. He called, and Ward told him to fly out to Las Vegas, where someone wouldl meet him and pick him up. He had actually fired Clyde, but the way the contract was he still had to sing with them until they got Jack ready. Jack got a chance to watch what Clyde did, although he didn't do exactly that. But he learned some of his mannerisms, how to work the song.'

Former Shaker Respess remembers when Jackie won: 'You'd think that Joe Louis had won a title fight, the way the city just went up when they heard that Jack won and was the new lead singer. The whole northside – where we lived around Oakland [Avenue] – people hit the streets, jumping and singing and shouting and screaming that Jack was the lead singer of The Dominoes. Oh, man! It was a festive occasion, everyone was singing and shouting, 'cause everyone knew him from church [from his Ever Ready Gospel group]. Everyone went bonkers.'

Ward became like a father to the 18-year-old. 'Billy Ward should get more credit than he probably has,' says Roquel 'Billy' Davis. 'He introduced discipline for the first time in his life. Jack didn't like discipline. Basically everything he had as a recording artist he had when he was 14. Billy Ward added discipline and polish. Who discovered Jack? I would say Billy Ward should have the credit. He gave him his first break, showcased him, took him on the road with him. That's what launched Jack. Billy Ward, a professional who was in a position to do something, recognised Jackie's ability. Without that he wouldn't have come to the notice of anyone.'

Jackie's stepfather, John Lee, had just procured a job for him at the Ford foundry on Woodward Avenue, close to the family home. When he was selected to join The Dominoes, he quit. Freda recollects: 'Jack had got a job at Henry Ford's, but only for two weeks. I picked up that pay cheque. He told me he was going to quit anyhow 'cause it was messing up his hands. He couldn't stand it. Jack told me when he was little he didn't want to do nothing else but sing; he was born to sing. He said he was going to be an entertainer – that was it. He wasn't going to do no hard work.'

The stories differ, but it is most likely that McPhatter only decided to leave the group after Jackie joined and after he learnt that Ward intended Jackie to share the lead tenor role with him. McPhatter had already clashed with Ward over his non-punctuality and drinking, and had a reputation for unruliness. Ward was a hard taskmaster and disciplinarian and, by his own admission, ran the group very much as a business. He had a saying: 'Two things destroy a man: booze and broads.'

Once Ward decided to sign Jackie up there was still a hurdle to be overcome. When Jackie had made the Dee Gee label recordings, he'd signed a management contract with Billy Mitchell, whose band had backed him on that unsuccessful 1952 recording session. Mitchell, therefore, could have made things difficult for Jackie. 'After Jack made the recordings with me, I had a contract on him,' he reflects. 'Billy Ward called me up. I said, "Yeah, I've got a contract, but if you want to use him go ahead."'

Regardless of his boasts, Jackie was captivated by Clyde McPhatter's expressive tenor voice. But Ward was adamant that despite the unabashed admiration 'he was never jealous of Clyde. Jack wanted to be somebody, and wasn't a dummy. Clyde had very bad diction, but Jack's was worse. I taught him how to pronounce syllables, how to appeal to an audience, soulfully. He was appreciative, but had a temper that wouldn't wait.' Ward taught Jackie voice projection and how to breathe while singing. From this point on, Jackie's articulation would be impeccable. In something of an understatement, Ward adds, 'Jack was a fine singer. I taught him; he was as good as anyone.' Jackie, using his nickname of 'Sonny', was at last receiving his big break under the influence of the strict disciplinarian and father figure he fondly referred to as 'Pap'. Although McPhatter remained with the group for a while after Jackie joined, there are no recordings featuring their voices together. In May 1953 McPhatter signed with Atlantic Records and formed The Drifters. Thereafter, Jackie took over as lead vocalist of The Dominoes.

Following an engagement in Las Vegas, Jackie shared an apartment with Ward in Greenwich Village. This caused some people to question Ward's motives and he remains very sensitive about this period; Jackie was 18, he was 31. 'Some people thought we had a thing going,' says Ward.

Among the changes he made, Billy Ward decided that the name Sonny, as Jackie was known, belonged back in Uncle Tom's cabin. He gave him the stage name of Jackie, which wasn't immediately appreciated. According to Ward, it was not until many years later that Jackie decided the name change was a wise one and thanked him for it. From now on in his career it would be Jackie, but to old friends and family he would always remain Sonny or Jack.

The Dominoes were especially popular amongst young black females. In New York City an active Dominoes Fan Club was headed by a vivacious and ambitious young girl, Harlean Harris. Harlean was born in White Plains, New York in 1939. She generally refuses interviews, but a lengthy one was conducted in 1979 by Al Duckett of *Sepia Magazine*, in which she says: 'I met him [Jackie] in 1953 when he became replacement for Clyde McPhatter, who had left Billy Ward And The Dominoes, and I started dating him in 1958. When we first met, I was the president of the Billy Ward And The Dominoes Fan Club – the New York chapter. I was 14 and there were 24 other pre-teen girls in the club. We were all positively wild about Clyde McPhatter, Billy Ward's lead singer.

'The Dominoes were coming to the Apollo Theatre in Harlem. All of our members became terribly upset when we learned that Clyde McPhatter was no longer with the group. The rumour was he had been replaced by someone named Wilson. We decided to show our resentment by going to the show and just sitting there up front and not giving The Dominoes the enthusiastic applause we usually gave them. We had made up our minds to stonewall it all the way in protest against the dismissal of our idol. We were determined not to accept this replacement. Being true McPhatter fans, we were just that adamant about it all. Needless to say, Clyde truly was one of the great talents. But I have to admit that when Jackie burst forth upon that stage, we forgot about Clyde.' Harlean described the first meeting with Jackie: 'I was one thrilled 14-year-old. When we went backstage, he was quite nice to us.' At this time she was having an affair with McPhatter. In Ward's own words, 'Harlean was Clyde's lady.' Harlean would come to play a big part in Jackie's tumultuous life.

Freda discovered that while Jackie was with The Dominoes, he and other entertainers were having affairs with underage girls. 'There was a lot of them out there,' recalls Freda. 'They were 13, 14 or 15. Their mothers would give them to the entertainers, because they wanted the money. These girls were serious, they didn't mind going to bed; they hoped they'd get pregnant. They wanted the money. Their mothers knew what they were about.'

Jackie got involved with one young model named Estelle 'Stella' Zuber, who is described as stunning. She would go on to be crowned 'Miss Empire State'. According to Freda, 'Estelle was another girl [and] Suzie was her mother. Estelle would fight with Harlean. Harlean would like to have torn her face up. I met Suzie; Suzie said she didn't know Jack was married. Jack lived in New York, he was always in New York. So Suzie gave him Estelle when she was 14. She told me this to my face. Estelle was mixed Spanish or something, but her mother was real black. She had short hair, but she tied it up in a pony tail. He lived with Estelle before he liked Harlean.' In fact, Jackie moved in to their family home at the invitation of Estelle's mother and would father her child. Another young woman that shared Jackie's affections was Juanita Jones. She would, some years later, become dramatically involved in a shooting incident that nearly cost Jackie his life. Juanita, Harlean and Estelle had a fierce rivalry over Jackie.

On 27 June 1953, a few weeks after his 19th birthday in New York City, Jackie recorded as lead tenor for The Dominoes for the first time with 'You Can't Keep A Good Man Down'. His next Dominoes session was at the King/Federal Studios in Cincinnati on 12 October 1953, where 11 tracks were cut, allowing him to display his phenomenal vocal range and phrasing.

In 1953, 'Rags To Riches' reached Number One for Tony Bennett. The Dominoes' version, with Jackie's lead vocals, made later that year, reaching the No Two spot on the R&B chart, but getting nowhere on the more lucrative, mainly white, Pop chart.

Another from the same session, 'One Moment With You', is a slow ballad in which Jackie's voice sounds like a young boy's or a woman's. Singing in the high female range was easy for him and the song is pure and powerful. 'Above Jacob's Ladder', 'Christmas In Heaven'and 'Until The

Real Thing Comes Along', which had previously been recorded by Ella Fitzgerald, were other tracks he sang lead on. He'd proven he was not just a good singer, but a major talent. Jackie was on his way. All he really needed was some exposure — which meant radio airplay.

In the early 1950s white radio stations generally did not play music by black artists, which was termed 'race music'. White groups and artists often made insipid cover versions of black artists' songs, but the audience had no opportunity to listen to the original music. However, musical crossover was not far away, and enabled tunes that were successful on the R&B charts (ie sold well in black record stores) to crossoverr chart well on the Pop charts (ie sold well in largely white record stores), where the real financial rewards lay.

Joe Glasser, who managed Lionel Hampton and Billie Holiday, also booked The Dominoes and kept them very busy on the gruelling touring circuit. In 1953, Jackie collapsed on stage during a performance with The Dominoes in Charlotte, North Carolina. He was suffering from chronic tonsillitis and had to be rushed to hospital. Freda remembers him being petrified lest surgery destroy his vocal ability: 'His tonsils were so bad we thought he wasn't going to be able to sing. They were ulcerated — there was pus and stuff. He would write notes instead of speaking, to save his voice so he could sing, and he'd be eating lemon and honey all day long. Show time comes. I said, 'You can't sing. 'He just looked me and smiled; Mr Wilson would sing just like a bird. What he was doing was resting his voice; he wasn't going to make no money talking.' They need not have feared; he sounded better than ever! 'He got his tonsils out at Sinai Hospital, but his voice didn't change. He was a happy person.'

Despite many recordings featuring Jackie's emotionally racked vocal treatments, The Dominoes had no chart success during 1954. Success for them came in the form of a two-year contract to perform at the Sahara Hotel in Las Vegas for an extraordinary 5000 dollars a week. They were supporting the popular Louis Prima and Keely Smith and played to packed houses, although not in the main room. Being black, they weren't permitted to enter the casino or restaurants and had to live on the west side of town.

Still, The Dominoes were becoming big time, in Las Vegas and elsewhere. Ward billed them as 'The World's Most Entertaining Vocal Attraction' and, by all accounts, they were a polished act with some very slick stage work and recordings, ranging from the earliest rock 'n'roll to great evergreen standards.

Ward ran a very tight ship and didn't fraternise with members of the group. He held himself above them, believing that this was the best way to encourage respect and discipline. As Freda says, 'Billy always looked after himself and tried to get the boys to do the same. If they disobeyed, they had a court session.' That discipline didn't exist in Jackie's private life. Before joining The Dominoes he had had two children with Freda, Jacqueline (Denise) and Sandra Kay (Sandy). During his time with the group they had another child, Jack Jnr, otherwise known as Jackie Jnr or Sonny Jnr, born on 13 February 1954. Another, Sabrina, was born in 1954 to Molly Byndon, a girlfriend from St Louis. The same year yet another child, Brenda was born.

Freda, generally with one or two of their children, lived for some time with Jackie in Las Vegas. 'White people rented their nice houses out to black entertainers, and they would go and stay somewhere else,' she recalls. 'They had washers and dryers. [Heavyweight boxer] Joe Louis lived down the street. Indians, all the different coloured people, stayed on the black side of town.' Freda has pleasant memories of their time there and saw plenty of Dominoes performances. She recalls proudly: 'When they came out they looked so pretty. They were wearing those suits with the long back jacket. Jack's eyes were sparkling. He was young and pretty. The girls were going crazy; they were screaming and screaming. Milton Merle and other Dominoes members were older than Jack. When Jack got through there wasn't a dry eye in the place; even the ones who were drinking the wine and talking. He was also excellent in the background. He sang first tenor-falsetto or second tenor; he could even sing a light bass, right down, if he wanted to. He was a good baritone and could blend in with the other guys. He learned a lot by looking and listening to other entertainers.

'We'd go to the Key Club. They'd be singing; Jackie'd be singing. First he'd do his thing, then Sammy Davis Jnr would do his thing.' When socialising with Jackie, Freda knew to remain in the background. If she did have any criticisms, she kept them to herself or made him aware of them when there was nobody around. 'I didn't know the other entertainers personally. Jack didn't like me to run around; you just sat down and acted like a lady.'

Ward correctly observes that 'Jackie had a temper that wouldn't wait'. He expected obedience and respect from his children, and from Freda as well. In 1955, when daughter Denise was only four, Jackie arrived home one morning after working at the Las Vegas Sahara all night. 'He'd learned something a little different and was anxious to practise it, but Denise interrupted him and he became angry,' Freda recalls. 'He told her to get out of there. He threw her across there to the couch; she was petrified.' Denise always maintained a deep love and fascination, to the point of obsession, for her father, but maintains that he expected strict obedience from his children. 'He used to tell me "Wilsons don't cry",' says Denise. 'He said, "You can breathe, I just don't want to see tears." He said, "Not in front of anybody. Go in your bedroom, or whatever. But if someone is looking, just because you got hurt or embarrassed, don't show that you're weak. Wilsons are not weak!"' The latter phrase sums up Jackie's philosophy on life; he had a ton of pride.

Jackie's sexual demands were still occasionally too much for Freda: 'When I'd just had Sandy, I was not going to let him. He said, "I just want to bring you something for the baby." He comes over there [to the hospital]; I tried to get rid of him.' Freda also became tired of being pregnant on an almost full-time basis and sought advice from a woman claiming she knew how to terminate an unwanted pregnancy. 'She told me to drink half a pint of turpentine, or sit on a hot pail of water – I did all of that – as hot as I could stand it. It made me get drunk and sick and throw up. The doctor said it would have killed me if I hadn't thrown up, but the baby probably would have been all right.' It was bad advice and not the episode was not repeated.

From around the same time, Freda recalls a beautiful event which typified Jackie and the esteem in which the people of the neighbourhood regarded him: 'One time my mother cooked a whole bunch of food. I said, "I'll give Jack my share."' Freda was pregnant at the time and, with Jackie's huge appetite, the food was never enough. 'He'd just walk in the BBQ place – it was on Oakland, too. He'd just put his hand up there and take the BBQ ribs – it was hot, too – and bring them home. He took so many ribs.' Jackie had not forgotten his theft from the small shop. Freda explained how he attempted to atone: 'So when he "made it" and he came back, we went up there to Oakland. He said, 'Miss M, how much do I owe you for when Freda was pregnant? All she wanted was BBQ ribs, and I know I took a lot.' She said, 'Jackie, you don't owe me anything; it's just so sweet that you remembered me and came by.'So he gave her 500 dollars anyhow. He said, 'You never came to my home and you knew where I lived; you never said nothing.'

Their first son, Jack Jnr, was born in February 1954. Freda recalls: 'When Jack Jnr was born he had grey eyes and red hair and freckles. My mother-in-law called Jack and said, 'You'd better check this baby out.' She said, 'I think it's mixed.' Now, I didn't even know he [Jackie] was coming; I was upstairs. Someone said, "There's a limousine outside." He didn't stop downstairs to say hello to his mother or anything. He bounced up those steps. He said, 'Get out of my way.' He turned the baby over and looked at its hands and fingers.' Apparently this convinced a suspicious Jackie that the baby was indeed his.

Whilst domineering at home, at work it was Ward who maintained strict rules about what group members could and couldn't do. But Jackie was never one for rules, as Freda knew. 'There was nothing Jack could do. Billy Ward had been a lieutenant in the army and he kept The Dominoes on the army routine: they couldn't drink, they didn't socialise with people, only each other, they couldn't be seen with this person or that person, they couldn't be seen over in the black side of town carousing around, they couldn't be going up to clubs and things there. Jack wanted to leave the motel, but couldn't.'

Once, Freda was staying in Las Vegas while The Dominoes were playing the Sahara Hotel on a six-month engagement. The discipline must have become too much for Jackie and he got bored. 'This particular time we were staying at a motel,' says Freda.

'I had Jackie Jnr with us that year. Jack worked days then, and alternative nights from six to twelve and twelve to six in the morning. He'd get off at night; he'd get up and put on black pants, black shirt, black hat, black shoes . . . black everything. One night I said, "Where you going?" "I'm going out!" That night, when he came back, I didn't say nothing. He jumped in the bed and he said, "Get back in the bed and if anyone knocks on the door, I've been here all night."

'Pretty soon there was a knock on the door. It was the police. They said, "Jackie Wilson in here?" I said, "Yeah." They said, "How long 's he been here?" I said, "Mr Wilson's been here all night." Someone said they recognised him in their room; he was taking a few things off the dresser. They were chasing him, he jumped over some fences. He'd been taking cologne, combs, any kind of jewellery . . . it wasn't worth nothing.' Freda became increasingly nervous about her husband's strange behaviour. 'I was getting scared. I thought Jack was losing his mind. I didn't want him to get in bad trouble – get shot, or something. Those people had guns out there.'

Ward wasn't fooled by Jackie's alibi, because he soon came to the room and said he wanted to see the 'black bandit'. He was most annoyed at Jackie's prank and called a meeting. Jackie said to Freda, 'Do you think I'm crazy? I'm not going to tell him I did it, and you better never tell him I did it.' Jackie needed Freda as his alibi, but she was nothing like the practised liar he was. She recalls, 'We had a meeting with Billy Ward; he was upset. Every answer Jack gave, Billy Ward was looking straight in my eyes. I was trying to look at his eyes, so my eyes were wavering. He said, "You shut up." So Jack shut up. "I want the truth; just what's the truth?" That's what he told me and I gave it to him. Billy always knew when Jack was lying, but he didn't want him screwed up down there. He sent me back to Detroit.' Ward believed that if Jackie didn't have his family around he could be kept under closer scrutiny.

But Ward wasn't able to completely eliminate Jackie's excesses; he continued to drink without Ward's knowledge. 'They say you can't smell vodka,' explains Freda. 'He always knew how to do good oral hygiene. He'd gargle and scrape his tongue with the bread knife; he'd work and work. They never smelled it on him for a long time, neither. He'd sing better and better.' This bizarre habit of scraping his tongue with a knife remained with him throughout his life. 'He conformed as long as he was with Billy Ward,' Freda continues. 'They were primarily in Las Vegas six months of the year, the rest of the time they were in California, some place like that. They only came back to Chicago, or New York to the theatres, like the Brooklyn Fox, and they did a lot of clubs. There's a lot of Irish people there – that's when he'd sing "When Irish Eyes Are Smiling" so pretty. He'd also do "Danny Boy", but he'd been doing "Danny Boy" all his life.'

Another incident, involving Jackie and Ward's fiancée, further tested the relationship between mentor and singer. Freda remembers it this way: 'The time he went out with Billy's fiancée, Jack was so mad at him [Ward]. Billy went out to California on a business meeting. Billy really loved that lady. She went out with Jack. I don't know how Billy knew it; I knew it, everyone knew it. Billy had a meeting that day; he interviewed Jack. Jack lied and lied. Billy got it out of her. Billy beat her up; he gave her some back-hand licks and said, "And I was going to marry you – I can't even trust you with my own people. You let him talk you into it; something like this destroys our lives, and you let it!" He wasn't mad at Jack. He was just a little person [Freda is not referring to Jackie's physical stature but to his social position, compared with the famous Billy Ward]. Why'd she go out with this guy? With one of his men, his young guy. It really upset him, it hurt him; he really liked her. She had a ring and everything. Couldn't she close her legs for a few minutes?' Ward broke off with his fiancée after that.

Jackie's desire to hurt Ward, as this episode demonstrates, sometimes caused deep hurt to others. But despite their differences Ward did a lot to bring out Jackie's full potential, a fact even Jackie later came to appreciate. Says Freda: 'Billy gave Jackie an autographed photo after he got to Las Vegas and it said, "For a rough hewn stone whom I am polishing into a diamond." He ran a very strict group and he did a good job with Jack. He cut out the drinking [well, to some extent]. He stopped everything. Jack thanked Billy Ward for a lot of things even though at the time he didn't appreciate it, because he wanted to do what he wanted to do.'

In later years, Jackie gave credit to Ward for grooming him into the performer he became. The four years he spent with The Dominoes were the best kind of apprenticeship he could have hoped for. In the New York radio interview with DJ Norman Nite, Jackie said, 'I can give full credit for that [my vocal style] to Mr Billy Ward; he was a vocal coach at Carnegie Hall. I studied under him for two [in truth four] years.' The only catch was, Jackie was not yet earning big money. For example, despite the 5000 dollars per week contract with the Sahara Hotel in Las Vegas, Jackie's share of that was only about 90 dollars.

The Dominoes played Las Vegas for many years, both with and without Jackie. Ward was not happy with the contractual arrangement with King Records in Cincinnati, but the contract didn't expire until 1955. Nevertheless some musical gems were recorded by them, with Jackie singing lead. His vocal gymnastics dominate on the ballads 'Until The Real Thing Comes Along', 'Love Me Now Or Let Me Go', 'Tenderly' and an up-tempo 'St Louis Blues'.

At that time the radio airwaves were dominated by white vocalists such as Guy Mitchell (who also grew up in Detroit) and Perry Como. The year 1955 was also the time that a white singer from Jackie's home neighbourhood, Bill Haley, led the vanguard of the social revolution that went by the name of rock 'n' roll. His record, 'Rock Around The Clock', remained No One for eight weeks. Haley was singing a form of music that, although new to whites, had been familiar to blacks for some time as rhythm and blues.

Despite the Dominoes selling millions of records, however, only one song featuring Jackie as lead made it into the Pop charts. The beautiful 'St Therese Of The Roses' reached No 13 in 1956, remaining in the charts for six weeks. It was Jackie's first hit and also the first single The Dominoes recorded on Decca, for whom he also sang lead on the 1930s Inkspots hit 'To Each His Own', since leaving King/Federal. Later they had a short stint on Jubilee where Jackie recorded two more singles, which didn't chart.

Jackie may well have listened to and admired Al Jolson, Mario Lanza, Roy Hamilton and blues master 'Good Rockin'' Roy Brown, but he didn't sound like any of them. There was no confusing Jackie's voice with that of anyone else. In Freda's words, 'Jack liked anyone who could sing, but he knew he was the greatest.'

In the eyes of his friends and fans, Jackie was now the star they had always known he would be and his homecomings were a celebration. A distant relative of his, Lawrence Payton, of The Four Tops, recalls, 'I remember Jackie when he used to come into town, when he was with Billy Ward And The Dominoes. It was always the highlight of our year. He was sort of our mentor, besides being our best friend and family. He was the guy we were all impressed with and made us want to be in show business. He came by the neighbourhood to get all of us, take us over to his mother's house on Cottage Grove and play all the things he was coming out with. He'd play his records for us and all that stuff. I remember the record "Jacob's Ladder". It was so amazing for us; it was more like a Pop hit. At that time everything was rhythm and blues, but that song had religious connotations. I thought, "What are you guys trying to do, man?"'

Around the same time, another major musical force was emerging. On 6 July 1954, Elvis Presley made his first commercial recordings at Sam Phillips' Memphis Recording Service studios, although it was not until the next year that he gained national attention. Elvis was a poor white boy who sounded and moved like a black, and was greatly influenced by the black gospel and R&B music he listened to on the radio or in local clubs. Jackie was only seven months Elvis's senior, but he had first recorded in 1952. He would have a somewhat harder slog on the road to success than Elvis.

At the Memphis Recording Service studios in December 1956, owner Sam Phillips kept the tape rolling while Carl Perkins, Jerry Lee Lewis, Johnny Cash and Elvis Presley – 'The Million Dollar Quartet' – were fooling around and singing a few of their numbers. On this recording, Elvis talks about a group he'd seen in Las Vegas: Billy Ward And The Dominoes. Elvis first performed in Las Vegas in April 1956 and had bombed with the middle-aged audience. Later that year he found time to go to see The Dominoes perform. On the recording, the impression that Jackie made on Elvis comes through not only in what he says about him (although he has no idea of Jackie's name), but also in the excitement in his voice and the fact that he returns to the topic despite others in the studio trying to discuss different matters. In Elvis's own words: 'I heard this guy in Las Vegas –

Billy Ward and his Dominoes. There's a guy out there who's doin' a take-off of me: "Don't Be Cruel". He tried so hard, till he got much better, boy; much better than that record of mine.' Elvis goes on: 'He was real slender – he was a coloured guy. He got up there. He had it a little slower than me . . . He got the backin', the whole quartet. They got the feelin' on it . . . Grabbed that microphone, went down to the last note, went all the way down to the floor, man, lookin' straight up at the ceiling. Man, he cut me . . . He had already done "Hound Dog" an' another one or two, and he didn't do too well, y'know; he was trying too hard. But he hit that "Don't Be Cruel" and he was tryin' so hard till he got better, boy. Wooh! Man, he sang that song. That quartet standin' in the background, y'know – ba-domp ba-domp. And he was out there cuttin' it, man, had all 'm goin' way up in the air. I went back four nights straight and heard that guy do that. Man, he sung hell outta that song, and I was under the table lookin' at him. "Get him off! Get him off!"'

Levi Stubbs, who has been lead singer of The Four Tops for more than 45 years, recalls how 'Elvis Presley used to watch Jackie in Vegas every night. Jackie was in the lounge at the Hilton, and Elvis would come down to watch. Jackie was one of greatest that ever did it; vocally . . . it just won't come along again.' Later, Elvis would get to know Jackie and they became good friends. Elvis went to see Jackie perform whenever he was able and used some of Jackie's stage techniques in his performances. Jackie would later say, magnanimously, 'I took as much from Elvis as he took from me.'

Another relationship based on mutual give and take was that of Jackie and his mentor, Ward. Late in 1957, Jackie informed him that the time had come, after four years with the group, to go solo. He was getting restless for a career of his own. Although Ward claims that he didn't try to hold either McPhatter or Jackie back from leaving the group, it must have been disheartening for him to see them go. Freda confirms that Ward didn't stand in Jackie's way: 'Billy Ward said he'd help him at anything he wanted to do. Billy felt that it was time for him to go and do his thing. Jack was sort of a driving personality and he wanted to do something himself, but he didn't want the responsibility. He was determined to succeed. He could do anything he wanted.' Ward was probably also losing control over Jackie. Says Freda, 'Jack was going to do what he was going to do.'

The Dominoes may well have been the first group in rock 'n'roll. Clyde McPhatter, Sam Cooke and Sonny Til (of The Orioles group), along with Jackie, should be recognised as having paved the way and set the standard for the many singers who followed them.

Interviewed in October 1972 by *Melody Maker* about his leaving The Dominoes in 1957, Jackie said, 'I'd learned all I could, and it seemed that Billy [Ward] wasn't aiming to go out any further than Las Vegas, which was where we were spending most of our time. I hadn't had a chance to play in the black field at all.' Las Vegas audiences were, in the main, white, as was much of the music performed by the group.

LEAVING THE SUCCESS AND SECURITY of The Dominoes was risky. Jackie had been part of a well-known group, yet was barely recognised outside the Detroit nightclub circuit. Solo, there was no guarantee that he would achieve the fame he sought. Freda explains some of the difficulties: 'When Jack got back from The Dominoes, he thought he was going to sing with Levi [Stubbs and The Four Tops], but his voice was too similar to Levi's, and they were already established. So he couldn't sing with them and the guys he used to sing with couldn't sing any more, except JJ [Johnny Jones]. The Four Tops had the smooth sound they were trying to push and Jack was still doing his blues stuff.' It wasn't going to be smooth sailing, as Freda explains: 'The Twenty Grand Club wouldn't let him sing there because he didn't have a group. So he'd sing at Phelps Lounge over on Oakland; when he'd made it as a star he'd still perform there.'

In the early 1950s Mario Lanza, an Italian-American, was amazing audiences worldwide with his extraordinary tenor voice. Lanza wasn't singing opera; he was singing American romantic ballads in pseudo-operatic style. Jackie was impressed and, what's more, he was able to sing with the same operatic quality, but with an even broader vocal range. Neither singer was better than the other – Jackie just sang with more raw soul and passion. Jackie took Freda to see the 1951 movie *The Great Caruso*, starring Mario Lanza as the Italian opera star, Caruso. Jackie immediately started emulating Lanza: 'Mario Lanza played that guy Caruso,' remembers Freda. 'Lanza was Jack's idol. Jack could almost break glass when he was practising his Mario Lanza stuff; he could make you cry doing that. So he got the [sheet] music, although he couldn't read music, but he'd remember how it sounded and then he'd find anyone who could play piano. He'd go down to Saint Antoine and have someone play this music.

> His chest really did expand about two inches. You could see it
> swelling when he was going to let all that power out; and then his
> voice would come all the way from his stomach. It was really
> fantastic and personally, at first I liked those songs better than
> anything else, because they showed his full potential. But like they
> say in the business, 'It's not commercial.' He still loved blues, that's
> why every chance he got they had to put some blues in, or he
> wasn't going to do nothing. That was his first love – blues, gospel,
> and then rock 'n' roll. But he really wanted to do Caruso-style
> songs: his diction was always good, and his enunciation . . .

Johnny Jones was now out of the army and, as usual, willing to assist his
friend, who he knew was going to 'make it'. As Freda puts it, 'JJ was
always there. He helped Jack get his stuff together. They'd pawn their stuff
– everybody pawned their stuff. When Jack got back from The Dominoes
he had a little money coming in, but we needed more. He needed some
[promotional] pictures of himself. He didn't want to look like he came back
from The Dominoes and didn't have nothing. Everybody was helping every
way they could, so that he would look good.' He mostly needed impressive
clothes, for both on and off the stage.

At the time, the Mecca of black nightclubs in Detroit was the prestigious
Flame Show Bar. The acts were generally black entertainers from Detroit
or elsewhere, such as 'Little Miss Sharecropper' (LaVern Baker), Ivory Joe
Hunter, Louis Jordan, T-Bone Walker, Dinah Washington, Billie Holiday,
John Lee Hooker and popular local, 'Singin'' Sammy Ward.

The Flame was owned by Morris and Sally 'Sal' Wasseman and run by
Albert 'Al' Green. All three were Jewish. Green also managed talented
singers; the white crying-crooning specialist Johnnie Ray, LaVern Baker and
Della Reese, who were regular and well-loved acts at the club. Green was
to become instrumental in the advancement of Jackie's career. The Flame
was luxurious, with a sunken entertainment floor and a long bar, and the
tables grouped around the stage in semi-circular fashion. The club also had
the unique custom of patrons expressing appreciation of each act by banging
wooden gavels on the table tops. Patrons generally dressed flamboyantly;
this was the place to be seen. In a word, it was class. There was a particular
Mob feel to the Flame, with many believing it to be owned by the powerful
Detroit underworld; certainly it had that association about it.

For more than 16 years, the band leader was the musical genius Maurice King (with his band, The Wolverines). The well-liked and highly regarded black arranger would later be influential in creating the Motown sound which would bring Detroit's musical talents to the attention of the world. He admired Jackie, and the two got along well. Working for many years under King was saxophonist Thomas 'Beans' Bowles, who was also destined to be a major musical force with Motown. 'They didn't let Jackie in the Twenty Grand [Club]; they wanted the Las Vegas, up-scale music style. They wanted to attract the middle-class blacks who had a little more money to spend, rather than the blues people. There were only a few blues people there at that time that made it in that circuit. BB King was on the fringes, but T-Bone Walker and Big Joe Turner were the guys that were drawing people.

'Al Green wasn't what you'd call a likeable person himself . . . a Humphrey Bogart type. He was very direct and didn't give a damn about nobody.' Still, Green appears to have been well respected and it required a particular toughness to succeed in the music business. 'He was a hard, upfront cookie, but he'd give you the coat off his back. He gave [jazz saxophonist and band leader] Charlie Parker a coat 'cause he was walking around cold in the snow just two weeks before Parker died [in March 1955]. He was a good guy, gangster type; we all got along well with him.

'It was common knowledge in them days that the Jews and Italians were involved [with each other] – cross-relations. Money and contacts were what they had in common. The outlet for entertainment has always been gangster-controlled. Nightclubs had always been under the auspices of the underworld . . . still are,' reveals Bowles. William Weatherspoon who, with Alonzo Tucker, wrote 'As Long As I Live' and 'Why Can't You Be Mine' for Jackie's very first album, plus some tunes with the founder of Motown Berry Gordy, relates: 'Al Green was like the Mafia; big cigar and all that. Al was probably fronting at the Flame Show for some other people. Al was very powerful; when he talked to men they acted like children.'

Fatefully, through the Flame Show Bar, Jackie reconnected with Roquel 'Billy' Davis, his friend since the early street corner singing days. The meeting would be fortuitous for both men. Davis was raised in the northend of Detroit. His first cousin, Lawrence Payton of The Four Tops, shared the same house. Jackie lived within two miles of Davis and was treated like one of the family. Davis was therefore familiar with Jackie and his singing talent. Davis puts it this way: 'Billy Ward might say Jackie was a 'diamond in the rough', but to his fans and the people he grew up with on the northend, he was the Hope Diamond. He gave hope to all of us who aspired to become singers. He was a true diamond.

'Jackie came back after leaving Billy Ward and played the Paradise Theatre. The emotion was always there; he could value one word – the word 'so'; and you'd understand exactly where he was coming from emotionally. [He had] impeccable phrasing, because he had such control over his voice. He could change octave anywhere in the song; that was total control,' Davis explained.

Gwen Gordy, sister of Berry (who later founded the Motown record label), worked at the Flame Show Bar where she had the hat check, photograph and cigarette concession with her sister Anna. Both were young, attractive women who established excellent contacts, later to be useful for their now-famous brother. Davis had a relationship with Gwen, and Green would let him use his office on Woodward Avenue for songwriting because the office had a piano in it. It was to Davis that Jackie first came when he set off to establish himself as a solo artist, and through Davis and Gwen that he was introduced to Green and granted an audition. 'It was my impression that Al Green was the manager of the Flame Show Bar and may have had a controlling interest,' says Davis. 'Green was quiet, reserved and strong, knowing a lot about a lot of things. He had a lot of connections due to Johnnie Ray and LaVern Baker.'

'Jack went to the Twenty Grand Club but they didn't want him without a group,' explains Freda. 'So he said, "I'm going to sing by myself." He went to the Flame and that's when Al Green listened to him by himself. Green had a good eye and ear for talent, and promptly signed Jackie, with himself in the role of manager. He advanced Jackie a little money to get some stuff to get himself together, because all his uniforms belonged to The Dominoes.'

As Davis establishes, Green's major client was Johnnie Ray. Born in 1927, Ray sang with the power-charged vocal delivery of a black soul artist (quite unimpeded by the hearing aid he wore). He hit the big time in 1951 with 'Cry', which held No One position for 11 weeks. It was a song which had an R&B flavour and was very much a forerunner to the popular music that soon followed.

LaVern Baker – who incidentally had taught Johnny Ray how to sing blues – was Green's second major client. Born Delores Baker in 1929, she began performing at 17 as 'Little Miss Sharecropper'. Baker had two local hits in 1952 before signing to Atlantic Records and achieving numerous R&B and pop hits from 1955 to 1965. As a performer, Baker was in many ways the female version of Jackie. She could make any song uniquely hers and had a powerful voice. She was also versatile, going from up-tempo R&B to jazz and Latin numbers with ease.

To help organise his roster of stars, Green had a few 'assistants'; Harry Balk and Irving 'Irve' Maconic, both always looking for an angle – a fast way to make a buck. Money also prevented Jackie appearing live as often as before, as Beans Bowles recalls. 'Jackie wasn't a regular at the Flame Bar,' reports the former Flame Show musician. 'He appeared there very little because, number one, he couldn't get the money he wanted and, as Al Green was his manager, he wouldn't let him on for no money. When Al got him Jackie'd just left The Dominoes; he had no hits, he wasn't a big star. But they asked a lot of [appearance] money for him because of The Dominoes work. His singing of 'Danny Boy' they still talk about.'

Investment in the act was working, however. On stage Jackie always looked the part, favouring tight-fitting suits and expensive silk shirts. In the fashion of the time, he had his hair processed to straighten it and also had it coiffed in a high style. 'Once his hair was processed it was fixed,' remembers Freda. 'It was done with a chemical [lye]; it would last a long time. He knew how to fix himself. His mother would get him some clothes and she'd make him look good.' The use of lye caused a burning sensation to the scalp which was quite painful. With hair cream to keep it in place, Freda said, it was 'as hard as a rock' to touch.

Having learned footwork in the boxing ring Jackie was a natural mover, although not a natural when it came to dancing with a partner. Freda recalls: 'He could not dance; we'd go to a dance or a party and do the foxtrot, just like they taught you; just straight up-and-down foxtrot. He didn't add nothing to it. He was glad when you could forget about what the lady was doing.' But most who saw Jackie perform on stage would agree that he was unsurpassed; pure grace. He would appear to glide out on stage and perform spins and splits with consummate ease, executed flawlessly after innumerable hours of practice.

In the 1940s and 1950s tap dancing was the rage and one of the best exponents around Detroit was Ziggie Johnson, who also ran a dance school. In later years he MC'd at the Twenty Grand Ballroom and the Flame Show Bar. Freda recalls: 'Ziggie Johnson was the MC at the Flame Show Bar. He was watching Jackie sing one night; he just came down to our table and he said, "Look, Jack, you need a little help on your dance routine, so why don't you come to my school?" I wanted to see what Jack did, but I said "no", he might be embarrassed for me to see. I waited until he got it together and had his stage routine together. He taught himself that little twirl.

'Ziggie helped him put his little routine together. He told him to do his boxing steps and taught him how to do the splits so it became second nature to him. He could do it without missing a note. He could always throw that mike around; I used to think, sometimes, when he was a little high, that he was going to miss it or fall off the stage, but he never did. Ziggie taught him to do whatever he felt comfortable with and try little things, and then put 'em all together. First he started with a single spin. Then he did the double spin. Then he did the triple spin, and I don't care how high he was, he never failed.' Their daughter Denise agrees. 'My father was not your average good-stepping black person,' she admits. 'He was out of step, out of tune. Nobody knows it.' Yet to see Jackie on stage was to see a graceful dancer; pure poetry in motion.

Jackie lacked only one thing at this stage – suitable songs that he could turn into hits, which is where Roquel 'Billy' Davis and Berry Gordy came in. Davis had been given a break in the most amazing way. In 1956 he had sent a tape of some his compositions to Chess Records in Chicago, sung by his Four Aims group. Davis explains the response he received: 'Phil Chess wrote back in longhand, "We like your tape of the Aims, we'd like you to come to Chicago and give me a call."' Davis caught a bus to Chicago: 'I called Phil Chess. What they really wanted were the songs, not for the Aims, but for The Flamingos and The Moonglows. Chess was an R&B company; they thought nothing of us as a group, or Levi Stubbs's marvellous voice.'

Davis's musical career further progressed when he combined his songwriting skills with those of Berry Gordy. Davis: 'Al Green, because of Gwen working at the Flame Show bar, told me Berry Gordy was coming to his office and had some songs. One Saturday Berry came to the office with his reel tape. He had six to eight songs. He was heavily influenced by jazz music and had early basic piano lessons. I said to Berry I thought he had some good ideas, but that he'd have to make his material a bit more commercial, melodically and lyrically. It was in the jazzy or blues – down, negative – vein, but he didn't want to change anything. So when he left that meeting he was a little upset, but he came back that Saturday, or another Saturday. I remember him coming up, no one there again but myself, but with a slightly different attitude. I said, "Have you written any songs?" "Yes, I've written a couple." But he was always suspicious. I was working on an idea when he came and we ended up working on a tune together. That meeting then led us to eventually writing together.

'There was a piano in Al Green's office. Berry said, "How are we going to do this?" I said, "Whatever chord changes come into your mind, play them. I'll work on the melody, you play what you want to play and I'll start singing words I think are going to make sense." We developed that kind of working habit: "Here's an idea" and "let's discuss the feeling of it." We'd hear something we loved and write that down . . . words, any words. We couldn't write music, so we either recorded it or remembered it. I can remember 150 of my songs; I can sing them all. Being street singers, we stored them all [mentally].'

While working at the Lincoln-Mercury plant and being a talented boxer, Berry Gordy decided he'd prefer to achieve fame and fortune as a songwriter. He was eight years older than Davis and four-to-five years older than Jackie. His sister Gwen evidently believed in him and there was a strong love between them. 'Gwen would give him money when he wasn't working. They looked out for each other,' says Davis.

Looking out for each other worked in other ways too. 'We both had a lot of songs, but we decided to become partners in every sense of the word,' Davis continues. 'We combined all of our efforts – all the current efforts became *our* effort. All the songs we wrote became ours, whether we collaborated on them or not, and it remained that way. I never tried, and Berry has never tried, to separate out who did what. I only get a third on some since we cut Gwen in, but seeing she never wrote a note, we didn't really have to cut her in. It [songwriting and re-publishing copyrights] only comes up once in 25 years, but I continued to cut her in on most of the songs; I have no regrets about that. The publishing rights I do have some feelings about, but I can't change one without the other. It means two-thirds of the rights, including two-thirds of publishing rights, go to Joebete [Berry Gordy's music publishing company].' Songwriters must share royalties 50–50 with their music publishers.

Jackie had the talent, they had the songs, but they all still needed the right connections. Eventually it came together, as Davis points out. 'I introduced him to the Chess brothers. They didn't like him. They naturally regretted it.' Even Chess were not infallible when it came to recognising great talent. Davis tried another approach. 'I took him to Al Green,' he says. 'Al signed him up.' Green had good connections with the New York recording industry and, equally, with the Mob. Davis and Gordy had the songs. Freda remembers, 'When they started off, just Berry and Jack would be rehearsing at Berry's father's little newspaper shop.' There was a piano at the print shop on St Antoine Street.'

Around Al Green's office at the time was a young man, Nathanial 'Nat' Tarnopol, who many thought was Al Green's partner, though subordinate is more accurate. In reality Tarnopol was little more than a 'gofer' for Green. He earned a living cleaning a car lot, selling tyres and, at one time, even selling ice popsicles. But he would soon assume a major role in Jackie's career, becoming his manager throughout much of it.

Nat was born in January 1931. In 1957, his mother died and he lived with his Aunt Lena. Tarnopol's son Paul recalls: 'At that time my dad was helping at Mercury [Records, where The Platters recorded]. My dad met Al Green at the Flame Show Bar; he was working for Al. His parents came to the USA from Europe. They were close to orthodox, very conservative, Jewish. Nat sold car tyres, but his love was the music business. He was into black music; he'd listen to R&B in the basement. Nat knew Jackie before he came to Al Green [this may be so, but there is no record of any relationship]. Al was nervous about taking Jackie on. Jackie was a wild card at times, even back then.'

Says Beans Bowles, 'At the first part of it, Tarnopol was a guy learning the business. He worked for Al Green. They eventually went into business together; I suppose Green must have sponsored him. He evolved out of his relationship with Al Green. Nat was just a fascinating, energetic young man. We kinda all liked him. He wasn't like he ended up being. He started dealing in the big money and it kinda distorted his thinking. People that are very aggressive are generally not liked very much anyway, but he caught on quick. As he got started he knew where to find the money.' Finding the money was what it was all about, as producing stars and recording hits was highly speculative.

Roquel 'Billy' Davis came to know Nat Tarnopol well: 'The Jewish people totally controlled the music industry,' he recalls, 'especially in those days. I didn't think Nat would recognise talent if it looked him in the face; but it was Green who was so well connected.'

First, in the new role of Jackie's manager, it was necessary for Green to arrange for him to have a recording contract. He had signed R&B singer LaVern Baker with the progressive Atlantic label, while Johnnie Ray had been signed to OKeh Records. Despite this, for Jackie, Green first approached Bob Thiele of Decca Records, in New York. Thiele had extensive music production experience, having worked with Teresa Brewer (who later became his wife), Pearl Bailey, The McGuire Sisters and Lawrence Welk. In 1957 he had signed Buddy Holly And The Crickets.

Green had previously taken Thiele to the Apollo Theatre to see Billy Ward And The Dominoes. Thiele vividly remembers seeing Jackie for the first time: 'I freaked out, "This kid is amazing!" Jackie was utterly fantastic. This guy was not only a great singer, almost in the James Brown style, but also a great performer. [Singers like that] are entertainers as well as creators. Jackie could do it all.' This is high praise from one who has worked with the best of them. Thiele claims he said to Green, 'I'd love to sign that guy Jackie Wilson' and that Green said, 'You've got him.' There is some ambiguity here: Roquel 'Billy' Davis is adamant that it was he who put Jackie in touch with Green – after Jackie had left The Dominoes. Nevertheless, there is no dispute that it was Thiele who signed Jackie to Decca. He continues: 'We prepared an agreement between Decca/Coral and Jackie Wilson through his manager, Al Green. Green was staying at the Taft Hotel. When the contract was ready to be signed, he said he'd meet me there the next day at 9 a.m. Everything was to be signed and Jackie would be on Decca/Coral at that point. So I rang up to his room and Nat Tarnopol answered the phone and said, "Al Green died last night." I said, "Look, I've got his contract." Nat came down and said, "I can handle it; I'll take care of things." Jackie must have signed it and Nat signed it. All of a sudden, Jackie Wilson was signed to Decca/Coral.' It was a most opportune event for Tarnopol who, at that point, had no artist management experience.

As Davis told Robert Pruter of Goldmine magazine, 'A lot of people thought Nat was Al's partner, but that was not true. He was around the office a lot and assisted Al, but by Nat having the image of a partner, he stepped in and assumed the management of Wilson.' In a radio interview on New York's WCBS (FM) with DJ 'Mr Music', Norman N Nite, Jackie discussed his involvement with both Green and Tarnopol: 'Well, actually I met Nat through Al Green, who was manager of LaVern Baker at the time. We were all from Detroit. Nat was a young, hot-headed kid who wanted to get ahead and was doing all the publishing for Al Green. Al Green took me when I left The Dominoes and he started to manage me. And he got me a contract, through LaVern Baker, with Decca, which was for Brunswick. And then, God rest his soul, he died and Nat decided he was going to try his hand. Although there was several other guys around, Nat just took me by the arm one day with his raincoat over his arm and just ran. I never will forget . . . we ran.'

Certainly, before Green's death Tarnopol, who at the time was still living with his aunt, had few prospects. In Freda's words: 'Nat didn't know hardly anything. He was sweeping the used car lot. At the time, Jackie was singing mostly at the Flame. Jackie said, "I don't know if he knows anything about the music business." But Jackie wanted to keep everything going.' So he entrusted his career to Tarnopol. And, having signed with Decca, Jackie and Tarnopol moved to New York. Eddie Pride recalls the period: 'Jack never had any education. When he went to New York, Tarnopol bought him an old 'raggedy' Cadillac and put some money in his pocket. Tarnopol robbed Jack blind.' Pride believed his childhood friend deserved better.

The conservative Decca management preferred rock 'n'roll singers not to record on the primary Decca label. 'The company didn't like the fact that he would be on Decca or Coral,' says Thiele. 'They probably didn't think a black singer should be on a white label. They felt it could look bad, so I remembered we owned the trade name 'Brunswick'. That's what I had to do with Buddy Holly. Decca thought that they were inappropriate to be with mainstream artists. We put [Buddy Holly And] The Crickets on Brunswick. Later we put Buddy on Coral and The Crickets remained on Brunswick.'

Tarnopol set up an office in the Brill Building on New York's Broadway. 'The Brill' is a beautiful, large and impressive building then totally occupied by songwriters, music publishers and people involved in the music business. It was the era's version of 'Tin Pan Alley', which formerly was located nearby. In the office next door were the Goodman brothers, Harry and Gene, who had the musical publishing businesses Regent Publishing and Arc Publishing, through which most of Jackie's hits were, and are, published. Another of the brothers was world-famous big band leader Benny Goodman. The Goodman connection with Brunswick is both long and strong; Gene Goodman, especially, was very close to Tarnopol and later they became directors on the Brunswick board.

Another who knew Tarnopol was Larry Maxwell. Maxwell went on to form his own record label, Maxx Records, and manage and record a young Gladys Knight. He also managed The Four Tops, recording them for Maxx prior to their signing with Motown. Widely considered one of the best record promoters of the time, when he first knew Tarnopol he 'was working at a garage fixing tyres', Maxwell remembers. 'A guy who used to manage a lot of shake dances gave him [Tarnopol] 50 dollars to go to New York.' Thus Tarnopol became involved in concert promotion and through this became a friend and colleague of influential rock 'n' roll pioneer DJ, Alan Freed.

On the surface, things were coming together nicely for Jackie. But Freda wasn't so sure: 'Nat had everything all set up just the way he wanted it, that's why Jack came out like he did – with nothing. That's why Nat got him away from Detroit as soon as he got a hold of him. Jack just wanted to sing; he didn't want any responsibility. I told him to get his own lawyer, not one of Nat's friends, but he said, "No, no, no, I trust Nat." Jack gave Nat power of attorney, first shot. Brunswick was created just for Jack.'

Jackie took his old friend JJ and another, Larry Frazier, along with him. They filled the roles of bodyguards, valets, drivers, procurers and plain 'pals'. In Freda's words: 'His best friend was Johnny Jones till the end. He knew him from childhood. Ralph Peterson was his friend till he couldn't function any more [due to illness]. Jack sent for him to New York and tried to get him ready to sing, but he could no longer sing.' Tarnopol had Alonzo Tucker move across to New York for his songwriting skills, but he also doubled as a driver for Jackie. Tucker, like Jackie, had a distinct fondness for women and partying and there was always a great respect and friendship between the two, despite their age difference.

In 1957 Dick Jacobs began a nine-year working relationship producing and directing for Jackie. At that time Jacobs, who was music director with Decca Records and director of artists and repertoire (A&R) with Coral Records, had an illustrious career in his own right. In a fascinating interview not long before he died, Jacobs related to Tim Holmes of *Musician* magazine (11 January 1988) his association with Jackie: 'One day Thiele called me in and said Jackie was coming in for his first sessions. We'd have to cut Jackie fast since he didn't have any money to stay in New York for an extended period. Since time was tight, I was concerned about the songs we'd be recording. Jackie was bringing in a couple of tunes penned by one Berry Gordy Jnr [and Roquel 'Billy' Davis]. Not only was the singer unknown, but who the hell had ever heard of the songwriter?

'When Jackie arrived, he was ushered into my office for an introduction and goddamn if he didn't look like he had just come in on a freight train. He was wearing jeans and a sweatshirt and seemed bedraggled and exhausted. In retrospect, this first meeting was entirely out of character for Jackie. I remember him being very fussy about his appearance. This was a guy who wouldn't appear on the street, or on a record date for that matter, unless every tonsorial detail was sculpted and perfect. He is the only guy I ever knew who could spend hours in shoe stores. Yet, on this first meeting, he looked like any other kid off the street.

'I asked him if he had the lead sheets of the songs he intended to record. He said no, I'd have to write them down as he sang them to me. I'd been down this road before with other vocalists, and as I wrote out the music for "Reet Petite" I began to feel some respect for the unknown tunesmith. "Reet Petite" had an unusual melody and a strikingly inventive chord construction; even before recording it, it felt like a new kind of hit.

'After I'd written down the music, Jackie and I sat down to figure out what keys to record in. I began playing piano chords in what I considered the usual male keys, but Jackie kept telling me to take it higher. I transposed the keys until they hit the female range, a full octave above where we'd started. Jackie explained that since he had laryngitis he couldn't sing along, but kept saying, "Take it higher," in a gravelly, phlegm-filled voice. I had no idea what he'd sound like in these upper register helium arrangements he insisted on.

'The whole set-up was making me very nervous. I went into Thiele's office and told him that Jackie's keys seemed all off to me; he hadn't sung a note and I really hoped we hadn't signed a lemon. Thiele – ever the philosopher – just said, "Oh, what the hell, we only signed him to get LaVern [Baker]. Do the arrangements in any key he wants." Bob always had good gambler's instincts. We'd just do the session and see what happened.' The mention here of LaVern Baker, the powerful R&B singer, is of interest. She was hot property and Green ad apparently dangled her as bait to get Jackie the Decca contract. However she was still contracted to Atlantic and, most likely due to the untimely death of Green, Decca never did get Baker signed.

Jacobs goes on: 'Jackie and I discussed the instrumentation. We hired Panama Francis on drums, Lloyd Trotman on bass, Ernie Hayes on piano, Sam Taylor on saxophone and Eric Gale on guitar. I figured that with all these seasoned pros in the tune, the session couldn't be too bad. We held the session at the Pythian Temple on East Seventieth Street in Manhattan. I passed out the arrangement of "Reet Petite" to the band and ran over it a few times to do the necessary fine tuning. The band gelled and purred like a Mercedes. Jackie commented that he liked the arrangement very much. Now it was his turn. I got him behind the microphone and said a silent prayer that this aerial key he'd picked to sing in would be okay, and that this guy was a reasonable approximation of a singer.

'Jackie Wilson opened his mouth and out poured that sound like honey on moonbeams, and it was like the whole room shifted on some weird axis. The musicians, these meat and potatoes pros, stared at each other slack-jawed and goggle-eyed in disbelief; it was as if the purpose of their musical training and woodshedding and lick-spitting had been to guide them into this big studio in the Pythian Temple to experience these pure shivering moments of magic. Bob Thiele and I looked at each other and just started laughing, half out of relief and half out of wonder. I never thought crow could taste so sweet. For years afterwards, Jackie and I often joked about my initial underestimation of his range. In fact, his vocal spread encompassed so many octaves that he could sing not only in female keys but an octave higher without a hint of a strained falsetto. "Reet Petite" came out and did very well, although nothing like the hits that would follow.' This took place on 12 July 1957. Jackie would soon be on his way as a solo artist in his chosen career.

When Roquel 'Billy' Davis turned his efforts to professional songwriting, he found it to be a craft with a formula, as he explains about Jackie's first hit: '"Reet Petite" was a common phrase used in connection with a fine girl. It was about this girl that was small in size and build; she was an actual person. It was also lyrically inspired by her. Musically, it was inspired by a riff known to everybody – a boogie-woogie riff. This being one of my early compositions; I was around 16.'

Davis had mixed feelings about the result at first: 'The first time I heard "Reet Petite" I didn't like it at all, because it had more big band and brass horn treatment than I ever imagined – or Berry. We viewed it as a lot simpler, predominantly rhythm, with Jackie being featured. Dick, of course, did this big horn arrangement, which didn't bother Jackie because there was no way of overpowering him.'

Some of the earliest Jacobs sessions were, for some reason, done at Joe Syracuse's United Sound Studios in Detroit. Says Davis, 'I was in on the early United Sound Studio sessions with Jackie. That was the studio Motown used prior to [Tamla/Motown's] Hitsville USA studio being built.' The first release, 'Reet Petite', in August 1957, did poorly in the USA, reaching only No 62 on the Pop charts and not making the R&B charts. In Britain, however, it held No Six for four weeks. The Guiness Book Of Records rates 'Reet Petite'as No 20 on the 'top 100 singles of all time' listings.

'Reet Petite' featured an interpretation by Jackie; a rolling of the 'R' in the word 'Reet' throughout. But Freda recalls one occasion when that distinctive 'R' embarrassed Jackie during a concert performance. 'He was appearing with Dinah Washington. Jack blew his two front teeth out singing 'Reet Petite'. It was his dentures. He did that thing [with the rolling of the Rs] and his two front teeth came flying out. He stopped singing right there; he wanted somebody to find his teeth. He wasn't going back on stage with no teeth.' Jackie's daughter Denise interjects: 'He said, "I'll never sing it again," and he never did. He probably rolled over in his grave when he learned it was No One in England and Japan [when re-issued in 1986–1987].' Jackie rarely performed the song on stage again.

DJ Norman N Nite, in his radio interview, asked Jackie about his first hit on Brunswick. Jackie answered cheekily: 'That happened through a young man, he's got a small label called Motown; Berry Gordy Jnr. He was doing the writing for us then. That's why I liked it, but I was very hoarse that day in the studio. I couldn't hardly talk because I'd been working that hard in the studio and on the road, and so I couldn't hit, as Nat would say, 'the bird', the high note [high C].' On all his recordings with Jackie, Jacobs used full orchestras. He didn't want Jackie to be a two-hit rock 'n'roll singer, with guitar and drum backing. Jacobs also used white back-up singers, receiving criticism for doing so.

One of the many affairs that Jackie had was with a stripper and dancer, Lee Angel. Angel was a gorgeous schoolgirl when wild rock 'n'roller Little Richard first spotted her in her home town of Savannah, Georgia. 'I was his choice, he was not mine,' says Angel. 'I was walking down the street and one of the girls said, "Little Richard wants to meet you." I said, "What!? Does he know I'm female?" I was 16 years old. I used to go and see all the concerts, but this was one I was not going to see; I didn't like his music.' Nevertheless, she met Little Richard and ended up following him on the road. More than that, she fell madly in love with him.

Angel, who stands five ft two in, is of white, American Indian and black descent. In 1957 she and Richard had plans to marry, but while on tour in Australia he gave up rock 'n' roll and took up Christian ministry. Angel was heartbroken; they had even set the wedding date. She became reclusive, living with her godmother on 116th Street in New York. Her godmother advised her, 'Get out of the house . . . go to the Apollo Theatre.' 'So I went to the Apollo', Angel says, 'and I met LaVern Baker, [comedian] Slappy White [later Baker's husband] and [blues singer] Jimmy Rogers.' They all went to see a new singer at the Baby Grand Club. That singer was Jackie. 'He was staying at the Teresa Hotel and working at the Baby Grand when we first met,' Angel adds. This was in December 1957, when Jackie had his first hit, 'Reet Petite'. Angel and Jackie had an affair that lasted, on and off, for a few years.

On one occasion Angel met with Jackie's wife; it was a meeting which led her to a deep admiration for Freda. 'I went bouncing into Jackie's dressing room in Richmond, Virginia. There was [singer 'Rockin'Robin']

Bobby Day, who I ran around with, his wife Jacqui, Freda and Jackie. I was introduced to Freda and I said right then and there, "It's nice meeting you. Bye." Jackie would not let me out of the dressing-room. I was trying to think of a million reasons to get out of there, 'cause I'd heard about Freda's tough reputation. Jackie was about to go on stage and I said, "Bye." He said, "Don't you walk out of that door." He turned to Freda and said, "Now if you don't want to fight tonight, don't let her go. If she disappears you know what's going to happen when we get back to Washington."'

'He left to go on stage. I said, "Goodbye" to Freda and she said, "Stop, I know who you are, I know all about you. But do me a favour, do not leave. I really don't feel like fighting Jackie tonight. Not only that, you tried your best to show me respect and he wouldn't let you. I like you for that." That's how we became friends.'

Jackie took a strong romantic interest in Angel. Whenever he was in New York he'd get in touch with her or send JJ and Frazier to call by the Alvin Hotel, on 52nd Street, to collect her. Angel claims, 'I was from the kind of family that if you belonged to one man, that man is supposed to belong to you.' She therefore spurned Jackie's advances. When JJ and Frazier arrived at the Alvin Hotel, the front desk would call to warn her. 'I had my room next to the fire exit, and I dressed running down that sparrow cage more times than you can imagine. I found out what type of person he was, and from there it was, "Leave me alone, Jackie."' She was referring to Jackie's well-known reputation for sleeping with any woman who took his fancy. 'I was avoiding him because of the womanising. I'd say Jackie loved every woman on earth. Jackie was one of these "do as I say, not as I do" people. Jackie wanted to mess with every woman on earth, but didn't want them screwing around with another man.'

Angel recalls: 'JJ and Frazier kidnapped me one time. I was getting on the elevator at the Teresa Hotel in New York. The moment I saw them I knew I was in trouble and they lifted me right up and said, "Jackie wants to see you." I said, "Jackie doesn't even know I'm in town." They have actually kicked in doors of mine.' Angel also remembers Tarnopol, though not kindly: 'Don't you believe that Nat was a nice guy – I was there! Nat did everything he could to get me into bed with him, but I never could get past his personality.' She had her own special way of getting back at Tarnopol: 'I couldn't stand Tarnopol, I disliked him intensely. Tarnopol used to tell me if I didn't go to bed with him, I couldn't see Jackie any more. I said to him, "I just won't see Jackie any more." I used to find out where Jackie was working, get a cab, have the cab park, and go right up front where Jackie could see me. He'd be on stage singing and I'd leave. I'd tell the cab driver, "Don't leave yet," and within five minutes Jackie would be off that stage and in the cab with me. I only did that when Nat Tarnopol made me angry. I used to tell Nat, "All you've got to do is leave me alone and I'll leave Jackie alone."' Angel commented on the relationship between Jackie and Tarnopol, 'Jackie didn't hate Nat in the beginning; he was so strung out on the coke and fame.'

While reckless in love, Jackie had many years behind him in terms of singing experience. As Jacobs explained in *Musician* magazine: 'Jackie was the consummate professional in the studio. He never asked to change anything on an arrangement and could get a track down in two to three takes max.'

Due to Jacobs having other commitments, the second recording session, in the final months of 1957, was directed by Milton De Lugg, the big band leader. Only eight tracks came out of the session. One was the beautiful ballad by Davis/Gordy, 'To Be Loved', which was given Jackie's silky treatment. Released in February 1958, the song was perfect for Jackie and reached No Seven on the R&B charts and No 22 on the Pop charts. It was Jackie's first Top 40 hit as a solo performer. In his radio interview, Norman N Nite asked Jackie about 'To Be Loved': 'That was Berry's idea too and his penmanship. He decided I could sing better than I could gimmick. He wanted to prove I could do both.' Roquel 'Billy' Davis says, "'To Be Loved' probably sold more R&B than anything, even though it was a ballad. It had more of that appeal. At that time R&B artists were not getting that much pop exposure on radio or television.' Most likely 'To Be Loved' was Jackie's most performed stage song.

He continues: 'The big sales of R&B artists began to happen more in the mid-60s. As the years went by, we [black song writers and artists] got more exposure and sales increased. Sometimes they became 'Pop' first. 'Night' was getting a lot of play on R&B stations. It sold well. Black fans knew he could sing anything. After 'Doggin' Around' came out . . . that was totally different for Jackie – there was a lot of talk about that. Wow! A lot of the pop jocks [white DJs] didn't think he could sing that bluesy.'

In the late 1950s, studio technology was still in the electronic stone age. Davis recalls: 'Three tracks didn't come along until 1962. At Chess we had one of the first three-track Ampex recorders in the mid-west. They didn't use it the way you'd think. They said, "Okay, well, put the voice on one, the band on the other – I don't know what we're going to do with the third track." That was the attitude for a long while.

'The band would came in and we'd run it down a few times to get the kinks out and then we'd start. The singer would then come in and [after] a few takes you'd have it. A small mistake and you started all over again. A mistake was great; that made the producer do his work.'

Band leader Henry Jerome had the responsibility of putting the huge studio bands together for most of the Dick Jacobs recording sessions. The back-up singers were talents in their own right; cousins Cissy Houston and Dionne Warwick, and Lillian Clarke. Jerome insists Tarnopol was only executive producer; which really means he had minimal involvement with the actual studio sessions, despite numerous record album credits.

Apart from the very early recordings, which were done in Detroit's United Sound Studios, two New York recording studios were used for the Jacob's sessions; Bell Sound Studios and the Pythian Temple, where the large hall sounds resulted. Henry Jerome not only put the bands together, he also did the mixing. Recordings were done live, so a mistake by anyone meant the whole song would have to be re-done from the start. Originally only three, and later four, tracks were used to record the huge orchestra, background singers and Jackie.

Incredibly, from where he sat in the sound booth, he could see neither Jackie nor the orchestra. When stereo recording started to come in, it was up to Jerome to work the levels in order to get the ultimate finished product. He relied on his musician's ear, because there was no going back later to alter the mix. Jerome speaks highly of Jackie as a performer and a man: 'Jackie was one of the all-time great acts, absolutely,' he says. 'A gentleman, a nice-thinking human being and an exceptional talent.'

Another black singer with ability from Detroit was Eddie Holland. With a very similar vocal pitch to Jackie, Berry Gordy would have Holland do the demonstration ['demo'] recordings so that Jackie could get a better feel for the song. Along with his brother Brian and Lamont Dozier, they formed one of the most successful songwriting and production teams of all time – Holland, Dozier and Holland – writing hit after hit for most of Motown's major artists. He recalls: 'My first recording session was done on Jackie Wilson's session. It was in New York. Jackie Wilson allowed me to take one of his session songs as a second cut. He allowed me to take some of his session time. The arranger was Don Costa; a great arranger.' Costa, although not credited, worked on many of the early recordings, also working with Frank Sinatra, Paul Anka and Sarah Vaughan.

Jackie sometimes did his own 'dubs' [demonstration recordings], recorded directly on an acetate disc. Late in 1957, Jackie and Gordy got together in the basement studio of Detroit DJ, Bristol Bryant and recorded two songs, 'To Be Loved' and a slow version of 'Lonely Teardrops', both of which featured a tinkering piano played by Gordy with Jackie's haunting vocal treatment. Luckily, quite clear copies of those rare demos are still around today.

Davis recalls the writing of 'To Be Loved' somewhat differently than Gordy: 'Berry tells a story in his book [*To Be Loved*, Gordy's autobiography] of how he came to write 'To Be Loved' and of course he makes no mention of anyone else. He states that he and his wife had a big falling out this night about his kids. He was upset, she put him out of the house and he discovered that she was suing for divorce. He came up to his sister Gwen's apartment. He was sort of lonely and in despair and upset because of what had happened. That's when he decided to write 'To Be Loved'.

'He says, and it's not true, that he started to write a song about his kids. As it developed, he discovered it was not just about his kids, but was about being loved by everybody. It went on to be a hit. That's the story he tells in the book. Actually, he arrived at his sister's house, where I was staying at the time. Gwen and I were soul mates at that time. I was there and asleep. I heard noise in the living room. There was a Wurlitzer electric piano there and Berry was playing on it. I went out and said, "What are you doing here this time of the night?" He went on to tell me that he and Thelma had this argument. We sat there talking and I said, 'If we are going to be here we might as well write a song about it.' He was doodling with some chords, but it was I who came up with 'To Be Loved'. You know, love is great, the greatest thing in the world and to have someone who really loves you – there's nothing like it. As we usually do, Berry started doodling with some chord changes, without melody, and I began to see what I could feel melodically there, what came to mind. That's how the song came to be written.'

Freda was friendly with Gordy's first wife, Thelma, who was also anxious for the success they both expected. Said Freda: 'Thelma and I used to cry on each other's shoulders: 'My water is cut off; what are we going to do?' Berry was screwing around with this girl [who] Thelma didn't know about. He always appeared very sincere. All the money was going right back in the business. They were both trying to get somewhere. I knew Jack would eventually – even though we stayed in the old 'raggedy' house, with no locks on the doors.' Freda recalls that Jackie held Gordy in high regard, but he too was getting impatient for success. Says Freda, 'Nothing ever happened. Jack said, "There ain't nothing happening there."

'Then, at last, we did get a little something. I was working at the Harper Hospital – I was pregnant with Tony. Then Jack called me at work, which he never did. "We've got a hit!" ['To Be Loved'] I ran down the hall screaming, 'We made it, it's a hit.' It sold 500,000.'

On the very same day, Freda took maternity leave from her job at the hospital. She was seven months into the pregnancy. Their second son and fourth child, Anthony ('Tony') Duane, was born on 21 February 1958. Jackie was again suspicious that this child may have had a different father. Tony had very dark skin and when Jackie visited the hospital he began inspecting the infant minutely. 'Why you doing that?' asked Freda, 'Checking the bone structure,' replied Jackie. Denise adds, 'He was like some kind of damned doctor. Because Tony is dark skinned like her [Freda's] side of the family, got a keen nose like hers, he had to have blood tests for the child.' Freda continues, 'He kept getting me pregnant and then he'd come and say, "Whose is that?" Acting like he was crazy. Fifteen times pregnant! I almost went crazy with the four children.'

Jackie's suspicions were, of course, more to do with his own weaknesses than his wife's. Freda remembers one unusual situation. 'This rich, white girl, Carol, took care of me and my kids,' Freda says. 'She was nice to Joyce [Jackie's half-sister], to Mama, nice to me. She bought us things. When I had Tony she sent everything. A basinet, a baby buggy, a stroller. She was so nice I didn't know she liked him like that for a long time. I was really stupid, I thought she was just a nice lady trying to help him out. Whenever I had a baby, something would come for Freda Wilson. I said, "I didn't order nothing." They said, "It's paid for." Baby things and basinets; all kinds of baby stuff, expensive stuff.

'Carol bought for Jack for a long time – even when he became famous. She used to come over and help my mother-in-law take care of the kids. She'd stay upstairs. She'd clean the house from top to bottom. She'd comb the kids' hair. Everyone in the house got an allowance. She never acted like she was in love with him. It took me years to realise there was more to it. Finally it dawned on me; she don't get no money back. I never did hate her like I did some of the other women.'

Possibly Freda really understood better than she let on, being aware Jackie had been a 'ladies' man' since he was very young. She knew there were other children he'd fathered, such as Brenda, to Suzie Johnson, and Sabrina, to Molly Byndon, both in 1954. Says Freda, 'Like I say, he was a busy man.'

He was just as busy professionally. The first opportunity for Jackie to be seen on nationwide television came with Dick Clark's popular *American Bandstand*. The show, which went out live, was an institution, especially with the young. To perform on it almost assured chart success, while it was also syndicated throughout Europe. Clark hugely admired Jackie and vividly recalls their long involvement: 'The first time I ever heard a Jackie Wilson record was in 1957 and that was "Reet Petite", and both that and "To Be Loved" were written by my friend Berry Gordy. We played him on *American Bandstand*. He was an extraordinary performer. I've always said he was the most exhilarating performer I ever saw.'

On Jackie's first appearance on the show, in 1959, he performed 'Lonely Teardrops'. The unwieldy television cameras didn't allow him to give full rein to his performance, as at his concerts. Over the years Jackie appeared on the show seven times, doing two songs each time. They are amongst the best visual records remaining of his smooth stage routine; however, they were lip-synced.

Roquel 'Billy' Davis recalls how vital the *Bandstand* appearance was for Jackie to gain exposure to white audiences. 'If it was not for Dick Clark, Jackie may not have been played on Detroit radio,' he says. In any case, Jackie's next few years were his peak, with non-stop touring and numerous single and album releases. From 1958 through to 961 he had 17 Top Forty hits, out of the 24 for his entire career. The money began pouring in for Jackie, Tarnopol and the others controlling them.

Following the show, Jackie's first album, 'He's So Fine', comprising eight Milton De Lugg-produced tracks and two from the first Jacobs session, was released. Jackie was now hot property and throughout 1958 there were four single releases, including the song that would be his signature tune, 'Lonely Teardrops'. It held No One on the R&B charts for seven weeks, even gaining No Seven spot on the Pop charts; his first Top Ten hit and yet another Davis/Gordy tune.

Jacobs explained to *Musician* magazine how the session went: 'Nat told me that in the future I would be Jackie's sole arranger, and that he and I would co-produce on the sessions. He handed me a lead sheet for another Berry Gordy composition, "Lonely Teardrops", and asked me to call Gordy in Detroit to discuss the arrangement. This would be the first of many phone calls over the years, but this time I had some questions. The chord progression of "Lonely Teardrops" struck me as being a little unusual and I asked Gordy if it was correct. He assured me that it was and we went on to discuss the arrangement in highly technical terms. Not only was Gordy a budding populist genius in terms of knowing the teen market, he was a brilliant and knowledgeable music theorist. The phone conversation ended with me inviting Gordy to New York for the "Lonely Teardrops" session.'

Davis and Gordy supervised the session, meaning they did everything from rehearsing Jackie to organising arrangements. They even helped to produce. The resulting *Lonely Teardrops* album, Jackie's second, included five Davis/Gordy compositions. This time, probably to ensure a more commercial product, no string backing was used and a reduced brass accompaniment. Jackie's uninhibited, supercharged vocal delivery was given full rein.

'Lonely Teardrops', the single, is believed to have sold more than one million copies, but Brunswick, like Motown later on, was not a member of the Record Industry Association of America (RIAA), so sales figures were not audited and they may well have been overstated. The common practice then was for the record company to provide the gold disc representing sales exceeding one million. In other instances, record sales were understated in order to defraud the artist.

Jacobs said in *Musician*: 'It was the flip side of "Lonely Teardrops" that really caused problems. Bob Thiele had left the company to become the head of A&R at Dot Records. The new head of A&R at Coral/Brunswick, Paul Cohen, came from the country department at Decca. To put it charitably, Cohen and Tarnopol hated each other with a passion. Cohen always wanted one of his, or one of his friends', songs on every session and Tarnopol objected vehemently. Cohen won the battle, if not the war, by issuing Nat a simple ultimatum: unless the flip of "Lonely Teardrops" was an old ballad called "In The Blue Of Evening", there'd be no session. Nat was furious and came up with an ingenious sabotage scheme. He told me to deliberately write the arrangement in the wrong key for Jackie. That way, "In The Blue Of Evening" would get so screwed up that we could pull one of Jackie's older sides for the flip. The scheme would've worked had it not been for Jackie. I wrote the arrangement in what I thought was an impossible key. Jackie, unaware of the subterfuge, took the arrangement and – without breaking a quaver – turned out such a beautiful performance that we were forced to use "In The Blue Of Evening". His rendition of this smouldering chestnut of a tune was the first clue we had to the incredible versatility of his singing.' Tarnopol, too, was generally anxious to have one of his friends' compositions on an album or single B-side, because songwriters' royalties were split evenly between A- and B-sides, or between all the tracks on an album.

As Roquel 'Billy' Davis explained, 'Lonely Teardrops' came out differently than how it was envisioned: 'It was originally a blues ballad and because of the cha-cha dance at the time, it inspired the rhythm to be changed. That was the one thing we didn't do.' Jackie's version of the recording of 'Lonely Teardrops' came in his Norman N Nite radio interview: 'It was supposed to be a ballad – a blues ballad. It was written also by Berry Gordy Jnr, and Nat and I flew in [to Detroit] from New York. We heard the song, liked it and took it back to New York. And then we did record it as a blues ballad, but we didn't like it. So then we decided to play with the guitar a little bit . . . we had a great arranger at the time, Dick Jacobs . . . we had him finagle with it a little bit and we played and we got a good tempo going, and it was like a chalypso [a cross between calypso and cha-cha], which at the time was very popular. . . we liked it. We brought it back and gave it to the disc jockey; it was hot off the press and we told him to play it. So they put the record on and Berry was there waiting patiently and everybody was just waiting. And they put it on and Berry said, "Oh, my God, you've ruined my song. What have you done to it?" And tears came out of his eyes.'

In February 1959, when 'Lonely Teardrops' was released, Jackie sent a touching telegram to Freda in Highland Park from New York. It read, 'DEAREST FREDA EACH TIME I LOVE YOU MORE AND MORE THAT'S WHY I LOVE YOU SO = SONNY XX.' It is partly in code, but was easily deciphered by Freda. 'Each Time (I Love You More)' and 'That's Why (I Love You So)' were two of the songs from the album.

Another song on the second album, 'The Joke', was written by Janie Bradford, although it lists Gwen Gordy as co-writer. In 1959 Janie co-wrote the enormous hit 'Money (That's What I Want)' with Berry Gordy and went on to have a successful songwriting career with Motown. Bradford claims, 'Before Jackie became a star, he could have been a comedian or whatever. He was charming, witty . . . just someone nice to be around all the time. That's if he liked you and if you were a friend of his. He was a charmer with the ladies. Jackie was such a loveable person. He was definitely a character. The way he could get down on the floor and do the splits. I still think he's the most amazing performer; I've never seen anyone to compete with him. Even though I love Michael Jackson, he still doesn't quite have the energy that Jackie had. Jackie was on fire, dynamite.'

In 1959 Berry Gordy's brother-in-law, George Edwards, was standing for re-election in the Michigan State Legislature. He needed a campaign song and so Davis and Gordy wrote 'Let George Do It', which Jackie sang. The catchy rock 'n' roll number became a minor hit in Detroit.

Unfortunately, it wasn't enough to have Edwards re-elected. Gordy later related the episode: 'Jackie thought it was a commercial song. He didn't know, he was just singing it. So they made it and it was on jukeboxes and all over town. People were dancing to it; they liked the beat.'

Driving from Detroit to New York for a session one time, Roquel 'Billy' Davis recalls, they all almost lost their lives. It would have been a tragedy for the music industry. Johnny Jones was driving Jackie's bronze El Dorado Cadillac and in the car were Gordy, Davis and Jackie. As usual, JJ was driving too fast and the roads were icy. 'Johnny loved to speed – we were all sleeping in the back, it was winter, snow and ice everywhere. Jackie would wake up and swear and say Johnny was going to get us all killed. Then we'd doze off again. Johnny lost control of the car and hit the centre guard rail and spun, out of control, into the path of a semi-trailer in the right-hand lane. The truck driver barely missed us. Jackie wanted to kill Johnny, but the car wasn't badly damaged.'

1959 was an excellent year for Jackie and another Davis/Gordy tune, 'That's Why (I Love You So)', reached No Two on the R&B and No 13 on the Pop charts. This was followed by 'I'll Be Satisfied' (No Six R&B, No 20 Pop). Jackie's third hit for the year was credited as his own composition. It was the song he'd sung in Alan Freed's rock movie *Go Johnny Go*, 'You'd Better Know It' (No One R&B, No 37 Pop).

However, there was simmering resentment between Tarnopol and his crack songwriting team of Davis and Gordy. It stemmed from a number of differences, but mainly from the songwriters' feeling that Tarnopol was underpaying them. Their belief is well borne out because, as well as the initial writing, the duo worked hard on the production side, as Davis explains: 'I was very impressed with Dick Jacobs; he wrote out a lead sheet faster than anyone I've ever seen before. We could stand up and sing a melody for him and before we finished the song he had it completely written. Berry and I were flabbergasted with his technical music ability as an arranger.

'Jacobs was the producer, but one might argue about who the producer was. It depends on what you think the role of the producer really was. I could say, Berry could say, Jackie could say: 'We are the producers.' We could say it collectively, we could say it separately. I don't believe Dick Jacobs could say he was the producer. He could say he was the arranger and when it got to the studio the instructions came from other people; what was right, what should be changed, and when the tempo was right. In the background, although we were songwriters, most people took their instructions from Berry and myself. I say to a lot of people, we were the producers in the sense of making sure that the song kept its integrity as it was intended, as deemed by us.

'Most of the time a tape was given to Dick Jacobs of the song already demo'd. He would take it from that and score it, in the same format it was given to him. He'd just try to capture what was there; what was there was generally what we felt. He would dress it up with horns, brass, strings to his style and try to recapture the rhythm that was given to him. It never came off as funky as it was originally, but it was different and so big that I was flabbergasted.

'Really the only time I saw Jacobs was during the sessions. Berry and I were not just writers. We wrote, arranged and produced. We did the whole bit; rehearsed Jackie to learn the songs in the first place, played a major role as producers and worked the songs out with Jackie. This music was a little different for Dick Jacobs. There were a lot of questions as to whether he should be doing the arrangement at all.'

Despite all their involvement in Jackie's success, Tarnopol would not consider paying Davis and Gordy for their contribution to the production of his records. Davis says that part of the dispute with Tarnopol involved the B-sides. 'He wouldn't put our songs on the B-side. Berry and I had separate meetings with Nat and we came away with the same conclusion. We told him, "Screw you, too."' Davis says that Tarnopol insisted on putting his friends' tracks on the B-side, so that they would end up with 50 per cent of the writers' royalties.

The second half of 1959 saw the rift between Davis/Gordy and Tarnopol lead to a final separation. Tarnopol didn't think he needed this successful songwriting team and they sure enough didn't need him. Davis and Gordy both went on to very productive and rewarding careers, Davis with Chess Records in Chicago, and music songwriting and publishing, Gordy establishling his amazing Motown label.

'If not for Nat Tarnopol, Motown would not have been given birth,' Davis opines. 'If he hadn't treated Berry and I like he did, Motown wouldn't have happened. We were used and misused and did not get paid for our production work. He wanted to put his name on our songs. We said, "To hell with that." Nat didn't get away with putting his name on our songs.' The fact that Jackie was instrumental in the foundation of the Motown recording empire is often overlooked; his hits provided part of the financial capital that such an enterprise required. It was Tarnopol's perceived underpayment that finally caused Gordy to take the enormous gamble that was Motown. On a happier note, Davis says of Jackie: 'He had a gold name bracelet made for me and Berry. A sort of "thank you". Jackie spent his money like it was all going to last forever. Of course, he didn't get nearly what he should have gotten over the later years. He had everything he wanted; he just wanted to be performing and singing, [and have] fancy clothes, fancy jewellery, a big car.'

Jack 'The Rapper' Gibson was an influential black DJ who would later take up an offer by Gordy to be Motown's first national promotions manager. He confirms: 'There wouldn't have been no Motown if Nat Tarnopol would have given Berry what he wanted. He went to Nat and said, "Can I get some points on Jackie?" Nat said, "Get points? You're just a song-ass writer. Just write the goddamn songs and don't worry about the points." So Berry said, "Fuck you" and he went and started his own recording company.'

Early in 1960 Jackie's highest charting record, 'Night', was released. It reached a credible No Four on the Pop charts and No Three on the black R&B charts.

The flip side was a bluesy song written by Alonzo Tucker, although not credited to him, called 'Doggin'Around'. The songwriter is listed as Lena Agree, Nat Tarnopol's aunt. It charted very well also, achieving No One on the R&B charts and No 15 on the Pop.

Dick Jacobs, in *Musician* magazine, remarked on the choice of material Tarnopol selected for Jackie: 'With "Lonely Teardrops" demolishing the charts, Jackie became a one-man hit factory with 'That's Why (I Love You So)', 'I'll Be Satisfied', 'Talk That Talk', 'A Woman, A Lover, A Friend', and on and on. But somewhere in his heart, Jackie Wilson really wanted to be taken seriously as a ballad singer. Like Johnny Ace before him, Jackie wanted to be the Black Sinatra, a Mario Lanza of soul. And he sure had the pipes to deliver any kind of record he wanted to. So Nat came up with a song called "Night", which was an adaptation of "My Heart And Thy Sweet Voice" from the Saint-Saens opera *Samson and Delilah*. We got a big orchestra with lots of swelling strings and Hollywood heavenly white voices and I wrote this lush lavish arrangement which critics to this day claim was too powerful for Jackie's voice. What the critics don't realise is that it was impossible to overpower Jackie Wilson's voice; you couldn't do it with a chorus line of Sherman tanks. Besides, that wasn't the point. This was the sound Jackie wanted and this is the sound I gave him. But what the hell, the record went through the roof and into the hearts of Jackie's fans, which is where the sound really mattered.'

Tarnopol provided other opera-based tunes for Jackie, and although they were rarely commercial enough for the buyers of pop records, they enabled Jackie to fully demonstrate his majestic vocal skills. In September 1960 'Alone At Last', with a melody based on Tchaikosky's 'Piano Concerto No One In B Flat', was released. It charted well; No Eight on the Pop charts and No 20 on the R&B. 'My Empty Arms', based on 'On The Motley' from the opera *I Pagliacci*, was released in December 1960. In 1962 he recorded 'My Eager Heart', the melody of which was taken from a Wagner opera, then, in 1966, his version of 'Be My Love' was released as a single. Mario Lanza previously recorded it in 1949.

Detroit nurtured many talented songwriters during the 1950s and 1960s. Two close friends, Alonzo Tucker and William Weatherspoon, knew Jackie from the earliest days of his career. Both started out with singing groups and together they wrote 'Why Can't You Be Mine' and 'As Long As I Live', both released on Jackie's first album.

Charles Sutton, previously with The Royals group, naturally knew Tucker well and, like everyone else, liked him: 'Those were lean days for Alonzo, particularly in Detroit. So they sent for him to come to New York and have him fool around with Jackie. He was paid a minimum amount. He was Jackie's chauffeur, but also wrote tunes for him.' Many of Jackie's recordings which credit the songwriter as J. Wilson, J. Roberts, N. Tarnopol or Lena Agree, were actually Tucker's compositions. Tucker didn't fare well at all, says Jimmy Smith, who became Jackie's touring drummer for ten years: 'Alonzo got messed around. He only got a free place to sleep.' Tarnopol supplied him with a house, from which his family was evicted when Tucker died in 1977.

Almost without exception. women found Jackie's mischievous smile irresistible. But there was one incident in 1960 which was temporarily to dent Jackie's rather large ego. At the time, he was playing at the Capital Theatre in Detroit. Raynoma Liles, who later became Berry Gordy's second wife, had an attractive, white friend named Judy who was being dated by Al Abrams who went on to head Motown's publicity department. Abrams picks up the story: 'At the time Berry was driving us there [to see Jackie's performance], and at the time he had a lot of difficulty driving. Anyway, we got to the theatre and Jackie was his usual self and walked up to Judy and gave her a hug and a kiss . . . not on the lips, but the cheek. She got really angry about it and came over to Berry and demanded, "Tell him to never do that again, and make him say he's sorry." Jackie was totally taken aback. She was probably the first woman who complained.'

Judy, due to her friendship with Raynoma, ended up working in Motown's office. 'Eventually I hired her to work in the office,' says Abrams. 'One time she was going through the drawers and she found a major cheque for 10 to 15,000 dollars in royalties made out to Billy Davis [not Roquel 'Billy' Davis], that Billy had never cashed. She absconded with it. We heard about it when she was trying to cash it at the banks. I had to fire her and put her out of my life, as well.' Doubtless, Jackie had a chuckle about this when he was informed.

Abrams recalls: 'Jackie would always pull women out of the audience. I remember he told me he always chose ugly women out of the audience to kiss. He said those were the ones who'd remember it most.' Abrams had begun to work with Motown's management team. 'I used to wind up with the younger sisters that Nat would date,' says Abrams. 'Nat used to have a pretty heavy line he'd lay on them, too – album covers! He'd say, "I'll get your picture on Jackie's next album."'

Around this time Jackie began taking on Jewish mannerisms, such as referring to people he met by the term 'Booby', which he would use in a fast, clipped manner. It is a shortening of the Yiddish word 'boobela', a pet name of affection. The expression must have been picked up from Tarnopol. Jackie also took to wearing a mazuza (a small container containing a Jewish prayer or Ten Commandments) and a gold Star Of David (Seal Of Solomon) given to him by Nat. Jackie claimed to be Jewish and said he was encouraged in this conversion by Sammy Davis Jnr.

His ability to look out for his friends is demonstrated in a small incident that had a huge bearing on the careers of The Contours. Sylvester Potts and Joe Billingslea, members of the group, describe what happened: 'In 1959 we went down for an audition with Berry Gordy. He wasn't very satisfied and advised us to come back in a year's time. Hubert Johnson was one of the original group. He suggested we go and visit his cousin, Jackie. None of us had any idea he was related to Jackie Wilson; he'd never mentioned it. We got in the car and drove over to Jackie's house on Cottage Grove – we had nothing to lose. We met his mother and found out Jackie was Hubert's cousin. Jackie came down and we were formally introduced to him. He asked what was the problem. We explained about the audition and what Berry had said.'

Jackie asked them to perform the same three songs, which they did a cappella. 'He said, "Sounds pretty good, man. Go back downstairs and I'll be down in a few minutes." So we went downstairs. We were glad that he liked it. His mother provided some soft drinks and we was there about an hour. I was getting impatient. I said, "This cat don't like us; he's just got us sitting around for nothing, let's go." Hubert said, "We're not going, he's coming back." I said, "If he didn't come in about five minutes, I'm going." Jackie came down and said, "Come back upstairs." We went back upstairs. He was on the phone to Berry, blah, blah, blah, he hung up and said, "Go back over, Berry wants to see you." So we drove back over there – right down to Motown. We sang the same three songs for Berry and he said, "You're great," and we signed a contract.' It was fortunate, as The Contours went on to record some big hits for Motown, starting with 'Do You Love Me' in 1962, which reached No Three on the Pop charts.

Although Jackie was charting well around the world, he was still travelling all around the country on what was referred to as the 'Chitlin' Circuit'. The circuit was gruelling, often involving doing one or two nighters, with everyone travelling by either car or bus, loaded down with instruments and sound equipment. Patrons generally paid two or three dollars admittance and generally got to see ten or so major acts. Freda was annoyed that, being at home, she rarely saw her husband. 'The first time he took me on the road,' Freda recalls, 'he said, "Come on, Mrs Wilson, you've been wanting to go on the road. Get your rags together." He told me to bring mostly slacks.'

She was in for a few shocks; it wasn't quite the fun she'd imagined: 'He had to haul that little thing up the back [referring to the small box trailer they towed behind the limo containing all their baggage, instruments and sound equipment]. He told me to stretch my legs. He'd stretch out and lay his head on my lap. You had to be in the next place the next night, and they had to get there as fast as possible. He didn't even have a chance to take a shower. If he had time, he'd stop at a motel just so he could have a shower and get dressed. He didn't have time to lie down. He was used to travelling. You do adjust to the inconvenience, but it ain't fun and I was ready to come back home.'

Freda was fast learning not only that life on the road was tough, but that being cooped up with the same people day and night tested the strongest friendship. Jackie had the added pressure of the adoring fans, fanatical females and sharp-talking hucksters who always had an angle. He had a passion for dogs and insisted on travelling with them, despite the inconvenience. At that time it was his little Chihuahua, Poochie.

Freda now witnessed Jackie performing and the hysteria he created. She says: 'They took off their panties and threw them on stage. I thought it was bad enough with "Mr B" [Billy Eckstine, who also caused the same phenomenon]. 'Jack'd look at me when he sang, and he'd look at someone else and they'd feel the same way. He did a lot of stuff [songs] that Sinatra did. He would listen to Frank Sinatra and then say, "I don't like it like that." He'd get it his way. And when he'd wink and say, "Come on . . ."'

She began to appreciate the demanding life Jackie lived: 'All those people, and those lights up there are so hot. People think it's so easy.' She remembers one very embarrassing performance where his pants split right down the back: 'Tight! I don't know how he got into them. It's just as well he was wearing those jockey shorts, that's all I can say.' The audiences would sometimes try to get their hands on him and take a small souvenir, too. 'They'd try to get his ring when he dropped his hand, or his shoes when he laid down. He was the only person I know who wore a suit all the time. That's why, when he got home and changed, he was always wearing jeans and a T-shirt.'

Jackie was the consummate performer and, like an athlete prior to an event, would never eat prior to a performance. He did, however, enjoy his food, although witnesses were often appalled at his table manners and 'wolfing' of his meals. 'He never ate until everything was over,' says Freda. 'He'd get it all in one sitting. He'd start with something light first. He liked BBQ ribs, black-eyed peas, greens, ham hocks and hot water corn. He liked hamburger, he liked gravy.'

Throughout his entire career he would run through the scales, limbering up for around one hour prior to a performance, while taking the long baths he enjoyed so much. Says Freda: 'Jackie would sing with a finger in his ear; singers can hear better that way. He would practise the scales. He listened a lot to himself [listening to records at home], listening for mistakes. He played Jackie Wilson music to see if it sounded the same.' Another pre-concert ritual was for him to do his own make-up, something he began after an unfortunate incident where he allowed someone else to do it and appeared 'looking like a ghost'. Freda: 'He did his own make-up all the time. He used bronzing powder and did his own eyes.'

He would also drink a whisky before he went on stage, possibly to calm his nerves. 'He had a Scotch on the rocks before he went on, but he never looked like he had a hangover,' his wife remembers. Hangovers would come later. Around Jackie there was always plenty of partying, usually of the sort that went on all night, or sometimes even for days. Freda drank but did not experiment with drugs, making her the minority. On one such occasion they were partying with The Four Tops, and either the pot was laced with something more potent or they weren't used to indulging. In any case, says Freda, 'JJ had got some pot and we laughed. They were all high, but then they got deathly ill; they were all sick. They'd go to these entertainment parties – they had cocaine there; marijuana, cocaine piles where you could help yourself. I used to go with Jack. New York was notorious for those parties.' Freda just didn't fit in, it wasn't her scene. She says they would ask, '"What does she do [use]? What [drugs] does she want?" I'd say, "No, I don't want to eat or drink." I was scared to drink any pop, because I was scared they might put something in. I'd sit [waiting] for two or three days.'

When Jackie performed in Detroit, family members would enjoy the show. Freda remembers one such show, early in his career, when he wasn't heading the bill: 'We went down to see the show and Dinah Washington was the star. She looked around, like she always does, checking the crowd out. We were sitting right in front. Everyone was looking around thinking "what's she looking at, a bird or something?" I knew it was Mama's hat, but didn't want to say anything. She [Washington] said, "Somebody get it out of here. Better yet, kill it!" Then my mother-in-law said, "Look lady, I did not come here to see you sing. I come to see my son."' Eliza Mae was never one to trifle with, no matter how much of a star Washington was. 'Mama loved Jackie,' Freda went on, 'You say something about her, or him, you'd be looking for trouble . . . I mean, he could do no wrong.' It worked both ways, of course. Since Jackie got much of his innate vocal talent from his mother, it wasn't unusual for him to call her up on stage with him. Says Freda, 'His mother could sing. She sang with him on stage when he was in Detroit. Joyce [his half-sister] can also sing, but she never wanted to sing professionally.'

When Jackie returned home to perform at some of the clubs where he started out, it could be a boisterous event. 'We'd be in a nightclub in Detroit,' Freda explains. 'He'd be singing his heart out. [Cousin] Beccy would be with us, and Joyce when she got older. [Step-father] Johnny wouldn't sit with us, he thought we was all crazy. We'd be shaking and shouting and banging the beer bottles hard on the table; screaming and howling and carrying on. Jack said, "You all didn't have to go to that extreme." But it did make him feel better.'

There were times, however, when she saw how overwhelmed Jackie became by it all. His lifestyle was physically and mentally draining. 'He used to like to go in his room for hours,' said Freda. 'He liked his silence; or he'd pretend he was asleep. Then he'd tell Frazier to put the people out. And I'd know to sit there; I always took a back seat, especially in public. If I didn't like something he did, I waited until later. I didn't want him to be embarrassed in public.' She knew that as his wife, it was her duty to remain in the background.

Back in the early 1950s, when Jackie started out, the music most white people listened to on their radios and record players was sung by Guy Mitchell, Frank Sinatra, Tony Bennett, Perry Como, Vic Damone, Dinah Shore, Jo Stafford, Rosemary Clooney, Kay Starr, Patti Page and Georgia Gibbs. But the start of something big was beginning to happen, and all this was about to change.

THE TERM COINED was 'rock 'n' roll'. It had been there all along, but was only played by blacks and was called rhythm and blues (R&B), more generally known as 'race music'. White radio stations wouldn't play it, believing that to do so was to commit ratings suicide. Leaving aside the question of which was the first rock 'n' roll record, suffice to say it was a rhythm and blues song, which, in turn, evolved from the blues. The Platters, with 'The Great Pretender', are generally considered to have had the first crossover hit in 1955. That year Chuck Berry (a blues artist) and Fats Domino also burst forth. The following year saw Little Richard and the music world was never the same. The cat was out of the bag – and the cat was black.

It is now known and accepted that Elvis Presley was totally influenced by R&B and gospel. He took it and mixed it with a few parts country (or hillbilly, as it was derogatively referred to), and what he was left with was rock 'n' roll. He first came to the attention of the world early in 1956, at the same time that Jackie, six months his senior, was in his third year with The Dominoes. Presley led a lot of people to black music, but in the beginning he was seen as rebellious and not a desirable role model.

Reacting to the shift in opinion, Tarnopol selected material and arrangements for Jackie enabling him to cross over to the Pop charts, where most of the money was. A close friend of Tarnopol's, Bobby Schiffman who ran the Apollo Theatre in Harlem, remembers how unusual this was. 'Most black performers at that time did not concentrate on crossover,' he says. 'They aimed their music at the R&B market and kind of resented the success of white performers doing black music.'

Credit for enabling black music to be heard by white audiences must be given largely to DJ Alan Freed. Using hip patter that appealed to his teenaged audience, Freed played a steady stream of R&B music, but as he was generally playing to a white audience, it was he who coined the term 'rock 'n' roll', making it more palatable. Eventually, his show became syndicated throughout the USA and Europe. He was to expose a huge, young, white audience to black music. He enabled black R&B artists to be heard by white audiences.

In the book *Big Beat* (Alan Freed's biography by John A. Jackson), it is claimed Freed's personal relationship with Jackie dates back to his days with The Dominoes. When Jackie went solo, Freed pushed his records. He perhaps went a little too far with 'I'll Be Satisfied', which Jackson claims Freed played for 45 minutes straight! His *WINS* program became *Alan Freed's Rock And Roll Show*. Freed set up shop in the Brill Building on Broadway. Better known as Tin Pan Alley, The Brill was also, of course, the office of his friend Nat Tarnopol and his publishing company, Pearl Music. Freed's name became synonymous with the term 'payola'.

Concerning payola, it is hard to find a more detailed account than the book *Hit Men* by Fredric Darren. He states: '"Payola" is a word the record industry has bestowed on the English language. The term's familiarity has led to a common perception – unfortunately true – that the business is full of sharpies and opportunists and crooks. But as crimes go, payola is no big deal if the government's enforcement effort is an indication. After Freed's commercial bribery bust in 1960 and congressional hearings on payola the same year, Congress passed a statute-making payola a misdemeanour offence punishable by a maximum fine of 10,000 dollars and one year in prison. To date, no one has ever served a day in jail on payola charges. The law is hardly a strong deterrent.

'The Payola scandal of 1960 destroyed Freed's life. He was indicted on 19 May, along with seven others, and charged with taking bribes to play records. Freed admitted he accepted a total of 2500 dollars, but said the money was a token of gratitude and did not affect airplay.' Darren concludes: 'Freed paid a small fine, but his career was over. By 1965 he had drunk himself to death.'

By 1958, Jackie was an established star and was included in the Alan Freed-sponsored *Christmas Holiday Show* at Loew's State Theatre in New

York. There were some other big names on the bill as well: The Everly Brothers, Chuck Berry, Bo Diddley, Eddie Cochran, Dion And The Belmonts, The Moonglows, Frankie Avalon, Jimmy Clanton, The Cadillacs, The Crests, The Royal Teens, Baby Washington and The New Tornados.

The broader public now witnessed Jackie's tremendous vocal range and stage performance. He loved to sing,whether there were ten or 10,000 people in the audience. Always impeccably dressed, he would glide out on stage, often with a cigarette which he'd discard, and do twists and spins and the fall back splits, which he had perfected, all while holding the microphone and never missing a note. His typically drawn out and impassioned song endings would have him on his knees, his jacket discarded and his tie loosened by this time, sweat pouring from him in a frenzy of emotion. He had the audience in the palm of his hand. At the end of a performance he would often launch himself headlong into the arms of hundreds of frantic fans, or lie on his back on stage, hanging over the edge, microphone in hand.

Jackie understood that performing was acting; it was the ultimate expression of pure emotion. He gave it his all. At times fans would tear at his clothes and body, much to the consternation of his handlers. It seemed that everybody, except Jackie, was in fear of his being torn apart. Typically, he would turn on stage and exclaim to his band, 'They sure do love me, don't they!' Although Jackie lived for these performances, they were physically very demanding and he would be exhausted afterwards. It was a brave act that would follow him on stage – the audience's expectations were just too great.

Jackie joined Freed's 'Rock And Roll Caravan' again in 1959, performing to sell-out crowds at venues such as Brooklyn's famous Fox Theatre. Others to share the billing with him were his friend Sam Cooke, Buddy Holly, Roy Hamilton, Fats Domino, Bobby Darin, LaVern Baker, Brook Benton, Ruth Brown, Frankie Avalon, Bobbie Rydell, Paul Anka, The Cadillacs and Duane Eddy. Freda vividly recalls this period of Jackie's career. 'Bobby Darin would come and sit in Jack's room,' she says. 'All these young white boys; Bobby Rydell and Frankie Avalon would also come around. Jack went all out to help them; like Fabian. He told them not to be shy. This is Jack, he likes people who don't come on strong. If he liked you, he liked just you; simple person that you were.'

Irv Nahan was another who organised concert tours at the time. He says, 'I go back to when he just left The Dominoes. I took him out as part of a package in the mid-50s; package shows after the various theatres. Irving Feld and I'd put the top ten on the road for thirty days. We were a part of the record deals as well. I was strictly black acts. I was part of the corporation that owned The Drifters, also I managed all the groups with Vee Jay records, all the 'bird' groups.' In 1957 and 1958 Jackie was with Nathan's tours: 'When we put the shows on down south, the whites had to stay in the balcony. It [the segregation] changed [improved] during the '60s. We had a special little book that showed the [blacks only] hotels they could stay at. On those top ten shows – ten top artists.

'Jackie was lucky to get 300 dollars a week. You make money selling the shows for 2500 a night. But if a group made 750 a week and went to 5000 dollars a week, they still wouldn't have enough to live on. They spent everything! Jackie was one of the best. He did his shows; I can't remember him missing any shows, either. He was crazy, but pretty reliable to an extent. He was one of the greats.' Typically, unlike concerts of today, stars like Jackie would perform only three or four songs.

In 1958, Tarnopol arranged with Alan Freed for Jackie to have a one-song spot in Freed's low budget film, G*o Johnny Go*. The plot, such as it is, centres around Jimmy Clanton as 'Johnny Melody', a teen idol. However, being a rock 'n' roll-centred story, the film did feature some considerable talent of the time; Chuck Berry, Eddie Cochran, Richie Valens, The Cadillacs and Harvey (Fuqua of The Moonglows).

Jackie performs only one song, 'You'd Better Know It', and was sensational, although it was a tame effort compared to his live performances. The 75-minute film was a bomb, but it did enable fans around the world to see Jackie perform. The movie exposure aided his record sales, 'You'd Better Know It' briefly held No One spot on the R&B Charts and No 37 on the Pop charts.

Some music writers were critical of the material Jackie performed. An example of this is Don Waller reviewing a compilation of Jackie's recordings in June 1983: 'With his glass-shattering falsetto, gospel-drenched phrasing and his ability to juggle octaves in the space of a single syllable, Jackie Wilson was a singer whose skills bordered on the superhuman. How could such a talent fall into relative obscurity? Wilson's own versatility was partly to blame. He could – and did – sing anything, from scorching rockers ('I'll Be Satisfied') to torchy blues ('Doggin' Around'), from transcriptions of operatic arias ('Night') to supper-club standards ('Danny Boy'). Unfortunately, Wilson's producers saddled him with some of the corniest arrangements in recording history, all powder puff choruses and oceans of soapy strings. As a result, much of his work sounds horribly backdated, even by '50s standards.'

Waller's opinion, if widely held, leads one to wonder how huge a star Jackie might have been had he recorded more 'commercial' material and been on a prestigious label, such as Atlantic, RCA, Stax or Motown?

5. A WOMAN, A LOVER, A FRIEND

On a cold evening in January 1960, 23-year-old Lynn Ciccone of Springfield, Illinois, was feeling miserable. She wasn't interested in rock 'n' roll, but that day something happened that altered her life forever — Jackie Wilson. For Lynn it was 'destiny'. Jackie had another name for it — 'kismet' (fate).

'I HAD TWO impacted wisdom teeth removed that day,' she recalls. 'My mouth was bleeding and swelling so I took some pain pills, laid down and took a nap. When I got up I was still in pain, so I laid down on the couch and turned on the TV. Dick Clark came on with Top Ten of the week. The next song was introduced as "Mr Excitement". Well, he comes out; you know that wink, nobody could do it like he did, twisting out there with one of those tight bolero outfits on. Those dark eyes flashed imperiously. His smile was soul drenching. He did his just-released "Talk That Talk". He dashed across the floor, winking, twisting, jumping, dancing and electrifying the audience. Before it was over I was sitting on the floor and had forgotten all about the pain. I sank to the floor in front of the set, hypnotised, a nameless force penetrated my body unnoticed, changing my life forever.

'When Jackie came back and did "Lonely Teardrops", it was like, "I love this guy, he's great. Who is he? I've got to find out." I thought, 'he's so handsome, and he's black'; the most beautiful black man I had ever seen. Jackie appeared to be singing directly to me.

'I woke up the next day and the first thing I thought of was Jackie Wilson, so I went to the record store and bought everything they had.' Lynn hurried home to listen to the voice of her new found idol. 'I decided to write a fan letter,' relates Lynn. 'I told him I thought he was great, and asked if I could have an autographed picture. I wrote a very long and personal letter and included my phone number and address. A week later, I got a phone call at work. The caller said, "Hi there, little lady. My name is Nat Tarnopol and I'm Jackie's Wilson's manager. We got your fan letter and we love it. I called to ask if you're interested in seeing Jackie perform live? He'll be in St Louis on 26 and 27 February."' Naturally, Lynn was delighted and accepted.

'Tarnopol went on, "Here's our phone number at Pearl Music. Call me back here next Monday." This was on a Wednesday. When I called, Tarnopol said,"I've got someone here who wants to talk to you." It was Jackie. He said, "Hi, doll, this is Jackie Wilson. Nat says you're my biggest fan. I won't send my picture, we are going to bring them to St Louis and I'll give them to you there. If you've got any albums, bring them down and I'll sign 'em."' Lynn needed some moral support on such a momentous adventure: "I asked my friend Louise, who thought I was crazy, but said she'd go with me.

'I had never been out of Springfield. It was about 100 miles from St Louis. If I had to divorce my husband, whatever, I was going to go to the show. I just flat-out told my husband I was going and he didn't give me any argument. He was too busy working on his car.

'I had to call back later and Johnny Jones [JJ] would tell me what to do and where to go. They were staying in the Hermitage Hotel, which was in a bad part of town.' When Louise and Lynn arrived in St Louis, they phoned JJ at the hotel. 'Oh yeah', he said, 'you're the chick that sent the letter. Tell you what, be at Kiel [Auditorium, aka Kiel Opera House] at 7:30. We've got two tickets for you at the box.' Arriving at the auditorium, she recalled, 'JJ came and took us backstage. Ike and Tina Turner opened the show. The Olympics, with their "Western Movies" hit, were on and a local, Sugar Pie De Santo, who I'd never heard of, and The Coasters. Jackie walked up behind me and put a hand on my shoulder as I turned around. With a voice like silken oak, he said, "Hi doll, you're much prettier than your picture."' She followed Jackie to his dressing- room. As he changed into another suit he asked, 'Why did you write that letter? How long have you been a fan?' Lynn explained, '3 January 3 1960, that's the first time I ever heard of you.' 'Man,' he said, 'I've heard a lot of stories from a lot of chicks, but I've never heard anything like that. I thought you were just another chick, playing games with me.' Jackie took her hands in his and kissed her on the lips. As they left the dressing-room Jackie whispered, 'I'd like to take off the red dress and see what's underneath. My imagination is going wild. Man, where did you come from?' He whispered in her ear, 'I got a feeling you may have a chastity belt under that dress.'

Lynn continued: 'When Jackie walked out on stage at the Kiel Auditorium and said, "Hi, ya all, I'm Jackie Wilson," pandemonium broke out. I'd just met him and I've never seen a performance like it! During the performance he just dived off the stage and terrified everybody. You didn't forget a performance by him – not ever.

'After the show, Jackie took me back to the dressing-room with him. He rested, then showered and dressed. Now he was a whole lot different – it was like nobody was around him. He asked if we'd like to go to dinner. We went in his limousine, where he held my trembling hand as he talked to the driver about dinner. After we ate, we just sat in the car and he was a perfect gentleman. They stayed with us till three o' clock in the morning, when the train was due to leave. When I went to get out of the car, he said, "I'm going to give you a number at Pearl Music" and he also gave me his apartment number. He said, "If you ever want to get hold of me, either Nat can get me or you can call the apartment." Both were New York City numbers.'

After this meeting they spoke on the phone several times and during each conversation Jackie told Lynn he wanted to see her again. Three months after they had first met, Jackie arranged for her to go to Chicago so they could spend a weekend together. JJ picked her up, with Jackie's driver, Clarence 'Pop' Watley, one of the kindest people Jackie had in his entourage. as he had a show to perform. Watley sensed her scepticism: 'Now, I'm gonna be somewhere close all the time,' he said, trying to reassure her, 'so you tell me if anything is wrong. Don't worry, Jack said you was scared. He'll take good care of you.' 'Thanks, Mr Watley, I am scared,' she said. JJ went inside and came right back with Jackie.

Jackie told her: 'I keep a small apartment here. I'm in and out of Chicago a lot. Mama stays here when she visits Aunt Belle Williams.' Lynn indicated to Jackie that she'd prefer to stay in a hotel. 'Okay,' he said, 'I don't want to scare you out of town.' He got Lynn a room at the Ambassador Hotel, then told her to call him if she needed anything.

Lynn closed the door and was soon asleep.

It was almost 1.30 a.m. when she woke, sat up and looked at the phone. She dialled the number and Jackie answered. 'Jackie,' she said, 'you tried to be a gentleman. You told me to call you if I needed anything. Will you please come and get me?' 'You aren't scared of me any more?' Jackie asked. 'No, I'm not afraid of you, but you are overwhelming,' she said. 'JJ will be there in 20 minutes, be packed,' he replied. JJ picked up Lynn from the hotel and drove her to Jackie's apartment. Lynn recalls: 'So it comes time to go to bed that night. He said, "You can have any bed you want." I went to bed and there's a knock on the door. I thought, "Oh, my God!" I was very nervous, partly on account of him being black.' But it wasn't too long before she relented and allowed Jackie to make love to her.

To this day, Lynn loves Jackie just as much as when she met him all those years ago: 'I can see him like it was today – he had beautiful skin tone, he really did. Photos make him look darker than he was. Those eyes, they'd flash, they'd light, they did everything. He totally mesmerised me.'

Jackie was equally at home in the environment of a raucous chitlin' circuit concert or high-class supper clubs like the Copacabana or Coconut Grove. As Dick Jacobs recounts in *Musician* magazine: 'Jackie always had the ambition to transcend being a rock 'n' roll singer and, as he put it, "go on to bigger and better things." So Nat Tarnopol booked him for an engagement at the Fountainbleau Hotel in Miami Beach, opening for the deadpan comedian George Jessel.

'The crowd at the Fountainbleau was mainly your basic Borscht Belt blue-hair-rinse set, who didn't know Jackie Wilson from James Brown. However, there was a sprinkling of hardcore Jackie fans at the shows. Jackie knew that the crowd was there mainly for Jessel, so he included an amazing punchline to his set: a knockdown, drag-out version of "My Yiddishe Momme". And when the predominantly Jewish crowd got an eyeful of this black sylph gliding across the stage like there's no such thing as gravity and there's no bones in his body at all, and he's crooning a mean, mournful and exuberant "My Yiddishe Momme" that would stop a bar mitzvah cold before sending everybody's heart right through the ceiling, this polite but sceptical crew of Jessel fans went berserk. As a kind of insurance policy, we threw a couple of other standards, like "California Here I Come", into the act and restricted the rock 'n' roll numbers to a long medley (to satisfy the real fans in the audience).'

As well as outfoxing the locals, Jackie arranged for Lynn to meet him in Miami, even though Freda was there as well. Says Lynn: 'He was the first black entertainer to appear at the Fountainbleau in Miami. That was April 1960; it was my first big concert. [The Fountainbleau was] one of the poshest hotels, with a mainly Jewish audience. Even then, although there was no screaming, hotel keys and notes from waiters were sent to him: "I'll get rid of my husband and meet you later." Women adored him.'

Lynn recalled one of his performances: 'Suddenly Jackie smiled devilishly, then dived into the sea of grasping, clutching hands before him. I said, 'Oh, God, Jackie . . . they'll tear him to pieces. Help him." "Help him? Hell, he loves it," JJ said, as he came running out to see what caused the uproar. I could see Jackie's arms and shoe-less feet thrashing about as the screaming young women tore at his clothes. When security helped him into the dressing-room his tie and shoes were missing. All the buttons from his white ruffled shirt were missing and the sleeves were torn. His normally perfectly coiffeured hair stood on end. Jackie sat down at the dressing table, laughing, as JJ hurried to him with a washcloth and towel.'

After another performance, at Harlem's Apollo Theatre, the artists and their entourages went to the Four Seasons Club. 'As they sat around the table, praising each others performances, the singer Dion Di Mucci came to the table and put a hand on Jackie's shoulder,' recalls Lynn. '"Hey Jackie, great show. I see Lynn is wearing out a chair here. Okay if we dance?"' Jackie still didn't dance well as a couple and appeared to indicate it was all right.

Sadly for Lynn, she'd done the wrong thing. 'When I came back he was drinking straight doubles,' she says. She knew Jackie's pride had been damaged and soon found out how annoyed he was. As Jackie unlocked the door to his apartment, Lynn started to tell him what a lovely evening she'd had. He slammed the door with fury. His eyes were filled with rage as he stood looking at her. 'Don't ever do that to me again, white girl,' he yelled. 'What did I do?' she asked. 'You're with me; I don't want anybody else's hands on you, got it?' Her eyes filled with fear as he moved closer, not knowing what he was thinking. Lynn ran into the bedroom and locked the door, crying and praying. She says: 'He began to pound and kick the door. Finally the lock broke and burst open, knocking me to the floor. Jackie grabbed my arms and dragged me to the side of the bed. He stood me up and flung me on the bed. "You hate me, huh, bitch? You are a spoiled, pampered little whore, and I made you that way, didn't I?" he said. Jackie raised himself astride me, placing his fingers around my neck. 'Jackie,' I whispered, 'are you going to kill me?' He removed his hands and sunk down on the bed beside me, sobbing. Slowly I moved to the edge of the bed and dashed into the bathroom, locking the door. I sat in the tub, rocking back and forth.

'After what seemed like hours, Jackie knocked softly on the door. "I'm sorry, Lynn, please come out, I won't hurt you, baby." I didn't move. It became quiet; I thought he was asleep. I cautiously opened the door and stepped into the bedroom. I felt his nearness at once. Jackie was sitting on the floor outside the bathroom, with his head resting on his knees. He looked pathetic. He sat there watching as I put on the pink gown and robe he had bought me. He went to the kitchen and returned with two glasses of wine. Jackie said,"I promise I won't hurt you again. I'm sorry."'

Around the same time, he had begun having a serious affair with model Harlean Harris, while still married to Freda. His career was at its peak and if he wasn't in the recording studio he would be constantly performing and, generally, on the move. Still, their relationship continued and, over a period, Lynn would accrue her work leave entitlements to rendezvous with him.

Jackie, as an adult, was reading *Captain Marvel* and *Tales From The Crypt* comic books — he had vast collections of them. He also loved old movies, particularly cowboy movies, watching them over and over. He loved his pet dogs, young children and 'old folks', who he was totally at ease with. In the body of the man there lurked a child. Lynn recalls one incident of Jackie's childish simplicity, when she visited him in Denver. 'It was very cold,' she says, 'and I slept with one of Jackie's sweaters on and socks. He had been in a happy mood all day. That evening, after the performance, he even ate cheeseburgers, my favourite food, to appease me. It was my birthday [22 March] and he had given me a beautiful pearl dinner ring, set in a musical bar. He had it made for me. I never cared for diamonds, but I loved pearls. He would laugh and say, "Not only are you dumb, but you are cheap."

'I was sleeping peacefully, when he began shaking me. "Get up! Come on, baby. We're gonna have some fun." It was snowing heavily and he wanted to have a snowball fight. What he didn't know was that I had been pretty good on the girls' softball team. I really pelted him! We were at a motel and we became so noisy that people got up to see what was happening. When they found out who Jackie was, some got dressed and came out to join in the fun.' They also made a snowman and despite Jackie having seen plenty of snow in Detroit, Lynn says, 'That time he made the snowman; he'd never made a snowman before! He reverted to a little boy.'

As he'd already proved to her, Jackie also experienced childish jealousy. When they went for the first time to the Copacabana in New York, with Nat Tarnopol and road manager, August Sims, and their wives, Lynn saw a side she had tried to forget. The feature act was singer Jerry Vale ('Pretend You Don't See Her'). Lynn recalls: 'I was enthralled with his performance. After the show we were having dinner and I was aware that Jackie's mood had changed. He put his fork down and said, "How come when that motherfucker sang you melted and ran all over the table? You don't act like that when I sing!" He shocked me. His ego was dying. I said, "Jackie, listen to me. He has a beautiful voice and he's a great performer, but what you saw was on the outside of me. When I look at you, all my feelings come from within." He looked at me for a moment and said, "Damn, I guess I should have stayed in school." Then he finished his steak.'

There could be as much frenzy around off stage. Once, when Jackie was appearing at the Lazy Boy Supper Club in Charleston, South Carolina. After the show they set out for dinner and Jackie and Lynn chose to walk a little, with Pop Watley following behind in the car. Lynn recalls: 'Suddenly a voice said, "Hey, you, nigger-boy, we wanna talk to you." When we turned around we were facing three huge white men. "Oh, he's one of those pretty niggers," one of them said. "Look, boy, you don't come down here and mess with our white women." Turning to me, he said, "You get yourself on home, white trash."

'I moved closer to Jackie and said, "I'm not one of your women, and I'm with him." "That's right," Jackie said as he removed his jacket and handed it to Lynn. "I own her," he told them. "Nobody calls me 'nigger' or 'boy' and she's not white trash, she's a lady." "Look, boy, we know who you are and we don't care. You take your white whore and get your black ass out of town," he told Jackie.

'As I started to speak again, Jackie put his hand up and said to me, "Shut up, mama, and get behind me. They're gonna eat those words." I dropped Jackie's coat to the sidewalk and took his hand. I told him, "I'll stand beside you, Jackie, but I won't hide behind you." At that moment, Pop Watley pulled the limousine over to the kerb. He stepped out with a tyre iron in one hand and a machete in the other. "Is there a problem here, Jack?" he asked. "Get back in the car, old man," one of the men said. "You wanna go?" Pop asked him. "I'm ready, and when we're done, somebody's gonna be hurt bad, or dead."'

Unbeknown to Jackie and Lynn, Jimmy Smith, Jackie's drummer, had been sleeping in the back seat of the limousine. Smith opened the door and stepped out. 'Put Lynn in the car,' Jackie told Jimmy. As he reached for her arm, Lynn said,'I'm not leaving you, Jackie.' 'Get your ass in the car and shut up,' Jackie yelled, but Lynn didn't move.

They were all squared off outside a tavern when three black men stepped out onto the sidewalk next to Jackie. 'Need some help, buddy?' one of them asked Jackie. 'I'd appreciate it, man,' Jackie said. 'Me and my woman here were just out takin' a walk before dinner and these bastards don't like it.' 'Okay, slick, you win this time, but if you ever come back here, you're dead,' one of the white men told Jackie. 'Hey, man, you got a deal, but tonight I'm takin' my girl here out to dinner and we're goin' back to the motel and we're goin't o bed,' Jackie said, defiantly. He gave the three black men some money and got in the limousine. 'Well, now,' he said to Lynn. 'You were gonna go all fifteen rounds with me, weren't you?' 'Yes,' she said, as he put his arms around her. 'Jackie, I'm sorry about the things they said to you.' Jackie replied, 'You don't have to apologise for white people, baby.'

Lynn says now, 'Jackie gave me self esteem I previously never had, I never knew I was entitled to.' But that journey towards self esteem included an amusing incident in 1963, which resulted in Lynn appearing on stage with Jackie, much to her chagrin. She had become pregnant by Jackie, but was afraid to tell him lest he dump her. 'I began avoiding him,' she remembers, 'failing to show up when I said I would. Finally, he told me to be in Houston or he was coming to my workplace.' So, Lynn met Jackie in Houston and, as she put it, 'It didn't take long for him to notice the problem. He said we would talk about it after the show.'

There were a group of people backstage prior to the show. Jackie's young keyboards player, Truman Thomas, had just told a joke and everyone was laughing. Says Lynn, 'Jackie was standing next to me while I sat on a chair. Then my hair was nearly waist length. I leaned forward against Jackie, laughing. My head was just above his belt-line. Jackie was laughing so hard he was twisting back and forth. His hands were in my hair. My hair became tangled around the buttons on his shirt and entwined in his belt buckle. Then it was time for his performance. Everyone tried frantically to separate us, to no avail. Finally Jackie said, "Well, baby, you're about to have your stage debut." He pulled me out on stage with him; I was dying of embarrassment. He was laughing so hard. He said, "Folks, I know this looks bad, but it isn't what you think. I'm not even going to try and explain." Somebody found scissors and freed me.'

Lynn's pregnancy was not something he found easy to discuss, but he raised the subject on one occasion. 'One afternoon, in Colorado,' says Lynn, 'Jackie and I were playing cards. I was four months pregnant . Out of the blue, he said, "Didn't you think that this could happen? Weren't you afraid? If you thought your friends didn't approve of you seeing me, how do you think they're gonna feel now? You ain't had trouble like you're gonna have." I just smiled at him and said, "I love you, and I need two cards." He shook his head and said, "Man, you're some kinda crazy chick."'

Gina was born in April 1963, but was 13 years old before Lynn informed her who her real father was.

Sadly, from his earliest years, a lot of Jackie's fun came from alcohol. Lynn relates one incident: 'After a big evening of too much Scotch, Jackie woke up at 1.30 p.m. with a terrible hangover. It was my job to bring him tomato juice and coffee. When I sat on the bed and handed him the juice, he said, "Don't jump on the bed and don't touch me!' I said, "If you think your nose is bad, you should see your eyes, or can't you see?' Jackie sat up and said, 'Don't yell so loud. After I feel better I'm gonna slap the shit out of you. You're always saying I don't look good."'

His day started at two or three in the afternoon and alcohol was forever present. 'Jackie drank Chivas Regal straight or on the rocks; he was hooked on that,' says Lynn. 'He drank a lot of stuff straight. He could drink and drink and not show it, but when he got drunk he would pass out. As for drugs, the only thing I ever saw Jackie use were these red capsules – uppers. He was also a first-rate cusser. At the same time, he had a lot of compassion.

'Sometimes, when he had a cold, he could be a bear like anyone else. "Don't touch me," or "I can't talk to you because my vocal cords will be swollen." He had to be taken care of when he was sick, but had no sympathy for anyone else when they were sick. Oh, no.'

Other women troubles were manifold. One of the subjects that few wished to talk about, and still fewer knew about, concerned Jackie's affair with Alona, the daughter of a notorious New York mobster. Her father was one of those who had a stake in Jackie's career. Just what problems this caused for Jackie, if any, could not be determined. Then there was a woman with the unusual name of Fadwah Peace, a Cajun voodoo from New Orleans. Jackie is said to have had two children by her and would often phone her from various parts of the country.

The recipient of many phone calls herself, Lynn had almost been ostracised by her own family on account of her relationship with Jackie. Their daughter Gina would come to know Jackie, though she was unaware he was her father. By the time Lynn informed her of the truth, Jackie had been stricken by a heart attack and would never speak again. Gina, now married, says: 'I do not have the fond memories of him that my mother can so ably recall. At best, I seem to remember feeling as if I were out of place when we were there with him. At times he had this need almost to hide us from certain of his acquaintances.' This observation is more than likely correct, given that he married Harlean in 1967 and was living in a de facto relationship with Lynn Crochet from late 1970.

Gina recalls that Jackie did show her affection on a couple of occasions: 'Mama and JJ left me with him once. We were playing a children's card game. Suddenly he threw the cards up in the air and they fell to the floor. He told me to pick them up. Then he got on the floor to help me. He laid face down, looking at me. After a moment he squeezed the end of my nose and said, "Yeah, you're gonna look just like your mama." Then he pulled one of my long curls and helped me pick up my cards.

'Another time we were sitting eating in the suite. I didn't want to eat. My mother was arguing with me when he picked me up and held me on his lap. He cut up his food and recited the old standard, "Through the lips and over the gums, look out stomach here it comes." I recall laughing and after each bite he would kiss me on the cheek.

'My other memories were not unhappy ones, but not necessarily endearing. He did exhibit genuine concern when I broke my leg at the age of seven while trying to imitate his acrobatics. He picked me up and was running down the corridor yelling for someone to help. But I also recall the smell of liquor on his breath when he would kiss me hello or goodbye. He only spanked me once. I suppose I was very spoiled. I kicked Mama on the leg in anger. He jumped off the bed, pulled up my dress and let me have it. Then he pointed at me and said, "Never again, get it?" I did.'

States Lynn, 'If I could have only one wish, it would be to be with Jackie again and look upon that beautiful face. I once said to him, "I love your nose and your face." He laughed, "Doll, my nose is my face." I dried and pressed nearly every pink rose Jackie gave me. Even with his many faults he became my salvation, my reason for being. And then I had Gina.'

Gina believes Jackie should have treated her mother better.'"I don't dispute that he is undoubtedly one of the greatest entertainers who ever lived, but I believe that is the sum total of the man. He certainly took mother's heart and soul with him when he went.' Although Gina cannot understand the enormous hold Jackie held over her mother, she is sure her mother would have taken better care of him: 'If Jackie was in mother's care he still wouldn't have recovered, but the quality of life would certainly have been maintained. She would never have allowed him to languish as he did.'

The black youth of Detroit were especially proud of their home-grown hero. Contours manager, Jack Ryan, who grew up in Detroit, says: 'Everyone knew the reason that many kids here wanted to be a singer; Jackie had proved he could make it. He was black and from Detroit, and he made it. It was like Joe Louis was to the boxers. He was proof positive that anyone could make it. You didn't have to go to a factory. I was a white kid and I knew what Jackie meant to Detroit.'

THE FALCONS, a Detroit group, had included such notables as Eddie Floyd, 'Sir' Mack Rice and Wilson Pickett amongst its line-up. In 1959 they had their one major hit 'You're So Fine', featuring the lead vocal of Joe Stubbs, brother of The Four Tops' lead singer, Levi. Stubbs discussed the tour they'd been on with Jackie, on a joint radio tribute to Jackie by WAEV-FM (Savannah, Georgia) and *Record Profile* magazine, broadcast in 1988, 'We were down on the road one time in St Louis — me, The Midnighters, Ruth Brown, Sam Cooke — whole lot of us were there. We did our show and came off. Jackie was last. He did his show and was coming off when a guy grabbed his coat and tore his pocket. So Jackie hit him and knocked him off the stage. Two or three more came up, so Jackie knocked them off. Billy [Davis, guitarist with The Midnighters] was playing for Jackie, too . . . Billy is a 'pug' [boxer]; hell of a guy, knock you out in a minute. So I got beside Billy Davis 'cause they were starting to surround us. People was coming up getting ready to come up on stage. We were backing out to the back entrance, so they came out to the back entrance. So Jackie and Billy started knocking out guys and I got to do a little hitting, too. We got back to the hotel and they started busting windows with bricks and we heard some gunfire. That was scary!'

With obvious respect for Jackie, Stubbs went on: 'Jackie was a good guy, he had a heart of gold. Jackie was the star of the show and I told him, "Hey, Jackie, see these people" — there was about 40 of them — "they ain't got no money to get in." Jackie said, "Let 'em all in."' Summing up life on the road with Jackie , Stubbs says it was 'hectic and chaotic'. It's no wonder that the name given Jackie by Alan Freed, and the name that stuck, was

'Mr Excitement'.

Singer and writer 'Sir' Mack Rice, also of The Falcons, went on to write some big hits, the best known of which is 'Mustang Sally' (made famous by Wilson Pickett). Rice knew Jackie well at the time, having been considered for The Dominoes' replacement position, which was taken by him: 'He was just a fantastic guy, man. Never saw him mad in my life; always had a smile on his face. He loved everybody, always kissed any woman, fat, greasy, ugly, whatever. That would make the women go crazy. He was the hardest working guy I ever met.'

Rice explains the rivalry between the talents of Sam Cooke and Jackie: 'That package show we were on, Sam Cooke was the star,' he says. 'Him and Jackie were star and co-star. They had a little argument about who was going to star and Sam won out in some kind of way, 'cause he had a hit out – all those big records – was smooth and all that. Each night, man, I felt bad for Sam, because Jackie would beat and destroy him. No one would follow Jackie on stage; Sam wouldn't either any more. By the time Sam came on, people [the audience] would start leaving. Sam had the clean-cut image, good guy like, while Jackie was nasty – he'd do all kinds of stuff. As an entertainer and a person, Jackie was one of the best I've met; best I ever met in my life. Couldn't beat his personality.'

As Rice found, with two of the greatest voices in contemporary music there was bound to be some friction. 'We went on this tour with Sam Cooke and Jackie Wilson together,' says Grady Gaines of The Upsetters band, 'all the major cities in the US. The way they had that billing, Sam Cooke would star in the show, the next night Jackie would be the star. Sam Cooke had four or five records in the Top Ten and one of them was No One. Jackie Wilson had some in the Top 50. Sam Cooke was just burning Jackie up with those hot records. They would both tear it up. That was one of the greatest tours I was ever on.' At the end of the tour, it was all smiles: 'In the beginning they were kind of worried, about who would star and all that. But when that tour was over they was the best friends you've ever seen,' Gaines remembers. 'I'm going to tell you, Jackie Wilson was one of the baddest cats that ever lived in show business. Sam and Jackie were bad and when I say bad, I mean good! If Jackie was living now he'd be all over the Pop charts.'

Gaines finds it incredible that Jackie didn't achieve greater recognition: 'He started everybody that's out there now; they all got something from him. Jackie Wilson had a voice . . . tormenting! That cat could go so high and do it with ease; I'm telling you, he had full control. I got along so good with Jackie. That was the greatest tour,' says Gaines nostalgically. 'He definitely lived hard and fast.'

In 1959 Jackie, a major headliner, earned only around two to three thousand dollars a night. With the average American man then earning only around 100 dollars per week, this would seem adequate, but out of that Jackie had to pay for food, accommodation, his entourage, travel costs and management. Typically Jackie took three musicians with him and, by pre-arrangement, picked up the rest at the venues along the way. For a time, he travelled with the hard-driving, brassy Chris Columbo band, another of the pioneer rock 'n' roll bands. Gil Askey, who played trumpet with the band, travelled with Jackie for nearly two years. 'I met Jackie when "Lonely Teardrops" came out in 1958,' he recalls. 'We did a show in Detroit: I think I was getting 30 dollars a night. We didn't fly in those days, we had a truck we travelled in. The whole band would get 200 dollars, and Jackie used to pay it out of his pocket.

'Jackie was so powerful, and we had to go to keep up with him. He'd do those splits, twirls, and we'd be romping – all we had to do was drive it home to him. Jackie never rehearsed. I used to write the horn parts out. The first guitar player was Billy Johnson [formerly guitarist with The Moonglows], then Dickie Thompson followed.' Earl Van Dyke, another member of the band and extraordinary keyboards player, would later become one of the famous Funk Brothers, the driving force behind the great Motown sound.

Although The Four Tops did not have their first hit record until 1964, by which time they had signed with Motown, they often were often on the same tours. 'We went out together with Jackie when he got hot,' remembers distant relative Lawrence Payton of The Tops. 'Those were wild times, man. We almost had riots everywhere. We were in southern Illinois one night. Everyone had arrived and we were waiting for Jackie. He'd always show, but he was late as a mother. They had us under siege. We tried to stave them off, but they were ready to kill everybody: "We want our money back!" Trouble followed Jackie, but he was up to it, man. He was one of the gangsters himself, he loved it. That was his life and those were his friends.' Jackie couldn't live life any other way but on the edge.

Saxophonist and flute player Thomas 'Beans' Bowles, during the 1950s, worked behind Maurice King at the Flame Show Bar as a member of his band The Wolverines, and so knew Jackie early in his career. 'I recognised Jackie as a major talent in the early days – absolutely,' says Bowles. Bowles was often on the early tours; he was with singer Marv Johnson in his early

Jackie with the vocalist he greatly admired, Roy Hamilton.

Jackie on stage in an early 1960s performance.

Left to right: August Sims (Jackie's manager), Simon Rutberg (a young friend and fan) and Jackie Wilson, backstage at the Count Basie recording session in Los Angeles in 1968.

Jackie and Count Basie at a recording session in Los Angeles in 1968.

Left to right: Billy Ward (Jackie's mentor of Billy Ward and the Dominoes group),
an unknown lady and Jackie, in the late 1950s or early 1960s.

Left to right: Jackie Wilson, Judy Garland and Count Basie in 1968.

Jackie's 'minder,' Johnny Roberts (at head of the table), and guitarist Billy Johnson (second from the left), at a nightclub with Jackie and his second wife, Harlean.

Group photo taken in Cleveland in 1961. *Left to right*: Billy Johnson (guitarist), Al Abrams (Motown promotions man), JJ (Johnny Jones, Jackie's best pal), Jackie, Berry Gordy (Motown founder), Robert Bateman (Motown producer) and (on his knees) performer Little Willie John.

Left to right: Jackie's touring guitarist Dickie Thompson, boxer Floyd Patterson and Jackie.

Studio pic of Jackie from the early 1960s.

Above, from left to right: Jackie's closest friend JJ, Jackie and an unknown man backstage. *Below*, from left to right: JJ, Zola Taylor (of The Platters group) and Jackie at a nightclub. From the early 1960s.

days with [organ player and band leader] Jack McDuff's band. Bowles witnessed the pressures Jackie endured: 'Every time I saw Jackie he was so tired; he was always trying to get into bed, and all these kids and these people idolised him and worried him to death. He was such a genial guy he let them do it. I found him one time in Pittsburg – I had to use the john [toilet]. There were two suites and an interconnecting john. I went into the room and tried to get in – it was locked, so I waited a while and tried again. Finally, the door opened and it was Jackie. He'd been in there with his puppy, a pretty little dog he carried with him. He was sitting in there trying to rest. I said, "Why don't you take my room?" He did, and slept for about eight hours. Nobody would give him a chance to rest. His room was full of fans loving him to death and it just wore him out. He'd have to chase them out – they'd stretch him to the limit.'

Touring by car was always a problem, as Gil Askey relates: 'Jackie would wait until the last minute before leaving for these gigs and then drive 110 miles an hour to get to the gig one hour before the next gig was over. I remember we were going to Savannah, Georgia one night. It was 285 miles. I was in the car with Henry Wynne, the promoter. They left after 8 p.m., but Jackie still got there on time. JJ and Frazier sat on 100-plus on the interstate. The cops pulled them over, but they still got there by midnight.'

A musician who backed Jackie on these gruelling tours says: 'We didn't like to see him surrounded by people who weren't musicians, but he needed them. They were takers and bleeders. They couldn't do nothing but drive a car and they had guns; they had pistols, 'cause of some of the promoters. You weren't living in the Hilton and the Holiday Inn and you might be carrying 3–5000 dollars. You could be in a violent area. The gun's a deterrent.'

Jackie occasionally stayed at the Forrest Arms rooming house in Atlanta. 'Jackie went mad there once and ripped out the toilet seat,' says Askey. 'He was despondent.' It wouldn't be the last time that Jackie vented his long-pent up rage in some room. At times he'd call his mother, speaking to her as though he were still a young boy. 'On one occasion Jackie refused to perform,' continues Askey. 'It was a huge audience and we were afraid there'd be a riot once the audience knew Jackie wasn't going to appear.

They wanted me to get up and make an announcement that Jackie wasn't going to appear. I said, "Man, I can't get up there and tell 'em that. They're going to be throwing shit at me." People had been waiting for two, two-and-a-half hours. So I got up and announced, "Mr Jackie Wilson has just arrived, so we're going to get off here to let Jackie's band set up." The other band was thrilled, because they thought they were going to be backing Jackie Wilson. We packed up the Hammond organ and speakers, drums and guitars, and loaded 'em all into the truck. Then we got out of there – in a big hurry! Naturally, Jackie got sued for non-appearance at times.'

Askey also recalls Jackie's affection for Poochie, his little Chihuahua dog: 'Jackie would sit out in the car with the dog for two, three hours. And he'd kiss the dog, he'd tongue it, right in the mouth! Jackie would say, "Dogs don't carry germs... people do."'

While his dog was well cared for, the four Wilson children, like all youngsters, desperately needed a father. But to earn a living Jackie needed to perform, which meant constant touring so he didn't get home to Highland Park often to see them. Though not exactly normal, but it was the life he had chosen since his earliest years.

In 1960, when Jackie performed at the Allen Theatre in Cleveland, Ohio, Freda and the children travelled to see him. Jackie called the three oldest – Denise then aged nine, Sandra aged seven and Jackie Jnr aged six – on stage to perform with him.

In the south, if audiences were not totally segregated, as they often were, bands would perform to blacks one night and whites the other. But Jackie's fans crossed the racial divide and he loved them dearly. Askey recalls one such gig in 1960: 'I remember how he was when he played for the blacks in Jackson, Mississippi at this place, out in the Jackson State College – it could hold around 2000 people. The kids were trying to get in the dressing-room to see Jackie. The cops were trying to push the crowds back. said, "No, no, don't push my friends, just let them in here, three at a time." He'd hug and kiss them like a lover, he'd tongue kiss them all. He had all this sweat on him . . . he had all this love.'

During 1960, at Toledo, Ohio's Civic Centre, Jackie's mother had come to see the show. Things got a little out of control, as Askey relates: 'During those days you had a dancing show, the band came on from nine till one. Maybe Jackie was due on at ten for about an hour. He would come on again at twelve till one. There was a walkway between the stage and the pit. A cop was walking around there, and we warned him, "You'd better get out of there, because when Jackie reaches the stage . . ." "Oh, no," said the cop, "I've got it under control."

'We went on at nine p.m., Floyd Smith on guitar, Jimmy on saxophone [band leader], Chris Columbo, me on trumpet and guitarist Dickie

Thompson [conducting at that period]. There were 2.5–3000 people, drinking and all. An hour passed, and we expected Jackie. We played for two hours. No Jackie! People were throwing bottles at us, so we took a break.

'Jackie was out in the parking lot, sitting in his Cadillac, with his Chihuahua dog. He hated to be doing this show. What was going on, I don't know. He just wasn't happy, but he came in about 12 and he said, "I better go on before these people wreck this place." Man, when Jackie hit that stage, people went over the rail and went straight over that cop. How they got up on that stage I don't know. They were cuddling him . . . they had him on the floor. They didn't care nothing about him being late! The organ was on top of the organ player. With all the chaos, Jackie was just smiling.'

Askey recalls things again getting out of hand in another town, Dayton, Ohio, at the Walpole Theatre, which seated about 4000 people. 'It was summer time – warm – they had this podium in the middle like a boxing ring, where Jackie was going to sing from. We, the band, were over the other side entertaining the people and we told the promoter that Jackie wasn't going to hear us from over there. They told us, "We've got it all set up, it'll sound like the band is there." We kept saying, "He's not going to be happy. Jackie likes his band right behind him."

'Jackie was back in the dressing-room, late as usual, and he was so close we could hear him talking. He kept stalling and stalling. By this time the crowd was thinking that Jackie was going to be up on stage with us and they massed right in the front of this space where we were. Anyhow, Jackie came out and they had to try to get him through the 4000 people and up to this podium. It took 20 minutes. We were being crushed – it was chaos. Jackie got up there and started, but he only got halfway through the first piece of music before he called out, 'I can't hear my band.'

'So now they were going to bring him back through the audience. They had pulled off his coat, his silk shirt had been ripped off – he never wore any undershirt – and he had nothing on but his pants. Jackie looked at up and laughed, and said, 'Boy, they sure do love me, don't they?' He wasn't worried about anything. He loved all of this stuff. He did his show; how he performed! Every time we played anywhere there was chaos, because the places were not big enough. Ninety per cent of our audiences were black.'

By most accounts, Nat Tarnopol encouraged Jackie to be constantly out on a financial limb. That way, Jackie would need to always sing for his supper. Their friendship became increasingly strained. Freda says, 'He never could break with Nat, but he did do a little something about it. He had been trying for years.' Freda was referring to 1961 when he changed managers from Tarnopol to Johnny Roberts, although still remaining bound to the Brunswick label. From Tarnopol's standpoint, Jackie was increasingly unmanageable. Numerous times he failed to appear for an engagement or recording session.

Nobody could recall exactly what contractual arrangements Tarnopol had drawn up with Jackie. Indeed, all documents pertaining to management fees and royalties appear to have been lost or, more likely, destroyed along the way. Tarnopol kept Jackie either in the recording studio or touring. Either way Jackie was earning large sums of money for Brunswick and Tarnopol. Jackie's earliest contractual arrangement with Brunswick was said to be royalties of only three per cent of retail, with a minimum guaranteed of 50,000 dollars per year. When Jackie and Tarnopol renegotiated the contract in 1968, his share became five per cent. Throughout his entire career, Jackie engaged Herbert Lippman as his lawyer. Lippman was the nephew of Jackie's original manager, Al Green, but more ominously was a crony of Tarnopol. Was this ethical, or advantageous to Jackie?

Freda recalls that it was not uncommon for Tarnopol to phone in the middle of the night, and Jackie would have to get up and go out to entertain some client. In the beginning, Tarnopol was like Jackie's shadow – never out of his sight. Brunswick was once more becoming a recognised label and he moved the operation to 888 Seventh Avenue, New York.

His son, Paul, believes it wasn't always easy for Tarnopol being Jackie's manager, though. 'There were major problems all through his career with Jackie,' he says. 'Jackie would wind up in jail, regularly. He would get into trouble with white women. Nat would get calls from all over the country asking to bail Jackie out. He'd be in a hotel with a girl when he should be on stage. My dad had to get a road manager, Augie [August] Sims, just to make sure he was in the right place at the right time, because Jackie just couldn't do it by himself. Throughout his whole life he was rebellious.

'At one time my father told him he had to stop doing this; stop getting into trouble and showing up late. Jackie would have cars, rings, furs; spending on people like crazy. One time he got a call from Augie saying, "You'd better talk to Jackie. He is not going to be up for the show." My father told him, "If you miss the show we're going to be up for a lot of money and you could end up in jail" and Jackie said, 'If I go to jail, I'll just give them an autographed picture and I'll be out." That same night, at ten p.m, dad got a call from a chief of police saying he was in jail. Jackie said, 'You've got to get me out" 'Dad said, "Why are you calling me? Just give them an autographed picture and you'll be out." Nat finally got him out.

'Nat and Jackie would often fight, and Jackie would say, "I don't need you any more." One time Nat said, "Okay, I don't need you," and tore up the contract. Next day Jackie was back. There were times when Nat and Jackie nearly got lynched [in the southern states] – partly because there were white women in the audience. There were shootings, too.'

Roquel 'Billy' Davis believes that Jackie would have had even more success in the hit charts with better guidance. 'All performers were in awe of Jackie back then,' he says. 'They couldn't be anything else but in awe of him. He had a great personality, charisma . . . unbelievable. You couldn't help but love him. Jackie didn't have anybody musically conscious to guide him. Nat thought he could, but though he always pretended he did, Nat didn't know one piece from another. He was totally out of step. Prior to Jackie, who was Nat Tarnopol? He was a 'gofer' for Al Green.'

American Bandstand's Dick Clark knew and liked Tarnopol. He says: 'Nat was a very colourful man – lots of rings and jewellery and loads of cash in his pocket at all times. I got along very well with him. Years ago, I went to see Jackie. He appeared in Atlantic City in a roller-skating rink – it was an all black audience – with a friend of mine, Al Wild, a little short guy, [a] fat, Jewish man, who was a manager. Nat was backstage, where Jackie had his hand maidens giving him rub downs, amongst the roller skates, and waiting on him like a king. It was a tawdry, squalid, awful atmosphere, with the empty gin bottles and broken glasses from after the show, but everybody was paying homage and court to him backstage. My friend Al Wild embraced Nat and proceeded to lift several thousand dollars from his pocket. Al said, "Wait till he finds out I took his wad." He gave it back to him, of course, but the joke was that, at the time, he was picking his pocket.'

Freda rues that Jackie trusted Nat Tarnopol so much he signed power of attorney over to him: 'Even I knew better than that. After Al Green died, I knew better. Green would have been fair with him.' Freda suggested he should proceed with caution, but Jackie was trusting and naive: 'I said, "Even if you gave me power of attorney, I might be tempted to do something. Especially if I got mad; I might take the money and put it in a bank account in my mother's name." I said, "Don't do it." Jack was having problems with Nat . . . with his money. Nat kept saying to us he was not taking his ten per cent [management fee]. Then, all of a sudden, the money that should have been in the bank wasn't there. Nat had authority to use his money in any way he saw fit.' In the beginning, Jackie relied totally on Tarnopol to take care of his financial affairs and the power of attorney claim is believed by many to be correct. Roquel 'Billy' Davis is one of those who believes it existed. 'They [Brunswick] even wanted power of attorney over Berry [Gordy] and I,' he reflects. 'I think Al Green, also, had power of attorney over Jackie.'

Aware that Tarnopol was holding back his royalty earnings, Jackie became increasingly unreliable, either appearing late or not at all. Many years later, when the legal system finally caught up with Tarnopol, it became known that he was selling Jackie's records 'out the back door'. It is likely that the Mob also benefited from these illegal sales, all to the detriment of Jackie's financial position. It is hard to believe that Tarnopol would have dared to short change them.

A classic example of Jackie's realisation that he was not getting his just desserts is a story related by Gil Askey: 'Jackie woke up one morning – he'd just come off a great three-month tour – and he called his bank to find out how much money he had in his account. They told him an amount, say "11.85". He said, "You mean $11,085?" They said, "No, I mean $11.85." Jackie fell out of bed, fell on the floor and nearly had a heart attack. So he went down to the bank and opened his safety deposit box. It contained a bunch of IOUs. Tarnopol had power of attorney and the key to his deposit box.' Of course, the sums quoted may not be accurate, but the situation was typical of what was going on.

His childhood friend Hank Ballard believes Jackie's real problem was desperate loneliness: 'I think most of the people surrounding Jackie were hangers-on and users,' he says. 'He knew why they was there. He had drug addicts, heroin addicts hanging on there. He was buying them drugs. He was just too generous. I think that's why he was so lonely.' Guitarist Dickie Thompson agrees: 'The thing I remember about Jackie was he didn't like to be alone. If he didn't have someone around, he'd go crazy. He would always have someone around in the dressing-room and if he didn't, he'd call me or find me. Jackie would pick up almost anyone off the street, get 'em a haircut and a brand new suit of clothes, take 'em on the road with him as a driver. They couldn't drive for shit, but they'd tell him, "Oh yeah, I can drive, man." He'd put them behind the wheel and 50 miles out of town they'd get lost.'

Thompson travelled at that time with Jackie and The Chris Columbo

JACKIE WILSON

Band. He says. 'I didn't really want the gig. I told them I couldn't read music too well, but I'd been around, played with everybody. So they said, "What I want you to do is conduct." So between Gil Askey and Earl Van Dyke [later to become one of Motown's rhythm section] they said, "All you do is keep time; you start the thing and you end it." Once you know the tempo, it's easy. He would change his vocals, but the back-up was the same. No rehearsals. Jackie always said, "Watch me, watch me." His basic show was the same ten tunes, so after a time I didn't watch him any more. Now and then he'd slip in an extra one or two songs. Jackie said to me one night, "You don't even look at me any more."'

Thomson went on, 'There were some scary moments, especially through the south. Once, around Jackson, Mississippi we got lost and it was the time the black boy was trying to get into the white college [James Meredith attempted to enter the University of Mississippi in 1962]. They had the National Guard out and here we are, lost, with two cars with New York plates! They gave us directions – took us to the town limits! Jackie knew what was going to happen and he pushed it to the limit. We got into brawls all the time.' But Thomson added, ironically, 'If he had so many true friends, how come he was always in trouble?'

Hank Ballard confirms one of the consequences of Jackie's success: 'We [the Midnighters] were the first to come out of Detroit with a hit record, but Jackie was the biggest entertainer to come out of Detroit and elsewhere. He was magic, man. He could go to Las Vegas and play those rooms; he was a class act. Off stage he was different, but on stage he was class. He was a party man. If anyone bruised him or violated him, you'd have to kill him – he would fight.'

He would need to. Being black and driving around the southern states in a Cadillac with New York licence plates could create problems, as band member Gil Askey explains: 'The way the times were, there were a lot of prejudices. We couldn't stop on the highway in Georgia or Alabama and go to the toilets in one of the roadside parks 'cause they had "Whites Only" signs. At filling stations in the middle of the night, we could buy gas but we couldn't go to the toilet.

'In 1960 we did a concert in Birmingham, Alabama. At that time you did a concert Sunday afternoon for a white audience and Sunday night for the blacks. Jackie refused to do the show for the whites. The next day we went to Florence, Alabama. The same situation prevailed, but he went on. These little white girls, five, maybe ten of them, moved upstage and Jackie would go into these gyrations, he'd do spins and flips and the girls would

103

scream, then they would stop real sudden because everyone was looking at them.' Well-behaved southern white girls weren't supposed to get excited over black performers.

'Sir' Mack Rice recalls touring at the same time. He also remembers seeing Jackie and JJ with some large amounts of money: 'I've seen him and JJ after a gig. They'd have a briefcase full of money and they'd put it into the trunk. A briefcase, just like the gangsters. Jackie was like Isaac Hayes – he cherished his friends.' Gil Askey, too, recalls the briefcase full of money that they had. 'Jackie never had any money on him, but JJ was there and had his little briefcase full of money. And it better be his money, 'cause he's supposed to send the other money back to the office in New York!'

One steamy July night in 1960, at the Municipal Auditorium in New Orleans, a riot broke out at one of Jackie's performances. Up to 5000 people were said to be present. Singer Chuck Jackson, a long-time close friend of Jackie's, was with The Dell Vikings at the time. He remembers: 'I was there when Larry Williams was performing. The police told us before we got there, "Don't come off this stage, black boy."

'They had police lined up all around the stage. Larry Williams had his foot up on the piano like Little Richard; he was doing "Dizzy Miss Lizzy" and he ran to the edge of the stage, but didn't jump off. He got down on the edge of the stage and women came forward – white women! Jackie was standing backstage and the cops took Larry and pulled him into the audience and started beating him with their sticks. Jackie came from backstage like he was Johnny Weismuller. He ran like he was Tarzan and he leapt, like he was leaping into a lake, into the crowd of policemen. When he hit the floor, he was like a little rabbit. He went down on his knees and when he came up, like he does on stage, he hit this cop, a big red cop. He messed him up bad. They beat him [Jackie] and nearly killed him.

'We finally pulled him out and had to take him to the hospital. They took him to jail and we got him out. It took us a matter of minutes to get out of town. They had his picture in the paper, where he hit the cop.' The riot received coverage in the newspapers, which stated that police laid charges which 'ranged from attempted murder to assaulting police and inciting a riot. Wilson was booked with disturbing the peace, inciting a riot and assaulting an officer'.

Also present was Midnighters' guitarist and friend, Billy Davis: 'Larry would jump off the stage into the audience. The police said, 'Don't you do that no more." The second the show started, Larry jumped out again. Jackie jumped up and the big cop pushed him back, then Jackie punched him out cold and Jackie could punch like George Foreman for a little guy. The cop was six foot one, 225 pounds; Jackie was 150 pounds and five foot nine. We were all locked up, but only for a few hours.'

With all the excitement of the riot and his being so keen to rescue Jackie, JJ completely forgot to look after the briefcase full of money, which he'd left unguarded in the dressing-room. Luckily, band leader Chris Columbo closed up the briefcase and took care of it. However, the New York office must have heard about JJ's blunder, because soon afterwards Johnny Roberts joined them on the road. Roberts formerly worked with Queens Booking Agency and had a fearsome reputation as a Mob enforcer. His role was to take care of the money, but also to provide protection for Jackie. Although he was usually the perfect soft-spoken gentleman, when he fixed his icy stare on someone they would become extremely nervous and do exactly what was expected of them. Certainly, with Roberts there, no unscrupulous promoter would consider short- changing anybody. After the show Roberts would take the money over to the Western Union office, where it was wired back to New York.

Johnny Collins, a singer who married Jackie's half-sister, Joyce Ann Lee, opened for his brother-in-law for a couple of years, and has vivid memories of the indignities Jackie suffered; such as one occasion when a southern sheriff had him beaten to pulp after white women had become interested in him. Collins recalls: 'When Jackie walked out on the stage after having his ribs cracked, he sang as hard as he did when he was fine. He heard things that would destroy you; the public have no idea what made the performance. The better the entertainer, the better the confrontation, the deeper the feeling. Jackie was the most honest. He gave all he could give. That made him special. Entertainers often start out as human beings and then turn into something else. Boxing and music were the two most violent games there were. He wanted to be a pro boxer, so he did it both ways.'

The Midnighters' Billy Davis recalls a near-riot situation which further illustrates Jackie's dedication: 'We were in Houston, Texas, at the Houston City Auditorium. There were Hank Ballard And The Midnighters, Jackie Wilson, Sam Cooke, The Flamingos; about 14 or 15 acts. They introduced Jackie and he came up there. The crowd went haywire. They had 10–15,000 people; you could feel the building move.

'Jackie was doing his usual opening number, "I'll Be Satisfied" when they sent for the chief of police, who came on stage and told him, "You cannot sing, we can't control the people." The cops told the audience two or three times, "You've got to sit down, otherwise there's not going to be a show."

The security guards took the mike and stopped the show. This went on for 20 or 30 minutes. They escorted Jackie backstage. He was furious because he could not sing. The promoter told him, "Jackie, don't worry, you're going to get your money." Jackie said, "It's not that, I just want to sing!" He just loved to sing.'

Another singer who came out of Detroit, a little later than Jackie, was Barbara Lewis. Famous for her smash hit 'Hello Stranger' in 1963, she remembers her fellow Detroit singer with fondness. 'I think Jackie Wilson was one of the finest performers from our era,' she says. 'Very charismatic on stage and unique in the way the audience became enthralled in his performance – they became a part of his performance. They would tear all his clothes off. That was not a common occurrence, to get an audience in that state of mind. His talent was so powerful, his voice was so powerful. I can't think that we've had another male entertainer of his magnitude. I can't think of any.

'Michael Jackson is great, but not in the same category. Jackie was charismatic. You either have that or you don't, it's not taught or learnt. What other entertainer do you know that had that? They were some of the hardest audiences, and he was put to the test. He came out victorious on stage. Many audiences don't show a lot of excitement. Naturally, he would transform them. Not many could do it. Sammy Davis Jnr could bring an audience to its feet. I've seen Wilson Pickett and Joe Tex and they'd get an audience to scream, but they never captivated an audience the way Jackie did. He was an entertainer's entertainer. When you're a singer's singer, you're something. You could hear within a song R&B, pop, opera, and blues. I think if he was doing today what he was doing then, there would be no one in the world who did not know who he was.'

Friend and vocalist with the successful Dell Vikings, Chuck Jackson, first met Jackie in 1957, the year the group had their three Top 40 hits. 'He started me as a single act, a solo artist,' says Jackson. 'That was 1959; I left The Dell Vikings in 1960. I did the theatre chain with him; the Apollo, the Uptown Theatre [in Philadelphia].'

There was rarely a dull moment travelling with Jackie, who mischievously often instigated it. Alcohol likely played a large part. 'One time we were in Texas, when I was only about 20,' says Jackson. 'I'm a mild man, I think. Jackie would always say, "You never get really upset." He was already a star, but I was trying to be a star and I had to watch my Ps and Qs. So we were in this place, a very small town. He was drinking and he said, "Chuck, punch JJ." I said, "I'm not going to punch JJ, are you kidding?" Don Harris was his bodyguard then; he looked like Jackie.

"Okay", he said, "I'm going to have Harris woop you." I said, "No, nobody's going to woop me." Don jumped up and we went to it. It was just one of those things we did at the time; we'd just try each other to blow off steam. I waxed him and nobody messed with me no more after that. When it had finished there was nobody mad. It was kind of fun.'

He recalls another crazy incident: 'I was riding in the car with him on the way to a gig on the same tour, and he had a gun. We were in the limousine, driving down the Texas highway shooting signs. If we came to a sign saying "Crossroads Ahead", we'd shoot the sign and it would turn. So if you had to make a left turn and saw that sign, you'd turn right! We were doing it one day and the gun went off. The window was still up and the bullet went through the window and shattered, and glass fell all over me. I was sitting facing him. It scared him to death and he never played with guns after that. When he hit the [driver] window, JJ almost turned the car over.

'One night, we were in New Orleans. Jackie and I were there with The Dixie Cups and their manager. We played the job that night and had a lot of fun. Their manager at the time was Jones; he wrote all their stuff. We sat up all night, then had to drive all the way to Macon, Georgia – 500 miles. The bus left with everyone early. I woke up about ten or eleven o' clock and, as Jackie was next door, I tried to wake him to say we had to get going. He was still asleep. We travelled together, his car and my car. I was trying to wake him, and finally JJ and Sims got him out of bed – at one in the afternoon!

'So we finally got in the car at two o'clock and he said he knew a short cut. Jackie Wilson knew a short cut, and he didn't even drive! He's the worst driver in the world! We were driving, flying, and we got stopped by the cops when we had about 200 miles to go. It was, say, six o' clock. Jackie's people gave 'em a story and they let us go. We finally pulled in about quarter to nine to this job; we were doing 120 [mph] most of the time.

'When we got there, Jerry Butler was on the show and he had sung "Your Precious Love" 30 times. The people were so sick of it. He was trying to fill in and we kept calling in [by phone] periodically, saying, "We're on our way, we're nearly there."

'When we pulled at the back of the place, Jerry Butler came running out of the back door. People had started throwing things at him. By this time, the audience were in a full state of riot. The police told us to get out of there. We ran and Jackie was trying to get dressed in the car. They were throwing rocks at the bus, it was incredible. We missed the job and I was mad 'cause I couldn't afford to miss a job.'

107

So what kind of a person did Jackson find Jackie to be? He answers without hesitation: 'He had a definite impact on people, he was completely different than anyone else of his period. He was good looking and he catered strictly to women. Guys loved him, but he loved women. He loved everybody. Jackie used to say, "Every woman is my woman." I used to say, "Every woman except mine!" He would steal women from friends. I told my wife, "I wouldn't leave my woman around Jackie for all the tea in China." It isn't that I don't trust my woman – I just didn't want to have to kill Jackie.'

Jackson believes that the only thing that prevented Jackie from achieving superstar status was his colour: 'Then again, Jackie Wilson was a pioneer in being the black lover-boy, and we don't fare too well in this country when all the women love us, being black. It's a shame, but it's the truth. It seems if you're not a clown you're not accepted. You have to be a clown [as a black person] to be accepted and be around for a long time, 'cause our talents don't do it.'

Jackson understood that some deep inner pain was eating its way into Jackie's soul. But being so proud and macho made it impossible for Jackie to express himself in words, even to someone as close to him as Jackson. 'The hate is all over the United States,' he says. 'and that didn't bother Jackie any more than it bothered Sam Cooke or Jerry Butler. I think what really got to Jackie was that he couldn't get over that barrier of acceptance.' Jackie knew no one could compete with him as a vocalist or performer, so why did he have to continually prove himself? Why hadn't he achieved the same acclaim as Sinatra or Presley had? And why was it that, despite the hits and albums and all the touring, all he had to show for it was a middle-class home on LaSalle Street in Highland Park and some jewellery?

Careerwise, 1961 was a excellent year for Jackie, in all likelihood his best. The five single releases all made it into the charts. The Mario Lanza-inspired 'My Empty Arms', co-written by Al Kasha, went to No Nine; 'Please Tell Me Why' reached No 20; 'Your One And Only Love' reached No Forty; 'I'm Comin' On Back To You' reached No 19; and 'Years From Now' reached No 37.

Two albums were also released; the first, *You Ain't Heard Nothing Yet*, in February 1961, was a 12-song tribute to Al Jolson, Jackie's idol. In a *New York Sunday News* interview in October 1961, Jackie said: 'When I was a kid and my friends were either Sinatra or Crosby fans, my idol was always Jolson. I don't know what it was about him, maybe it was because he was such a showman that he got to me. I played his songs over and over. Then

JACKIE WILSON

I'd sing his songs in my own way, not imitating his voice; but I got a kick out of his gestures, I'd seen them in the movies and watched people who imitated him. I copied his getting down on his knees when he sang – I still do it. I love that flashy kind of stuff and made it a regular part of my act.'

Dick Jacobs, in the *Musician* article, explained the Jolson album: 'Jackie Wilson was a super fan of Al Jolson. Jolson had a profound influence on Jackie's singing, which I found very apparent in his renditions of pop songs. When Jackie decided to do an album of all Jolson songs, we went ahead and did it. Since Jackie knew and loved the songs so well, we were able to cut the record in two sessions, recording six tunes per studio block. If there's one record in the Jackie Wilson catalogue that demonstrates his amazing versatility, this is it.'

In New York, he performed regularly at the Brooklyn Fox and Brooklyn Paramount theatres, the swanky Copacabana and the Apollo. Harlem's Apollo Theatre, the black equivalent of Nashville's Grand Ole Opry, was started by Frank Schiffman although his son Bobby ran it during Jackie's period and showcased most of the great black performers of the time. For a black artist, if you hadn't 'made it' at the Apollo Theatre, you were nobody. As Bobby Schiffman explains: 'The Apollo was a prestigious date and it was probably only the breakdown of discrimination by the entertainment business that sealed its fate. In its heyday, black performers couldn't play the white establishments. They couldn't play the Paramount, downtown smart clubs or theatres.

'Headliners earned 50 per cent of the gross, and the performer paid for the show, ie. the band and other acts and kept the difference. Headliners who didn't get a percentage made about $2,500 a week. Jackie was always on the 50 per cent and earned much more.'

The Apollo audience could be pretty rough if they didn't get the show they expected. Guitarist Dickie Thompson remembers one time when Jackie failed to excite his audience: 'We had just played the Copacabana, doing typical Broadway tunes, with Sy Oliver conducting a big band full of strings. But they made the mistake of taking the same show to the Apollo, where it went down like a lead balloon. The audience hated it. The second Apollo show Jackie did was back to 'soulville' and voilà! He left them screaming for joy.' The Apollo was hard work. 'We worked five shows a day on weekends and holidays,' Thompson adds. At the end of the tour, Jackie called the band in and handed out six men's diamond and onyx rings. He had selected a special one for Thompson. 'I still have it and treasure it highly,' he says proudly.

JACKIE WILSON

According to Apollo's Schiffman, 'Jackie was for a long time the biggest attraction we'd ever had. For a long time, we welcomed him with open arms. Billy Eckstine was terrific in his time, but he never had the excitement of a Jackie Wilson on stage. Jackie Wilson was exciting to watch. He hit the stage like a fighter. From an economic standpoint, he was a big home run for us at the Apollo.' But, as Schiffman says: 'Jackie was trouble. He was unpredictable and was therefore tough to work with. Sam Cooke was clean, a perfect role model, dependable and reliable, and a pleasure to work with.' Cooke, like Jackie, had a fondness for the ladies but hid behind those innocent good looks, while Jackie always had that wicked look in his eyes. Jackie definitely had a 'bad boy' image. Never known for reliability, punctuality or responsibility, he was a 'wild card', but once on stage was never accused of not giving his best shot.

Schiffman was a close friend of Nat Tarnopol and sees Jackie and his friend through different eyes. He, more than most, credits Tarnopol with much of Jackie's success: 'He seemed to have the ability to keep Jackie in line. He made Jackie fulfil his obligations to his fans and to the promoter. Nat made Jackie happen. It is possible that someone else might have done so, but there was Nat doing it every day. Jackie had his difficult times off the stage: his health was always a question, sometimes we didn't know if he was going to make it to the stage or not.

'It's also costly when you have musicians sitting around for a session and the performer doesn't show up. I know that Nat Tarnopol loaned him a tremendous amounts of money – that's what Nat told me. He was a perfect gentleman and dealt with me in a straightforward and honest way. I had nothing but the greatest respect for him, despite what they were saying out there on the streets. I'm not sure about Jackie being ripped off, but I do know that at that time artists were very high livers, spending money on all sorts of pleasures.'

Simon Rutberg who had known Jackie for 15 years. The two had first met while Jackie was touring Los Angeles in 1962 and they struck up a friendship that lasted until the singer's death. His extraordinary story illustrates the humility of the man. Rutberg was Jewish, white and, at the time, 15 years old. 'There were very few people in the world that I really admired; I mean *really* admired,' says Rutberg. 'When I saw Jackie I knew I had to meet this guy and become his friend. I walked right up to him and became so tongue tied I could not get one word out, just a few odd sounds. Then he responded to me and invited me back to the dressing-room.' Says Rutberg, 'I know some heart- warming stories; how nice he could be to people he didn't know and how he could make his fans feel, because he worshipped his fans.'

Whenever Jackie performed in Los Angeles, Rutberg was there backstage. He would spend hours in Jackie's dressing-room, either talking, giving Jackie the rub downs he enjoyed or fetching him his favourite chicken soup from the Jewish restaurant on Fairfax Avenue. 'Sometimes, at two or three in the morning, he'd send me out for chicken soup from Canters. It was not a glorious life when you were on the road, and in those days you were always on the road. He'd leave the club at 3 or 4 a.m. and go back to his hotel room. He'd be tired. In those days, if he wasn't working, he wasn't earning.'

He confirms the rituals that the singer practised before a performance: 'Jackie would be in his hotel room about three hours before show time. He'd be bathing and preening and he would warm up his voice before the show, running up and down the scales and hitting high notes constantly – while getting dressed – slowly, casually.

'Once he was on stage and singing he was it – as confident as could be. Getting up there was hard... always tense, nervous, always scared to go up on stage. He'd come off stage looking like wet rags; his shirts would be soaked. Jackie wore great black silk shirts with his name monogrammed on them. He would often get his clothes torn, if the women got their hands on him.'

Rutberg, too, was aware Jackie wasn't a natural dancer, either with a partner or on stage: 'Jackie couldn't dance; I never told anyone he was a great dancer. He was a great mover. What he does on stage . . . people who dance on stage, such as Michael Jackson, are performing. People will be applauding the moves and not listening to the music. Jackie, on the other hand, punctuated the music. He lets the moves underline the singing.

'It was so great, so exciting. The first few times I ever saw Jackie, well, you know how when you're in a race and the guys are in the starting block – 'On your mark, get set, go!'? With Jackie, it was as if somebody tied a rope around him; he was running, but couldn't move because of the rope. Then all of a sudden someone cut the rope and he'd be gone.'

Many times the performing and adulation became too much for Jackie. His young friend, Rutberg, provided Jackie with the space he needed: 'I knew Jackie well enough to know if he wanted to be bothered or not bothered. I'd see him be nice to people and after they left he'd say, "That motherfucker." Would-be stars would come around Jackie's dressing-room. There were a lot of hangers-on, people there who'd come around because they wanted to use that for something. They were draining him [mentally].

I would go to make myself scarce and he'd say, "Don't leave. You can't leave yet." So I had to stay. I'd sit there for four hours and he wouldn't say a word. Then he'd say, "Well, Sy, bye. I've got to go; I'll see you later."' Young as Rutberg was, he realised Jackie was deeply troubled: 'He'd talk to me and before you knew it he'd be crying. He wouldn't let the other guys see that, because of the black 'macho thing. It's an ego thing. Like, if you slap women around and people see you, it's like "He must be a big star".'

Rutberg closely observed Jackie's complex personality: 'Jackie had many faces. He could look tough or sweet. He had one look in which he looked like a cute little boy, a choir boy. Such an innocent sweet little kid. I have a picture of Jackie where you cover one side of the face and then the other and it looks like two completely different people. He had one of these pictures, and he covered one side of the face and said, 'You see that, Sy? That's my father. You see that? That's my mother.' It was two totally different looks.

'The thing about Jackie is he had a foot in both worlds. He was just a guy from the neighbourhood. Then he was taken out of the neighbourhood and placed in high society. He was above the rock 'n' rollers. Take the way Jackie dressed, in a suit; he was sharp. Put a suit on him, and he looked like he was raised in elegance. Yet at the same time he was a ghetto boy. He'd get up on stage and start swinging at the cops and also at his audience. It's one thing to fight, but you don't beat up on your fans! A fight would break out in the audience and Jackie would jump off the stage and get right in, because he wanted to fight. In some ways he was like a stupid little kid who never grew up. Literally, a punk.' Yet as macho as Jackie was, or pretended to be, he also had another more endearing trait to his nature. 'Jackie had a thing; he loved his mother,' says Rutberg. 'Whatever she said was law. He'd call her on the phone and say, "I love you, honey, how are you?"'

The schedules and performances were gruelling. 'Nat Tarnopol tried to get Jackie working every night of the year,' recalls Rutberg. 'That's how they made their money.' It would have seemed logical for Jackie to have toured the world; certainly he had an enormous following throughout Europe. 'He didn't go on overseas trips because he hated to fly,' Rutberg explained. Travelling constantly throughout the USA, Jackie always went by limo and had a chauffeur. Rutberg: 'He was the worst driver in the world. I heard it said that to give Jackie a new car was like giving a child a loaded gun. He cracked up every car he had.'

Having observed more than 150 of Jackie's live performances, Rutberg can truly claim to be an expert on him. He rates Jackie as the all-time greatest contemporary artist and was backstage often enough to observe

Jackie's dedication to his chosen career: 'He'd stop eating, say, six hours before the show. A real artist does that. He was like an athlete and to sing at your full potential, you can't have a full stomach. He was absolutely professional; I have no doubt that he got this from Billy Ward.

'Jackie could do everything, and I always thought that he figured, "I'm doing all this and I'm good, but I'm not stretching myself enough! And the record album sales do not reflect what I want, therefore I'm not doing enough." He knew he was good, but there came a point where he just thought, 'whatever! It's good enough.' He became lazy. He didn't seem so to anyone else, but to me it was. Perhaps it was because he was working for Nat Tarnopol, so thought 'who gives a shit.' That was the late 1960s. Jackie knew he was good, but I don't believe he knew how good!'

Roquel 'Billy' Davis knew how Jackie loved to perform. 'When he wasn't headlining, he still headlined, no matter whether he was opening or closing,' he says. 'Jackie had a lot of pride. He would have suffered twice as much when he wasn't headlining. The stars of the show would ask,"Put him as far from me as possible." 'Jackie loved every minute up on that stage. That's how Nat Tarnopol got away with murder – with his money. Jackie just looked forward to his next performance . . . seeing his name and his picture, and his fans screaming at him, and his continental suits and rings.'

Another popular black group of the late 1950s and early 1960s, The Dells were often on the same Apollo billing with Jackie. Chuck Barksdale, who sang bass with the group then and still does more than 40 years later, says: 'Jackie Wilson, of the artists that came out in the '50s, was the most talented we had.' Barksdale recalled Jackie's performances: 'Having worked with Jackie 100 times or more, it's like plucking a leaf of a tree; which one's the prettiest? That's how it was with his performances; it all came off the same tree.

'At the Howard Theatre in Washington DC, a theatre very dear to Jackie and The Dells before it closed down, we were on one of many, many shows with Jackie. On this occasion, Jackie was a little under the weather for one reason or another. He was hoarse. We finished our bit and got off. Jackie used to stand in the wings and watch, so as we moved into the show he was getting ready. He smoked his cigarette and had a little shot of whatever. He'd knock that whisky down – boom! He'd go out with the cigarette still in his hand; it was part of the act. I thought 'he ain't going to make it.' He could barely speak. I guess it's like Sammy Davis Jnr used to say, "All I've got to do is open a refrigerator door and I automatically do 20 minutes." That's what happened with Jackie. He hit the stage and the spotlight grabbed him over by the curtain. By the time he hit the middle of the stage and went through his bit, doing the gyrations and putting the cigarette out, it's like God had said, "Voice, open up."

'The people had already been informed. It seeped through the audience: 'Jackie Wilson can't sing; he's hoarse, he's not feeling good.' Bullshit! Jackie had them on their feet from the opening. His opening was fantastic enough, without him singing a word – and the women would just get hysterical. He'd shake his head and the hair would fall over his face; it had been wet before he went on stage.'

With such a wealth of experience of the great man's performances, Barksdale is well placed to sum up Wilson's position among the all-time great live acts. 'Jackie was a true, true, true showman – all the way. It's unbelievable. That's Jackie; wonderful man. It was indeed a pleasure and honour to know him and a talent like that we will never see again.'

The home Jackie's family had resided in since his earliest years, 248 Cottage Grove, Highland Park, was very ordinary. He and wife Freda shared it with his mother and stepfather and, up until around 1960, that's where the extended family lived. For all its memories, Freda remembers the place as a dump. 'We never locked the door [some report there were no locks],' she says. 'I had told Jack there were some rats in there. We were lying down one time, and Rebecca [Pitt], his cousin, was sitting on the side of the bed. All of a sudden this big rat came running in and jumped right across the bed. Jack said, "What was that?" I said, "A rat." He had Johnny [Roberts] come over.' Freda didn't say what Roberts did with the rat, but he did own a pistol.

NATURALLY, SHE WAS ANXIOUS to have a new home, something more suitable for their present social standing. But while Freda was living in such conditions and struggling to get by raising their four young children, Jackie was living in his luxury 500-dollars-a-month residence at the Sire Arms Apartments on West 57th Street, off Broadway, in New York. He kept telling her, 'We'll get a house next time, baby.' She finally told him that if he didn't get her a house very soon she was going to move and live with him – kids and all. The threat worked, and he got her a new and spacious house.

In a *New York Sunday News* (22 October 1961) interview, Jackie talked about his family and the new house: 'I am also sending my wife to modelling school; I want her to make the most of herself. But I think the thing that gave me the biggest kick was buying a 45,000 dollar house for my family in Detroit. My mother and stepfather live in it with Freda and our four children. There's Denise, who's ten, Sandra, eight, Jackie Jnr, seven, and Tony, who's three. The only fly in the ointment is that I don't get home very much. It's gotten to be a sort of a gag, with the kids to rush into the house yelling "Ma, here comes Jackie Wilson!" when they see me coming.'

The new home was a huge, two-storey house on tree-lined LaSalle Street in northern Detroit. Certainly, it is an upper-middle-class home, but nothing compared to the stone mansion Berry Gordy Jnr bought for himself, only a mile or two away on prestigious Boston Boulevard. There may even be some exaggeration on his part regarding the price he paid for it. In Freda's words, 'I bought the house; Jack gave me the money. I didn't even like the house. I paid 30,000 dollars first time.'

The new house seemed to satisfy everyone for a time. 'We were well supported by Jackie for a while and, for a while, we thought we were rich,' remembers Freda. 'Before that we didn't have anything. We stayed in Cottage Grove; they tore that house down. At LaSalle, his mother [and stepfather and Joyce Ann] lived downstairs and we lived upstairs.' Although she had a new home, Freda's role never altered. 'Jack believed in keeping me barefoot and pregnant,' she reflects. 'He didn't have to worry about me, I was too busy breeding. Every time he came home it was one of those things. You was married, it was your thing to have babies.' Birth control wasn't a priority.

He had many close relatives living in Detroit and nearby Pontiac. Most had moved from Mississippi over the years. Sadly, there was a degree of dysfunction within the family and Freda was not universally liked. Jealousy was part of the problem. In any case, one of the female relatives began acting in a very bizarre way. Freda explains: 'She used to tell me to get out of bed. She used to try and get in bed [with Jackie] – she'd be drunk. Some of the family on Jack's side, they were nuts. They hated me, and I was his wife!' The woman relative was so infatuated with Jackie that she seemingly had intentions of usurping Freda's position as Jackie's wife.

It was while living in New York that Jackie took up residence with Harlean Harris. They'd first met in 1953, when Jackie had just joined The Dominoes. According to Harlean, in the 1979 *Sepia* magazine interview, Jackie later noticed her photo on the cover of a magazine and got in touch with her: 'He got in touch to congratulate me, and that's when our love affair began.' At this stage, in 1958, Jackie had become a solo act.

At 16, Harlean began modelling and became a cover girl on the prestigious *Ebony* magazine. By 17 she was chosen as 'Miss Press Photographer, New York'. One person who knew her at the time described her as 'the most pretentious thing you ever saw'. However, there is little doubt that Jackie was captivated by her.

Singer Tommy Hunt was a confidant of Jackie's at the time and recalls, 'He'd even think Harlean was doing things behind his back; it was driving him crazy.' Harlean rarely went on the road with Jackie and sexual fidelity was not one of Jackie's strong points in any case, so Harlean could hardly be blamed if she too had an occasional fling. And, after all, they weren't yet married. Jackie plied Harlean with jewels and furs, while at the same time Freda had difficulty getting payments to support the children. However, at times, Jackie could be rough with Harlean, who he referred to as 'Harris', so the relationship was tempestuous. The major problem between them was Jackie's numerous affairs, over which Harlean proved she could be rough and vindictive.

In February 1961, Jackie was 26 and hot property in the entertainment industry. In the preceding months he had some of the best hit successes of his entire career: 'A Woman, A Lover, A Friend' had reached No 15, 'Alone At Last' No Eight, 'Am I The Man No 32, and 'My Empty Arms' No Nine. Life for Jackie couldn't have been better.

Apart from Harlean, he had a three-year affair with a 28-year-old woman, Juanita Jones, from Harlem, New York. Quite possibly Juanita had become pregnant to Jackie. Regardless, she was insanely jealous and madly in love with him. Jones was a former WAC in the US Army, so had received weapons training. Around 3 or 4 a.m. on the morning of 15 February 1961, Jackie and Harlean returned from a late show to their swank Sire Arms Apartments in mid-town Manhattan. Juanita was waiting for Jackie, a pistol concealed in her slacks. Exactly what took place is probably known only to the three people who were present, but Jones confronted Jackie as he was about to enter his sixth-floor apartment and shot him twice – once in the abdomen and once in the buttocks region. It is quite likely that Jones's intended target was not Jackie, but Harlean.

Possibly Jackie lunged at Jones to disarm her. Incredibly, despite severe injuries Jackie managed to seize the gun from Jones and stagger downstairs to the street.

Freda remembers what happened after Jackie was shot: 'That's how they got him. He was running down the street – he had took the gun and had it in his hand. Pretty soon the police saw him.' Jackie was fortunate that a passing patrolman, Donald Roberts, noticed his condition and rushed him to the nearby Roosevelt Hospital in a police car. 'He was in a critical condition. He was lying down there in emergency for a long time – they didn't understand it was Jackie Wilson the rock 'n' roll singer,' says Freda. A close friend, Linda Hopkins, who had performed with Jackie that night, has a similar account: 'JJ told me that when Jackie got shot and was taken to Roosevelt Hospital, he was laid out in the hallway for ages. They finally got a doctor to come from Long Island to take a look at him. JJ said he had to argue with all the hospital people.' Freda added: 'They [his management] didn't know until Harlean finally got in touch with Nat. Nat got the Mafia on the case and they were the ones who said, 'Get all your best doctors, for he's a great star – he's Jackie Wilson. Do whatever it takes to save his life. They did.'

'The chief neurologist, the chief neurosurgeon – the chief everything – attended to Jackie, in case anything was wrong. They had the neurologist present in case of nerve damage, because the bullet was near the spine: if it moved and hit the spine he would be paralysed.'

Jackie was operated on, having one bullet removed from his buttocks region. The second bullet was lodged so close to his spine that it was deemed too dangerous to remove and was left where it was, to be with him for the rest of his life. Jackie remained on the hospital's critical list for six days and, fortunately, fully recovered, albeit after the removal of one kidney. It was a very close brush with death.

Tarnopol and Jackie's lawyer Herbert Lippman, who also happened to be the nephew of the late Al Green, Jackie's original manager and another crony of Tarnopol's, concocted a story that would save Jones from being convicted of attempted murder and preserve Jackie's reputation as a devoted husband and father. Legal authorities were persuaded that the demented Jones had come to Jackie's apartment with the intention of committing suicide. Jackie, in trying to wrest the gun from her, had taken the two bullets.

In a subsequent radio interview with New York DJ Norman N Nite, Jackie put it this way: 'I was shot in the stomach. Actually the bullet is still in there, but it's in a safe place. It's in my back, but it hasn't moved. It's not a nice story, but it's not a bad story. The young lady, she wasn't shooting at me, she was shooting at herself. That's why we didn't prosecute her. When a person's a little off at the time they are a little stronger. I grabbed the pistol, but I'm the one who got shot.' The concocted story was apparently believed, as Jones was arraigned in the Felony Court and charged with felonious assault and violation of the Sullivan Law (to do with weapons possession). She was granted $2,500 bail. At the police station a dejected and sobbing Jones was photographed by the newspapers and reported as saying she was 'all mixed up and didn't mean to hurt him'. She said, 'I love him, oh, Jackie!' And so the falsehood was maintained.

Dick Jacobs, in *Musician* magazine, vividly recalled the shooting. At this time Jackie was a frequent visitor to his family home. He relates: 'Then, one morning at about 6 a.m. the phone rang. On the other end was Coral-Brunswick vice-president Marty Salkin, soberly informing me that Jackie Wilson had been shot and was in Roosevelt Hospital. That was all he knew.

'Juanita sure wasn't alone in her ardour for Jackie. Considering the numbers involved, hell hath no fury and all that, the most remarkable thing was that Jackie didn't have a whole lot more slugs in his rump. Jackie had lots of company in the hospital and seemed to take the whole thing in pretty good spirits, cracking jokes about having an extra asshole, etc. I set up a movie projector for him and he whiled away the time as he made a speedy recovery.'

Jacobs may well have made light of Jackie's wounds, but either of the two bullets could have easily taken his life. No doubt Jackie's physical fitness and tenacity helped pull him through.

In the *Sunday News* (22 October 1961) interview, Jackie said, 'I want to forget the incident and get on with my singing. I'll probably carry the bullet for the rest of my days – it's too dangerous to fool with – but I have no malice. I forgave the lady who shot me right after it happened, and I didn't want to press charges. I want to forget the whole thing and just get on with the show.' That's an understatement, as he was reportedly grossing around $350,000 a year at the time.

At the time of the shooting there was another woman with whom Jackie had renewed his association; Angel Lee, international stripper and former girlfriend of Little Richard. Angel now worked for Ben Bart's Universal Attractions Booking, which specialised in contracting black acts. Angel remembers that the shooting resulted because of Jackie having terminated a long-term relationship with Jones. 'Juanita Jones had two or three kids with Jackie,' Angel says. 'She was supposed to have had a miscarriage and Jackie decided she had aborted: he accused her of having got rid of his child and was mad. And that's when he stopped seeing her.'

Back in Detroit, Freda had just returned home that morning, having been to Chicago. Jackie's friend, Freddy Pride, was there. Freda recalls, 'My mother-in-law said, "They say Jack's been shot." A few minutes later there was a knock on the door; it was the police. They said, "Freda Wilson and Eliza Lee?" I said, "Yes, I'm Freda Wilson." They said, "We have a telegram here. If you want to see Jackie Wilson alive you better get the next plane out." They said, "If you need any help, let us know."' When Freda read the telegram to Eliza Lee, she was totally stunned by the news and sought some solace: 'Frank Gruman had gave us a case of VO [the best brandy],' she says. 'That's what Eliza Mae was drinking at the time – she drank almost half a bottle. She said, "Now, I've never been on a plane, but we've got to get on that plane and go and see about him."'

Freda believes Eliza Mae and Jackie were so close that a transcendental bond existed between them. Says Freda, 'She knew he was hurt bad. You could tell when something was going wrong; her heart was hurt. You could see her up that night tapping her feet and humming. Jack was in trouble somewhere. When we were married and he was not in town, she'd come and say, "He's in trouble again, I hope it's not too bad." Freda went on, 'The police told us, "Don't bring nothin'." We didn't take no clothes.'

In New York, they went directly to the hospital. 'We walked in the hospital and there was so many people. There were people on their knees on the floor, crowding around in the hospital. These were fans. Somebody said, "That's his wife and his mother." They were grabbing our clothes; we could hardly get through.

'He had just come out of surgery. His mother was standing on the other side and we was praying. He opened his eyes and said, "Pee Wee [his pet name for Freda]." He looked up and said,'"Hi, Mama," and took her hand. We were all crying. He held on to our hands.' There was no discussion of circumstances: 'Around that time Jackie was shot at a lot. I didn't count the times,' Freda says.

The first operation had taken two hours, and within 24 hours he'd had one bullet removed from his buttock. Being a nurse's aid, Freda was fully aware how serious his injuries were. She continues: 'Pretty soon they had taken the X-ray pictures. Three times they took him back for major surgery. The kidney was perfect, but the tube [ureter] that connected the bladder with the kidney was blown apart. They had to re-route it to the other side, and they had to go in and get that kidney out. They took that and made an ileostomy tube [this is an opening from the bowel, through the abdominal wall, which allows the faeces to drain]. A gun shot is very painful. Besides, he'd had all these major surgeries and a bullet was floating around. We just sat there all day and all night.'

Despite requiring bags taped to his body to take care of his bodily functions and horrendous unhealed body wounds, Freda found Jackie's rampant sex drive undiminished. 'Even when he got shot that time, we did it,' she says. 'He told me to go in the bathroom and bend over. I said, "So you can be all over me and I'll fall in the bathtub, and you'll be on me and I'll be dead! I'll hit my head." I was scared he was going to have a problem or something with the stitches. Then he was hurting.'

Until the shooting, Freda seems not to have been fully aware of how great a star Jackie was. She says, 'You'd be surprised. The letters; from Frank Sinatra, Elvis Presley, people he didn't even know well then, and people who had just heard of him. Baskets and baskets of flowers, fruit, champagne, cheeses, all that stuff. We really had never seen stuff like this.'

A constant stream of visitors arrived to help lift his spirits. One visitor was the American Bandstand host Dick Clark. Some visitors reintroduced him to one of his bad habits. 'People were bringing him cocaine and stuff in the hospital,' says Freda. He'd survived two bullets and now he faced another threat. There was real concern that if Jackie took drugs the result might be that which the bullets failed to achieve. But Jackie was at his peak, with a big future ahead of him: the Mob were going to make sure he remained alive.

'I didn't want him to get addicted like some of these other entertainers had,' Freda says, after being asked to fetch more drugs by Jackie. 'That's when the Mafia came over to watch him around the clock, after he almost OD'd – they ended up moving into the hospital. Nobody could come in except me and his mother, and then they suggested that his mother go home because she'd asked the nurses to give him some more pain medication.'

A devoted Freda joined Jackie at the hospital, with a roll-away bed in his room. 'I'd bring [the dog] Poochie; I'd put him in my big purse,' Freda remembers. Up until then, as Freda left, Harlean would come on in. Now she was refused admittance. Lynn Ciccone remembers the operation to keep the women apart: 'They had to do some fast shuffling when he got shot to get Harlean's things out of the apartment before Freda got into town.' But things went wrong and whilst Jackie was recuperating, Freda tidied up his apartment. 'I was just cleaning up . . . the things I learned, I learned by accident,' she says. 'There were bags and bags of pictures and things at the apartment. That's how I got the pictures of him and Harlean in the bathtub.' The pictures involved more than bathing.

Freda was understandably angry. After all, she was the one who had made the sacrifices early in his career. Her pay cheques had helped to buy clothes suitable for him to perform in. She had done without so that he could be Jackie Wilson. In her anger, she hurled a good few of Harlean's fine clothes from the apartment's sixth-floor window.

'When I was looking through those things in his apartment,' says Freda, 'he was already on drugs. I was scared of him because of that, because his personality would change. Everything that somebody did to him, he felt me and his mother and family were doing to him. He thought we were working, especially me, for the FBI. It would come out of a clear blue sky; he'd be laughing and talking and then he'd say it. It would be something real simple I'd say, and he'd say, "Why'd you ask me that? The FBI want to know that, too?"' The drug taking was causing Jackie to have paranoid delusions.

After five weeks of excellent care, Jackie was well enough to be discharged. Newspapers and national TV pictured the beaming smiles of Jackie, his mother Eliza Mae and Freda as they left the hospital. Freda says, 'He was sick when he left the hospital.' She had the task of nursing him back to health. However, being only a nursing aid, she wasn't as qualified as she had led Jackie to believe. 'I was washing the thermometers in hot water – pop,' said Freda, 'I didn't want Jack to know I didn't know what to do.'

Another revelation to Freda, on his release, was that despite being at the peak of his career, Jackie apparently had no money. 'When he got out of the hospital he wanted to get a new car,' Freda reminisces, 'because he didn't want people to think he couldn't sing no more.' Rumours were circulating to the effect that because the second bullet could not be removed, Jackie's singing days were over. Jackie thought that buying a new Cadillac would help dispel those rumours.

Shortly after his release, Jackie left the apartment for a period. When he returned, Freda noticed his bandages were wet and set out to renew them: 'They had to prepare a tube and make him an ureterostomy, because back then they didn't have the urinary bags they hook on now. They would show me how to do the padding, all the dressing and stuff. Nobody had changed the bandages since he got out and it was soaking wet. Anyway it had ruptured and he didn't want me to see that… I knew he'd been with some woman. He'd been gone too long. He went to see Harlean, because she couldn't come to see him. The activity had caused it.' It was enough to necessitate a return to hospital for additional treatment.

Fully recovered, late in 1961, Jackie was involved in his second and last movie, entitled *Teenage Millionaire*, again starring singer Jimmy Clanton. The black-and-white rock 'n' roll musical was, if anything, worse than the 1958 movie, *Go Johnny Go*, Jackie'd sang in. Jackie performed two songs, 'The Way I Am' and 'Lonely Life'.

In the *Sunday News* (22 October 1961) interview, Jackie appeared pleased with his life and career: his latest single disc was 'Years From Now', which boosted his earnings in the coming year to a probable $500,000. Jackie stated in the interview: 'Well, a chunk of the money goes in annuities, but I'm having a ball with the rest. I buy nine or ten suits a month and about as many 30-dollar shirts – they get torn off my back regularly. I've also got a New York apartment, because I love the Big Town. Let's see – what else? I love jewellery.'

In 1961 Nat Tarnopol's son, Paul, wasn't yet born, but his father later related to him his version of events concerning Brunswick Records and Jackie. Paul later got to know Jackie, albeit while a young boy. 'Nat agreed to let Jackie go because he had his hands full with the label,' says Paul. 'But he wanted Jackie to have a professional manager. In 1961 my father was 30. His partner [in Brunswick Records] – at that time it was Decca – was Lew Wasseman [later to head MCA] and those guys.'

Paul went on, 'About 1961, when Jackie got shot, it came to a head. My father was doing more for Brunswick than he could do for Jackie. I think while he was in hospital he was befriended by Johnny Roberts. Jackie had perhaps one complaint with my father regarding money; there was never money being hidden. Jackie and my father were together over a decade, and there was only one incident, over the $80,000 for the house. It was regarding money that was advanced for a house or something like that. Nat tore up the contract . . . Jackie pleaded with him, "Don't!"'

'While they were working that out, Jackie went to either Johnny Roberts or Tommy Vastola. Vastola had Queens Booking Agency and Johnny was managing artists, that type of thing. They were around. The industry was almost all in the Brill Building at that time. My dad knew who Vastola and Roberts were and to that point he had nothing to do with them. It was obvious who they [Vastola and Roberts] were involved with. My father pleaded with Jackie not to let them take over his management or get involved, but Jackie took it upon himself to do this. So they decided to end the management with my dad. Dad could look after Brunswick and Jackie could have separate management.'

Paul also explained his how his father was given the opportunity to own 50 per cent of the Brunswick label: 'Around 1960, Jackie was the only artist on Brunswick. Lew Wasseman and Sid Shinberger [who were high executives at Decca records: Brunswick's principal] controlled the independents [subsidiary labels with Decca]. Wasseman took a liking to my father in the late 1950s and asked my dad to run the label for him. My dad was the right person, as he knew black music better than black people could. He worked very hard. Lew said, "I want you to run Brunswick." Dad said, "If you want me to run Brunswick and there is nothing [meaning no artists signed to it] in it, I want half." They agreed. The deal was that if he developed the label and signed the acts, did the promotion and got the writers, they would give him half the label.'

Tarnopol accepted the Decca offer, which gave him a 50 percent share of the one-artist label. Rightly or wrongly, Jackie believed he owned a half share of that share, along with Nat Tarnopol. Freda and others believe the deal was that Jackie and Tarnopol held equal shares of the 50 per cent, but no evidence of this could be found.

In managing Jackie and Brunswick, Tarnopol had a conflict of interests that would not be legally tolerated today. Furthermore, by having signed over power of attorney to Tarnopol, Jackie effectively cut himself off from his believed proper shareholding. Jackie, a poorly schooled singer, was far from being an astute businessman and had put his total trust in Tarnopol, being the only artist on the label; Jackie was Brunswick.

Although always linked to the Mob, it was without doubt the shooting of Jackie and its aftermath that marked the watershed in the relationship between Tarnopol and Jackie. Lynn Ciccone puts the fault at Nat's door: 'After Jackie got shot in New York, Nat cleaned out all the money and left town. Jackie went to them [the Mob] for money, and that's when he really got in.'

Up until then, the Mob had control over Tarnopol and had been involved with Jackie's bookings and promotion. They may well have been earning money from recordings sold out the back door and therefore not accounted for. The move, therefore, must have been one of desperation by Jackie. Nevertheless, it was to Tommy Vastola that Jackie turned. He decided that Vastola and Roberts could offer him a better management option than Tarnopol and so this was arranged. Roberts would often accompany Jackie on his tours, with his primary function being to ensure the promoters paid up promptly and then to send the money to New York. Roberts had been out on tours before, the first time in July 1960 when a New Orleans concert erupted into a riot, with Jackie one of the main protagonists. His attendance at that time would have been at the behest of Queens Booking.

Both Roberts and Vastola were reputed to be Mob figures, involved with booking and managing black performers. One well-known singer of the time says of them, 'The crooked-nose guys? That was pretty much the nature of the business back then. ABC [Associated Booking], Queens, whatever . . . they were involved with those people. You were engulfed. Roberts left a whole lot of hurt knees and legs back there in New York.'

The Mob had always been involved in the entertainment business, particularly nightclubs, booking agencies, record distribution, promotion and record pressing. The fact that a lot of cash was involved, along with the risk, appealed to them. Another reason was that, like the rest of us, they enjoyed being around entertainers; it was a thrill. And, of course, they genuinely liked the music.

Tarnopol knew Detroit Mob figures from his earliest days as a gofer for Al Green. The mixture of black artists, Jewish promoters and managers, and Italian Mob guys seemed to work. The blacks had marvellous singing and musical skills; the Mob were willing to risk their cash and had the muscle to ensure their artists were treated favourably; while the Jews had business acumen and an inherent feel for music. The relationship relied on the premise that they all needed each other.

Tarnopol was a huge fan of the Yankees baseball team and often went to their games. Moreover, he was convinced that some day he would be the owner of the team. As Carl Davis, Chicago record producer and later vice-president of Brunswick Records explains, it was through baseball that Tarnopol became involved with the New York- based Mob: 'I think what happened was that Nat Tarnopol wanted to be a tough guy, but he wasn't. He was fortunate that one day he and a friend, a doctor, went to a Yankees game and there was a guy possibly having a heart attack. Nat and this doctor friend went over and did whatever they had to do to help the guy. The ambulance came and took the guy to the hospital. He turned out to be the Godfather. He appreciated what had been done and he kind of put his arm around Nat, which gave him the liberty to do things he might not ordinarily do. He probably assigned a couple of guys to look out for him. Johnny Roberts happened to be one of them. Johnny was kind of crazy; he's all right, but he has no concept of finesse. It's either "right" or "left".

'You can become enthralled with the idea that you're dealing with these people. Then, once you get involved, you find them saying, "We are going to put someone with you – you pay him a salary – he's one of us. If there's ever a problem, then this is the guy you go to and he'll come to me and we'll straighten it out." They can make things not happen that might be supposed to happen to you.

'You know, later, Nat Tarnopol abused all of that and it was Nat that went out and got these people to keep Jackie in place. But then there was a guy above Johnny, this Tommy Vastola guy. I think that he may have owned Nat, but not Jackie. Tommy wasn't the kind of guy to screw Jackie around, because he felt like . . . you don't screw your moneymaker. 'Cause he also had Sammy Davis Jnr. He saved Sammy from being killed.'

Davis is clear on how such an arrangement might come about: 'If you were Sammy Davis and you were out there and you were making money, let's say you were making; $200,000 was a lot of money. So I came to you and I said, "Listen, how much do you think you can earn in a year?" Actually. you know you can make a couple of hundred thousand, but you say, "I can make $500,000." So he says, "I tell you what, you sign this little agreement here and I'll give you a million dollars right now – cash, no taxes – this is yours. When you go to work from this day on, everything you make comes to me, except your expenses. Your hotel and yourself is all going to be taken care of, but your salary comes to me." Sammy [Davis Jnr] jumped at it and somewhere along the line, he started spending their money. They sent somebody to blow his brains out, and Sammy found out . . . somebody told him they were going to do that. He asked around and was told, "You've got to go and see Tommy Vastola."

'When he went to see Vastola, Vastola said, "I'll tell you what. They are going to show up, you know. You just tell them that you got to see Tommy Vastola. So they did, they showed up. They were going to take him for a ride, and Sammy said, "I'm with Tommy Vastola." The guys just stopped; they made a phone call and clarified it. From that point on, that's who his manager was. I think that also got Nat and Jackie and that whole ball of wax.' The connection with Jackie and Tarnopol is not clear.

Ruth Bowen also had dealings with Vastola. Having formed Queens Booking Agency along with Dinah Washington, she became sole owner when the singer died aged 39: 'After Dinah's death I wanted to go on, because she had that much faith in me, and I finally got another partner, Irv Nahan. He had a percentage of the company. The reason I joined forces with Irv is that he had the acts I needed. We made a good team. We were together many, many years, but I was the major owner of Queen's. Irv had stock, Jerry Butler had stock, Curtis Mayfield and Gene Chandler had stock.

'I've known Tommy Vastola 20 years, but he didn't have a percentage of nothing. He used to own a nightclub on Cony Island when I first met him. We met him through George Rhodes, who had the band at his club out there. That was 35 to 40 years ago. Tommy asked Dinah to do him a favour and come out and work, because he needed a boost for the club. She did, and he paid her. They became friends and I've known him and his familyever since.'

Bowen is a highly regarded woman and a superb booking agent, but the statement that Vastola owned no part of Queens isn't credible. She also omits Carl Davis, who owned a share too – the stock-holders seem numerous, for such a small company.

Bowen continued: 'From that point on, Jackie's management was with Johnny Roberts and, I think, Tommy Vastola as well. Tommy was the booking agent. There is obviously a conflict of interest with this arrangement [because of their involvement with Queens]. A lot of shows were paid for in cash.

'Till that time everything was fine; they were both earning good money. Jackie had plenty of money, but he didn't invest; he'd fill safety deposit boxes in the diamond district. [Even] Harlean didn't know where they were. Jackie would get cash and he'd run down town and nobody knew where it was.' In fact, ·Jackie was grossing over 300,000 dollars per year in the early 1960s, an enormous income.

Morris Levy may not be a household name, but in the era that Jackie was performing everybody in the contemporary music industry knew him. Levy was feted by the major record corporations. He was from a tough eastside neighbourhood of New York City and was very useful with his fists. Despite being Jewish, most of his childhood and adult friends were Italian. His closest business associates were known figures in organised crime. Levy also had a record company, Roulette Records.Of much greater importance, he had excellent record distribution and he controlled a chain of record stores called Strawberry. For a song to become a hit record required more than a good tune; it also needed expertise and contacts, which Levy could provide. Jackie considered Levy a friend.

Levy was the largest distributor of records in New York. He also had a 'cutouts' company, whereby he bought bulk unsold records at ridiculously low prices from the major record corporations. These were either unsold warehouse stocks or records that retailers had been unable to sell – 'returns'. The financial paperwork involved with their sale was minimal and, although the risks were great, so were the rewards. From his childhood years, one of Levy's closest friends was Tommy Vastola. A friend of both men said, 'If you grew up on the eastside [of New York], where every day was a hustle, you had to learn to fight, run and steal.'

Nobody who had anything to do with Johnny Roberts forgot him. Born in 1922, his real name was John Robert Tardibuono. He was described by one who knew him as having 'a face like an ice cube; cold as ice. A person not to be messed with.' He didn't need to shout in order to get cooperation; all he had to do was give you one of his icy stares. Musician Gil Askey recalls, 'Johnny wasn't little – about five foot nine, but around 220 pounds. JR was a plain guy. He didn't look fancy or nothing; no fancy clothes. When he walked your way you'd move out of his path. But he was polite; he was a nice dude. He was like a bodyguard; solidly build, a light heavyweight. He was changing his shirt one day . . . he had all these marks on his body – bullet holes, stab wounds.

'If a guy didn't pay his debts,' continues Askey, 'you'd send someone like JR to collect. He meant business. He didn't fear anything. If you killed him, he expected that. He was immune to fear. They are trained; like a soldier is trained for war. Yet he could walk into the Waldorf Astoria, just like Rockefeller.'

Askey relates, 'I remember one time Jackie was on stage and there was fighting out there [in the audience]. Jackie did one of his splits and Johnny Roberts picked him up: "Come on, you son-of-a-bitch, don't you see 'em fighting?" He picked him up with one hand! JR was smiling all the time – you never saw weapons or anything. Roberts looked after the money and it wasn't uncommon for him to collect 10,000 dollars for a night's work – in cash.'

It is wrong to think that the likes of Levy and Vastola were the parasites of the music industry, reviled by everyone else in the business. These people were the ' movers and movers' who put up large amounts of money to help produce the hits and promote the artists. One black artist put it this way: 'I grew up on all these people; I came up that era. In this business you had to go through and by these people. And I went through and by them and, believe it or not, I never met such wonderful gentlemen. I don't know what they did to other people, but they did nothing wrong to me. It had nothing to do with us, we didn't know nothing about it.'

The most accepted explanation to the complex question of who actually owned whom has it that Brunswick Records was controlled by one Mafia family, while Jackie's management and bookings were controlled by another. Undoubtedly, there was an amicable working arrangement between both families.

With Vastola and Johnny Roberts replacing Tarnopol as Jackie's personal manager, Jackie had the protection needed in the rough business he was in. They ensured he would not be ripped off by some of the sharks who booked the acts – for a price.

It must be said at the outset that Jackie generally got along very well with Roberts and definitely needed someone with his skills to keep him out of trouble. It was Roberts who in turn employed the intimidating black individual, August 'Augie' Sims. Sims, who weighed around 230 pounds and stood five foot eleven, had formerly been a bodyguard/masseur for world champion and legendary middleweight boxer Sugar Ray Robinson.

Sims first met Roberts and was recruited to work with the Mob in 1963. 'I knew Johnny Roberts when I was with Sugar Ray Robinson,' he recollects. 'He used to come to the Chandu [an after-hours club in Harlem]. He wanted to be bad at the Chandu; he hit a nigger there. I told that nigger, "Why you let that man hit you, man?" He said, "He's the Mob." I said, "I don't give a goddamn if he is the Mob."

'That's how he got to me. He wanted me and I was bad. I was doing all this old crazy stuff and I didn't pay it no mind. I didn't care about nobody; I'll woop you, shoot you, too. Johnny came to me and said, "We want you to work for us," and Jackie said, "Yes, we do." I never let Johnny bug me . . . Johnny was scared of me.' With that, Sims became the muscle needed both to protect Jackie and to keep him in line.

He was adept at his role as Jackie's road manager and masseur. Around 38 years of age, he wasn't one to argue with. Sims was under instructions to 'keep Jackie in line', admittedly not an easy task. When Roberts wasn't there, Sims was responsible for ensuring all the money was sent immediately to New York. His first duty was to fire some of Jackie's entourage, including JJ. 'I fired every one of those sons-of-bitches,' explained Sims. ''Cause all them guys are supposed to be your friend. You were raised with them guys, and those sons-of-bitches were robbin' him more than anybody in the place. That's when they went to work for me.' The explanation is ambiguous, but probably means that after they were fired they took their orders from Sims rather than Jackie. Sims went on, 'I said one time, "Hey, Jackie, the white folks are stealing from you." He told me, "You crazy." I said, "You motherfuckers is."' Most likely they both were.

There is no doubt that Sims was tough and could take care of most problems they were to encounter, touring with Jackie for around a decade. 'Nat had to toe the line with the Mob,' he reflects. 'He couldn't do nothing with me 'cause I was with them. Nat couldn't do nothing but go along with the program . . . I'd send money and he'd say, "Did you send Schwartz [at Queens Booking] his money?" I sent them money all the time . . . made sure I sent the money. I used to keep track of the money, too.'

Freda remembers the new arrangements: 'Nat had got out of town. Then they had Sims – he had just got out of prison. When Jackie got hot, Sims knew how to give him a shower and massage and stimulate his nerve endings. He'd do all that stuff. Johnny Roberts was the one who collected the money. The Mafia like family – they are family people. He [Jackie] was just one of the family.'

Another area of controversy is who actually wrote many of the songs that Jackie recorded. A typical example of this is 'Singing A Song', which lists as the songwriters 'J. Wilson, E. Wilson, F. Wilson'. Quite obviously, Jackie, his mother and his wife had little to do with it. Still, Jackie has his name on 88 songs listed with BMI, the main organisation responsible for the collection of airplay royalties. Many of these songs appear never to have been recorded by anyone and most are co-written with others, in particular Alonzo Tucker. A common practice was to buy songs and have them published under the buyer's name. Many of Alonzo Tucker's songs met this fate; many of his bear the name of Jackie, his half-sister Joyce Lee (e.g. 'Please Tell Me Why' and 'Sazzle Dazzle'), Tarnopol and his aunt Lena Agree (e.g. 'Doggin' Around' and 'Passing Through'), and even Morris Levy and Johnny Roberts. Tucker may not have been defrauded, having agreed to sell the song for 50 or 75 dollars, but he surely was duped. 'Doggin' Around' became a No 15 Pop hit and is certainly one of Tucker's, as he was singing it years before Jackie recorded it.

1962 marked another professional achievement. At that time, to be invited to work at the Copacabana meant a singer had really made it. The Copa was white cabaret, yet Jackie proved he could entertain there with ease, as Dick Jacobs described in *Musician* magazine: 'Tarnopol managed to book a solid week of Jackie Wilson shows at the Copacabana in New York. It was perfect: the Copa was the hottest club in Manhattan [therefore the world] and Jackie Wilson was headlining. We even planned a live record, *Jackie At the Copa*. I had prior commitments, so Sy Oliver wrote the show and conducted the band. The Copa was packed for every show and Jackie surpassed everyone's expectations. The album came out and, unfortunately, was not one of Jackie's biggest sellers: it has become highly collectible.'

Jackie's Copacabana debut didn't go unnoticed and a New York newspaper review by Gene Knight, headlined 'NEW COPA STAR IS BORN AS JACKIE WILSON SOARS . . .' wrote:

> A new sound has been found. Also a new nightclub star. He is Jackie Wilson, syncopated singer with a seething style. Practically unknown, he opened last night at Jules Podell's world-famous Copacabana. And stirred up such a storm of hand-clapping that the rest of this boy's career will be history.
>
> Last night, Jackie Wilson came into the Copa with his own conductor, a pianist, two guitarists, three violinists. Plus a vocal trio. This was his crack at the big break. Mr Podell crossed his fingers and hoped for the best . . . Jackie began to sing. Surprise, surprise! He's got rhythm. He's got style. He's got a new way of singing even old songs. And he's got new songs, too.
>
> 'What has Jackie got that other singers haven't got? Well, he is a male coloratura. He can change the pitch of his voice with an inflection that becomes a falsetto. He runs to flexibility and trills that amount to vocal gymnastics.
>
> Good-looking Mr Wilson opened with 'Tonight', 'Body And Soul', 'I Apologise.' I loved 'Can't Help Lovin' That Man' and 'My Beloved'. He even put new life in that tired old ballad, 'Love For Sale'. Delivery is dramatic. His songs are sung with the spirit of a spiritual. He has the gusto of a gospel singer, which is the coming thing in nightclub entertainment. In an eruption of emotion Jackie got down on the floor and sang his heart out. Not since Johnnie Ray first hit New York have I seen such a passion-packed performer . . . Wait till the word gets around. He is electric!'

At that time it was usual for *Variety* magazine to review R&B singers, so it is worth relating their critique, written by a Mr Gros, concerning Jackie's Copacabana debut. The review reads:

> Jackie Wilson has several tricks to give his tune, culled mostly from his disk repertoire, and some okay visual values. He loosens his bow-tie for the casual ballad approach, he takes off his jacket for a spirited rhythm mood and he gets down on his knees for the fervent gospel appeal. It's overly dramatic and somewhat hokey at times but

at least he's trying to put on an act and not just duplicate his disk
licks sound: the Copa crowd can't help but appreciate that.'

Freda recalls the debut: 'Sammy Davis Jnr was sick and Jackie went on for
him. A lot of people hadn't heard of him then. When he came out and
sang 'Night' he got a standing ovation. They didn't know him by 'Lonely
Teardrops' except, amazingly, there were a lot of high school graduates
there . . . they knew. He got another standing ovation. Next thing we
knew, they wanted him back at the Copa. They loved him.' Jackie was also
thrilled by the experience, saying, 'I thought I was Sinatra Jnr.'

Sammy Davis Jnr had given Jackie his break at the Copa by not
appearing, but that didn't stop Jackie embarrassing him. Jackie's friend,
drummer Jimmy Smith, recounts the incident: 'Jackie embarrassed Sammy
Davis Jnr onstage at the Copa; he took the mike out of his hand and finished
the song off for him. As a result, Frank Sinatra jacked him up. Sinatra "put
a lock" on every club.' For a time, Jackie couldn't get bookings in any club
in the country. Smith went on, 'Not for long. All Jackie had to do was
apologise. Johnny Roberts got all that straight.'

Like many artists, paying his income tax was one of the furthest things from
Jackie's mind. He always left it to others to take care of the details. Freda
recalls: 'Our financial problems started because of income tax. See, Nat was
supposed to take care of that 'cause he had power of attorney. We'd signed
all the papers, me and Jack, and they let us think everything was okay. Any
mail [from Internal Revenue Service] that Nat was getting he didn't say
nothing about, so the first we know was when the IRS got in touch with
us and the next thing you know it's 'in the name of the United States
government we now seize this property'. They can take everything you've
got.

'The tax was way behind and he didn't have the money. He couldn't
pay it all at once and had to make a deal. "How much you can pay
quarterly?" Then you're on the road till you pay it.' It was a very shameful
moment, as Freda remembers: 'I asked the men to please not put the
[repossession] sign on the front door. They agreed and put a sign on the
side door, but told me not to cover it up. It was so much [we owed], I
can't remember how much. Even when Internal Revenue came they said
they believed us that Nat Tarnopol had the money; he'd lied about paying
taxes on the house.'

So the Wilson's family home was put up for auction and they had to buy it all over again for a higher amount. 'My house on LaSalle was auctioned off twice,' explained Freda. 'The second time, when I got it back from the IRS, I paid more, but I can't remember how much.' While, at the time, Jackie was an international superstar!

In an unusual statement, Freda remarks how 'Nat said he was not taking his ten per cent, but he was living good. He had his own apartment. When he started he had nothing. He was taking him some money so he could dress good, he bought him a pinkie ring. He did everything he wanted, but Jack never checked behind him. I told Jack, "Get your own accountant, your own everything. These are [all] Nat's friends.'

'Lippman', another crony of Tarnopol's, 'was our lawyer at the time. The accountants, too; the tricks they used . . .' Freda was clearly annoyed that Jackie was making so much money for so many people, while he couldn't pay his taxes. 'Jackie was the one that was practising all the time; it was hard work. They gave Jack an office. He was the vice-president. The company was Pearl Music – Pearl is Nat's aunt. All of those records that say 'Pearl something'; she ain't wrote nothing. The lady can barely speak English. She's very Jewish. She's very nice, but don't know nothing about records.'

Jackie's accountant and close friend of Tarnopol's, Isidore 'Izzy' Silverman, was also criticised. Generally, there are two sides to everything, and so it was with the subject of whose fault it was that Jackie had no money, despite earning what was considered to be huge amounts at the time. Isidore Silverman says it was totally Jackie's fault: 'We did his income tax work throughout the 1960s. He was a gifted artist, the man had tremendous talent and a phenomenal personality, but he spent money like it was a bottomless well. To Jackie, money meant nothing; it was just another day. He loved being with people and entertaining.

'We parted company [with Jackie] only 'cause we couldn't control him. We told his business manager [Roberts] that, as much as we loved Jackie and Nat, he wouldn't follow our advice and his record-keeping left much to be desired. It was difficult. You can only advise if they follow that advice. If they ignore what you are telling them, you can't be by their side 24 hours a day. He was earning well over a quarter of a million a year, but it was a wasted talent. He could have been sitting on top of the world.'

Jackie's concept of investment was fur coats and diamond jewellery. But around this time he decided the best way of putting money aside was to store it, squirrel-like, in safety deposit boxes in the diamond district of New York, an area introduced to him by the Mob. 'They [the Mob] took me down to the diamond exchange in New York,' recalls Freda. 'You have to know somebody to even get in. I came in and sat on the couch with trays and trays [of diamonds] . . . I didn't even know they had yellow diamonds, green diamonds – all kinds! That was fantastic. I said, "I like green." And they gave me a charm bracelet with sapphires and rubies on it. Later, getting out of the cab, I lost one of the charms with the sapphire in it. I just called them up. They sent me one, free, from Johnny Roberts. They gave Denise a black-and-white pearl ring. They gave Sandy a white pearl and they gave Jackie Jnr a watch, and Tony was so little, they gave him one of those magic games.' Roberts told Freda, "You will profit by helping me." It was important to have Freda 'on-side', in the hope that she would help keep Jackie controllable. It was to prove a forlorn hope.

Drummer Jimmy Smith remained with Jackie for ten years, despite having no written contract. 'During the time I was working with Jackie I didn't know how much I was making,' he reflects. 'I only knew I could do anything I wanted to do, buy anything I wanted, go anywhere I wanted. He just picked up the tab and kept money in my pocket. He looked after my family.' Smith had a wild, crazy streak and was probably the wrong person to be around Jackie. He was easy going and good looking, with great timing; he could second-guess Jackie's every move on stage. Jackie's daughter, Denise, puts it this way: 'They were like lovers, right on the button. Jimmy could hit it right on time. He [Jackie] owed Jimmy Smith a whole lot of money, but Jimmy loved my father 'cause he took care of his family in Houston.' Freda added, 'You see, that's the kind of person he was. He didn't want nobody's family to be wanting.' The problem was, Smith drank way too much.

The substance abuse meant that Jackie and Smith would often perform on stage when they were very much 'under the weather'. Smith sometimes went off the stage mid-performance. Smith explained, 'That happened quite a few times. One time I fell off – it was at a theatre – they had a drop curtain, and all of a sudden I fell off into the orchestra pit. I couldn't get back up because of the curtains.'

'You'd have to push Jackie out when he was drunk,' says Smith. 'He couldn't stand up in the curtains, but once you put him on the floor, it was just like you'd wound him up. He was like a robot. He'd go through his whole routine.'

On the occasions when time and distance didn't allow them to drive between engagements they would fly, but Jackie and Smith preferred to be drunk first. 'One time we had a big fight up there on the aeroplane,' chuckles Smith. 'Jackie and I were flying from Cleveland and we always had to have whisky. We was late, [which happened] all the time. It was on a Sunday and everything [meaning the liquor stores] was closed. The airline told us they was going to serve liquor on the plane, but they lied to us.

'We got on the plane expecting liquor. The plane took off and we were waiting for them to serve us our drink. Nobody showed up. So Jackie hit the light [for service]. They came and told us they can't serve us no liquor, 'cause in the State of Ohio they can't serve liquor on Sundays. At first, Jackie sent Sims to get us some liquor. He came back and said, "They won't serve no liquor."

'Jackie took the seat and snatched it away from the little old lady sitting in front of us. Her head was going every which way! Jackie just went to the liquor cabinet. He told them, "I'm going to shoot out every window.' I said, "The ones he don't shoot, I'm going to kick out – the sons-of-bitches." The captain said, "Go and get it out of the cabinet and give it to him."' Jackie got his way, but could well have been in serious trouble.

On another occasion he did a stupid thing on board a flight out of Atlanta. Says Smith, "Jackie always carried pistols in shoulder holsters. Well, he took his coat off and the stewardess has seen the pistol. She went and got the captain. The captain said very nicely, "Mr Wilson, I have to have that pistol." So Jackie said, "Gladly, but I ain't going to give you but one." You see, the guy didn't see the other one.

'The captain went right back to his seat, the plane turned and landed back in Atlanta. Shortly we heard over the speakers, "Mr Wilson, we are the FBI and we're coming aboard." In court it cost him ten grand for each pistol. You see, the captain knew him. All he had to do was give 'em up.'

Life with Jackie was anything but dull. Smith related one remarkable event that could well have lead to all of their deaths: 'We played in Minniapolis and our next engagement was Philadelphia with Stevie Wonder. We was coming down the turnpike and [driver, Pop] Watley took a shortcut through the Ohio Valley. The National Guard had warned us, "Don't you try to make it through in the snowstorm." But Watley was the type that didn't listen to nobody!

'Watley was driving the limousine and the El Dorado was following with the band – The Upsetters. There was me, Jackie, Billy Johnson and this girl Jackie was going with, Carla. We was going down this two-lane country road and we ran into this snow plough. It had sunk down in the road. That caused us to turn around. The El Dorado was in front and we tried to get back to the turnpike. The El Dorado got stuck in the snow drift. We told the guys [promoter Henry Nash and The Upsetters band] in the El Dorado that we were going back six or seven miles. It was so cold you couldn't stand outside; it was a blizzard. I said to Jackie, "There's a house way across the field. I'm going to go to that house for help." You could see the light, 'cause it had got dark by then. We would have froze if we stayed in the car. I got in the trunk and got me about four pairs of pants and some coats and went running.

'I got to this house and knocked on the door and, man, these people came to the door and I'd never seen nobody look like that in my life! This was the mountain folks, and this style had just come out! They had long hair and long beards. Scared me to death, but it was so cold I went into the house and the lady said, "Well go ahead and get the rest of them, 'cause you cant stay in the car." So I goes back and said, "Jack, these people are crazy-looking." Jack said, "We're going." I carried the briefcase. I said, "If anyone falls down we can't stop 'cause we'll freeze to death." I heard Billy Johnson holler, "Oh Lord." He done dropped his marijuana. We get in the house; there was an old man, a woman and about eight boys.

'We'd been in the house about two hours and got warm when the old man came and called Watley and took him out the back. Then he got Billy Johnson, and carried him in the back of the house. He was taking 'em out one at a time and they weren't coming back! So when he came and got me, I was scared to death. We went out to the kitchen and he opened up the floor. He had a whisky still down in the cellar — moonshine. Boy, Jackie and them were just singing and drinking whisky. All the boys were musicians. I have never heard Jackie sing "Danny Boy" like he did that night. We stayed in that house for a whole week! We finally got to a phone and had them look for that car.'

Late in 1962 musician/arranger Gil Askey got a call from Jackie, whom he knew from 1959-1960, when he travelled with him as a member of the Buddy Johnson Band. In Askey's words: 'Jackie called me and asked to meet me backstage at the Brooklyn Paramount, where he was working the *Murray "The K" Show*. He gave me a tape of a rough "Baby Workout" with, perhaps, a female voice and piano-playing. Jackie asked me to score the music for it and take it to Decca Records reception. Jackie said, 'Hey, man, see what you can do with this tape?"'

Askey scored it extremely well. The big band-style dance tune was catchy and right on the money, and the horn arrangements were superb.

Released in March 1963, it zoomed to the No Five spot, which was second only to 'Night' (No Four) in terms of Jackie's overall charting successes. 'Baby Workout' credits Alonzo Tucker and Jackie as the songwriters. It certainly had Tucker's R&B feel, while Jackie sure moved well to it when on stage. To this day, the song remains a dance classic.

Gospel singer Linda Hopkins, born in 1924, was living in New York city in 1963 when she came to the attention of Nat Tarnopol. Says Hopkins, 'Nat Tarnopol was the one who thought Jackie and I should do the album together.' Tarnopol invited her to record with Jackie and the results were some powerhouse delivery duets. The first was a single, 'I Found Love', in March 1962. Naturally, it had a gospel-style delivery. The singers' powerful voices compliment each other well. The release reached only No 93, but for Jackie's fans it was a chance to hear and enjoy another style. In 1963 Jackie's only duet album, entitled *Shake A Hand*, which included gospel no only, was also released.

In 1964, after the success of 'Baby Workout', Jackie recorded the wonderful *Something Else* album, which comprised great R&B tunes written by Alonzo Tucker, many co-written with Jackie, again arranged by Gil Askey. 'I went into a studio with just him [Jackie] and Alonzo,' Askey says. 'He [Jackie] just made up these songs. He was constantly watching his watch. He was working at the Copa at that time and he had a date with one of the dancers. He was trying to get out of there. He was all dressed up and ready for his date. I guess he ran through all of these songs in 30 to 40 minutes. They had a beat going, these chords going, they just made up the lyrics as they went along – most of them. He said, "You got it, man.''' Askey makes the whole creative process sound so easy. When it came to the date for the recording session, Askey says, 'Jackie comes to the recording session and I've got to have all the lyrics ready for him, 'cause he don't remember nothing.' It's an extraordinary story, because there were 12 excellent tunes on the album – all written and arranged in less than an hour!

Although Askey worked on the album with the assistance of Jackie and his friend Alonzo Tucker, none of them are credited on the back of the album. Instead, the album states: 'Produced By Nat Tarnopol And Dick Jacobs'. Askey remembers the event this way: 'Dick Jacobs didn't have nothing to do with *Something Else*; Jackie produced that on his own.'

Sadly, this album, which deserved to do well, sold only moderately and Askey believes it was as a result of the ever-changing public taste in music: 'The "British Invasion" came in 1964 and changed everything. And Motown came along as well, with a sound equally palatable to both black and white audiences.'

Eddie Singleton, too, became involved with Jackie's recording career in New York, working with him until Jackie went to record in Chicago in late 1966. Singleton went on to produce four of Jackie's albums; *Shake A Hand* (with Linda Hopkins, the only duet album Jackie ever did), *Soul Time*, *Spotlight On Jackie* and *Soul Galore*. They were all beautiful recordings, but the *Spotlight* album enabled Jackie to really show off his vocal skills. On it he did many of the old standards – the 'evergreens'. The Dick Jacobs arrangements were perfect and the result was, for those who had yet to be convinced, that Jackie was an all-time 'great' vocalist, without peer. All of those tunes had been done by the best singers of our time, yet Jackie was still able to embellish them with his own style and set them apart. His singing is racked with emotion, straight from the heart.

Singleton, who later passed the production gauntlet over to Carl Davis in Chicago, says of Jackie: 'I worked with a few evergreen guys, but nobody could stand head and shoulders with Jackie Wilson, the performer, because he had the instinctive gospel singing relationship with an audience. He knew when to do what with his voice, and not just his voice; he was just as tricky with his feet. He was the whole nine yards. There was no escaping Jackie Wilson. If you sat in the audience he'd find you. He'd find the place you lived, no matter, whoever you were.'

In 1965, LaVern Baker ended a long association with Atlantic Records and, at last, the two talents of Jackie and Baker got together in a New York studio, with Singleton given the honour of producing the session. It was a great success, but also a lot of fun. Surprisingly, there was only one single release from the duet, 'Think Twice', backed by a moving 'Please Don't Hurt Me', on which Baker excels. It was released in December 1965, reaching No 37 on the R&B chart and No 93 on the Pop.

However, the fun part came after the session was completed. '"Think Twice Version X" was at the end of the night,' laughs Singleton. 'Jackie said, "I've got some ideas on this thing." He was joking with me. I said "Great, let's hear 'em." LaVern came over to the mike and they started. I fell apart. It was ad lib, Jackie had had a couple of drinks and the musicians were on their way out. Matter of fact, I was doing some sweetening [working on the recording mix]. It was a spontaneous thing. It was my session – both the songs. I produced it and mastered it and everything else. I never kept a copy of it.' The 'Version X' recording, which was done with the full orchestral backing of the original, was an extremely bawdy exchange of crudities between the two singers.

Jackie's relationship with Vastola and Roberts didn't help relations with Nat Tarnopol, as Singleton maintains: 'Around 1965 the relationship was just beginning to go downhill. There were many influences around Jackie at time. Some were friendly to the camp, others were inside the camp but weren't necessarily there to protect Nat. Nat was a character in his own right. Jackie respected Nat for the history, and for what they were able to accomplish together. So there was a lot of camaraderie between them that could not break up. When they fell out it was on their own terms and for their own reasons. Nat was very successful in creating a little dynasty around Jackie Wilson, and Jackie always felt he didn't share proportionately in the bounty of all this goodness, 'cause Nat took control and Nat ran the operation, which is how it was set up to be.'

If Singleton is correct, Jackie was also becoming increasingly aware that the money wasn't going to last forever and had begun to seriously hide it from the women in his life. Singleton explained, 'Like I say, Jackie and I were real close, in private and professionally. We were neighbours – off of West End Avenue and 72nd Street. He didn't give it all away [his money], he had safety deposit boxes in the diamond centre. They are in the jewellery shops. I went down there many times with Jackie, when he'd come off the road. We sat there many times and played with the money. Boxes and boxes of it– there was over a million in cash. He was saving up for his retirement. Nobody knew about it; Harlean didn't know. Everybody had some inkling that he had something, somewhere. I knew where, that's how close I was with Jackie. There was a considerable amount of cash there they never got a chance to spend. No one, because he never thought he'd be leaving [dying] that soon.' Singleton says fondly, 'Jackie was larger than life; he was a Daymon Runyon character straight out of the book, and he lived it. Live fast, die young – that was Jackie.'

Paul Tarnopol confirms Singleton's contention: 'Jackie had plenty of money. Jackie didn't invest; he'd fill safety deposit boxes in the diamond district. Harlean didn't know where they were. Harlean had jewels and furs, but 'Petey '[John, the son Jackie had with her in 1964] sold all that stuff when he was.'

In May 1964 Jackie again performed at Harlem's Apollo Theater, where he'd always been favourite of the crowd. Jose, of Variety magazine (20 May !964), reported glowingly of the performance: 'Wilson takes some unusual liberties on stage. It's odd for a performer to place himself in a position which virtually invites femme onlookers in the first pews to participate in the routine. Wilson, during the latter part of the act, works into a horizontal position. The youngsters may or may not be his stooges, but a group of girls approach him to mop his brow and later come to the foots to kiss him violently and with feeling. He made no attempt to move.

'BUT PRECEDING THIS DISPLAY, Wilson proves an excellent singer despite his proclivities for over-colouration. He has a vocal spectrum which ranges from a baritone to a falsetto. He works in bold, imaginative tones with warmth and vigor. He's extremely effective here.'

The domestic side of Jackie's life was less rosy. In May 1964 Freda, after being married to Jackie for over 13 years, decided she'd had enough of his philandering and filed for divorce. Jackie's friend guitarist Billy Davis put it this way: 'Jackie and Freda had a special love, but there came a time when they had to part. Freda never really stopped loving him; the feeling was always there.'

In January 1965 the Circuit Court in Detroit, in a default judgement – Jackie failed to appear or to contest it – granted a divorce. The settlement gave Freda the family home on LaSalle Street, while Jackie was ordered to pay $10,000, plus $200 a week ($50 per child) to Freda for support of their children. Considering Jackie, as claimed on his tax return, grossed $231,862 in 1963, it seems Freda hadn't done especially well. She often said that seeking the divorce was the biggest mistake she'd ever made in her life. Freda, quoted in the *Detroit Free Press* (11 January 1976), said: 'I didn't know what I was doing. I had this dream of his being a knight in shining armour. And when he wasn't, I got all upset and just wanted to get out of it . . . We had cars and cars and cars; Cadillacs and Broughams and Thunderbirds. We had three cars at a time. I used to buy all these clothes, to feel comfy. He liked me though. That's why he sent me to modelling school. He wanted me to learn how to sit, how to stand, how to eat cake. He was so proud of me when I learned.

'He told me not to get the divorce in 1964,' claims Freda. 'I just didn't see us doing anything; we weren't going any further. He was on the road, but when I wanted to see him I'd take some or all of the kids . . . When he came home, he just came home.' When it came to divorce or abortion Jackie was old fashioned. He didn't condone either.

Fortunately, she had some welcome assistance, as Freda explained: 'His mother really liked us and she helped us a lot and, when Jack got a chance, he'd get us some money.' It wasn't that he was mean spirited; Jackie was just irresponsible.

For Freda, it was a difficult time. She faced the daily reality of raising their four children without the help of a father and with the money generally not coming through. She wasn't coping and turned to the Catholic Church for support. Jack'd say, 'I'm a Jew and you're a Baptist, and the kids are Catholic. What a screwed-up family.' He wouldn't go to mass. He wanted to be something different. When I enrolled the children in Catholic school, he said, 'How can they be Jewish and Catholic?' I said, 'You're only Jewish because you wear a Star of David around your neck.''

Freda defended Jackie's lack of his involvement with his children this way: 'Jackie loved all children, but he loved to kiss babies – especially when they were little and didn't argue. Jackie loved children, but he didn't have a lot of time. He was always thinking about his business, which was singing. But he loved kids. He'd lie down on the floor when he was home and watch the cartoons and eat popcorn and potato chips. He loved his comic books and bought and traded them while he was a grown man.' Jackie loved babies and old folks; they weren't a threat.

Tony in particular had almost no relationship with Jackie, being only five when the divorce was granted. Denise had a much closer relationship, being 13 when the divorce occurred. She had a father fixation bordering on the unhealthy, and loved Jackie from the bottom of her heart.

Typical of Jackie's irresponsibility was that he was constantly in arrears with the child support. Says Freda: 'Jackie never caught up with child support payments. The Michigan Courts wouldn't get together with the New York courts. Each time I'd go down they'd say, "Nothing this time." I had to work two jobs just to exist. The children were used to certain things. Clothes were most important. When you step out that door, you'd try to look good so people didn't know how poor you were.'

JACKIE WILSON

By March 1966, Freda filed a complaint for non-payment. A non-support warrant was issued reporting that Jackie had fallen $7,500 behind in his $200-a-week child support payments.

The divorce and absence of a father figure helps to explain why the children would later have disjointed lives. Freda sought solace by drowning her heartbreak in alcohol, only making matters worse.

In December 1964, Jackie was performing in Las Vegas when he got word that Sam Cooke had been shot dead in highly controversial circumstances. Cooke had been one of Jackie's dearest friends in show business. Later that year Jackie failed to appear at an engagement at the Palladium Nightclub in Houston, Texas. The press reported that an angry crowd of 200 vented their fury on his $8,000 Cadillac, which they wrecked. Reportedly Jackie had been taken to hospital with a 105 degrees temperature, requiring a month's rest.

Drummer Jimmy Smith, who was with him, explained that the true explanation for their non-appearance was simpler: 'We didn't make it – we had a party.'Smith recalled a similar occurrence in Baltimore, Maryland: 'Jackie wouldn't go out [on stage]; he didn't feel like going out there. They had to escort us out of town.' Besides the exhausting routine of his stage act, Jackie was never kind to his own body, being a heavy smoker and a morning-to-night drinker, while taking innumerable 'uppers' and snorting cocaine. It was taking its toll.

DJ Norman N. Nite in his New York radio interview with Jackie asked him who he admired most. Jackie answered: 'I'll catch just about anybody, but I love Sammy Davis. I just love to watch him. And when Sinatra was around, I'd always get me a front row seat. In fact, he done me a great favor one time. I was playing Las Vegas and was at the Riviera in the lounge, and he was at The Sands, and we went down to see him one night. After he finished the show; I'll never forget it . . . after the show was over, he walked off and he came back out and he said, "Hey wait, sit down, wait a bit. What's the matter with you, I've got something to tell you. There's a young man sitting in front, his name is Jackie . . . Jackie Wilson: you go see him. I'm coming down. You'll dig him.' And it was great. No more said and no more done. He walked off, and you couldn't get in the place! They came down . . . everybody.'

Jackie and Elvis Presley were born six months apart. Elvis had been a fan of Jackie's since he first saw him performing, while still with the Dominoes in Las Vegas, in April 1956. Likewise, Jackie greatly admired

141

Elvis and they became friends. Sonny West, who was a close friend of Elvis's and one of his inner circle for many years, said: 'Elvis loved Billy Ward, Billy Daniels, Billy Eckstine, the Inkspots – he loved all of them. He took something from all of them and it all came together in his voice at different times. Jackie was rhythm and blues; Elvis would tell you that the influence of gospel singing and rhythm and blues helped form his style of singing. And what came out was rock 'n' roll. . . somehow they got together and you had rock 'n' roll.'

Jackie first gained national exposure due to appearances on *American Bandstand*, *Shindig* and *The Ed Sullivan Show*. His first TV appearance was on *American Bandstand*, hosted by Dick Clark, in 1959. *Bandstand* had a coast-to-coast audience of over 20 million people and, remarkably, went live-to-air. Jackie appeared six times on the show. The only disappointment was that Jackie's TV performances were tame compared to his stage routine.

In January 1962, he guest starred on the hugely popular *Ed Sullivan Show* in New York. The show appealed to a more mature audience than *Bandstand*. He performed two songs; 'Lonely Teardrops' and 'Danny Boy'. Freda summed up how Jackie felt about the Sullivan appearance; 'He was happy just being on. He had made it another rung up the ladder.'

Former fellow Shaker Gang member with Jackie, Harry Respess, was involved with promotion in Chicago when he again reconnected with him in the mid-1960s. 'At the Sutherland Hotel, Jackie went up to see Little Willie John and they got blasted out of their minds,' remembered Respess. 'Little Willie John kept telling me, "Make me high." I said, "You're already high." He said, "Make me higher." They really got bombed. It was all snorting . . . cok.'

Jackie had always flirted with cocaine, but now he had a full-blown habit. When high, Jackie could be somewhat different. As his friend and confidant, singer Tommy Hunt recalled: 'He snorted that stuff and got crazy. He knew he was a star and everybody loved Jackie, but he didn't love himself. Sometimes he'd go off his mind. He'd be so high off of coke. He'd be on the streets cussing and screaming at people. I said, 'You're a star, man, you don't have to act like that. What's wrong with you, man?' But he was so high. When he wasn't high, he was the most beautiful person you ever wanted to meet. Nicest guy in the world. When he got high he was a fireball, a thunder-stick. He was doing those things because he was lonely; I thought he was lonely. He thought he was strong enough to control the pressures he was under. He couldn't control them. He used to call me, just to talk with me and cry over the phone. He'd even think

JACKIE WILSON

Harlean was doing things behind his back, and it was driving the man crazy.'

Saddened at Jackie's worsening condition, Hunt explained, 'Jackie did what he wanted to, but he just got hooked up in the wrong circles, I think. Like I say, in those days you didn't know who you'd be hooked up with – you just knew you were going to be on stage, doing what you wanted to do, making those girls scream. That's what he wanted.'

However, Jackie's drug of choice was always alcohol. Says Jimmy Smith, 'He drank Jack Daniels [whisky] and vodka. He wouldn't buy fifths, he'd buy pints. His chauffeur would buy two pints every night, 'cause he didn't want to drink a big bottle.' This is probably on account of his long-time habit of never drinking from a pre-opened bottle. In 1965, after their divorce, Freda noticed the changes in Jackie's personality brought about by his excessive drug-taking: 'The lady [supplier] in Detroit had changed . . . she was not giving him cocaine; Jack could handle that. She was giving him heroin. Jack was snorting the heroin. He thought it was cocaine. When he went to somebody else, he was getting cocaine. All of a sudden it was mixed up. And he was smoking his special blend of marijuana. Then he was drinking.

'At Christmas time he came home.' Even though they were now divorced, Jackie still treated Freda as his wife. Freda went on: 'I was feeling real bad; I had a virus. I said, "I don't know if I want to see Jack." He came in. He seemed OK, but his eyes kept shifting away. He would talk about one thing, but you knew he was thinking of something different . . . . in his own world.

'His mother noticed something was wrong 'cause she asked me, "What's the matter, is he all right?" I said, "I don't know, I think that stuff has done something to him." Sure enough, they had stopped at this woman's house [to buy drugs] on the way to the house. It was bad. He took me, he said, "We'll leave the kids here, I don't want to be bothered right now." That wasn't unusual, the first day.' By staying at a hotel with Freda rather than the house, Jackie could get some peace and quiet.

Freda continued: 'When we jumped in the limo, Mr Watley asked me if I was sure. He said, "I'm going back to Philadelphia tonight." He told me, "There's something wrong with Jackie, I've never seen him like that." We went to the Sheridan Cadillac [Hotel, in Detroit]. That's when he blew, really blew! I wasn't saying nothing. He got real agitated. He ordered some Creme de Cocoa for me, and he ordered Scotch. He had stopped and got my record player and was playing Etta James, the same song over and over

143

— I hate her records.

'Then he called JJ: "Why don't you come down?", he said.' Jackie sent Watley in the limo to collect him. 'While Jack was talking [on the phone] to JJ, he wanted to speak to Pop [Watley]. He asked Pop, "Where is my limousine?" Pop said, "Parked in the driveway." He said, "You're a liar; shake them keys." He had Pop shaking the keys on the phone. I knew he was not right then.'

Watley, too, seemed aware that JJ was headed for trouble. Freda explained, 'Mr Watley, he told JJ not to come down. But JJ got in the car and came down.' Freda believed that Jackie's bout of paranoia meant he quite possibly planned to kill both her and JJ. She continued: 'He had laid his guns up there on the top of the chest-of-drawers, and, had he not been on the phone, he'd have probably shot me right then.'

As Jackie waited for the limo to return, Freda's misery continued: 'Jack was not saying anything much at that time,' she says, 'He just told me to keep playing that record, and he was standing over there by the window. He said, "You let the record stop. Put it back on!" I said, "Oh, God." He said, "Here I am, right here."

'Jack said, "You take off all your clothes and give them to me." I did. By then JJ was knocking. Jack opened the door. I pulled the cover up on me . . . on that bed that I was sitting on. JJ said, 'Hey, my man, where's the party?" I never will forget that smile freezing on his face. Jack looked at him like he looked at me. He jerked him into that room and he said, "Here's the party, motherfucker!" He was beating JJ and he pulled him down a little bit, he was beating the living daylights out of him. He was killing him. JJ never hit him back.

'I didn't say nothing. I was keeping the record going and thinking about how I was going to get out of there. He had put the chain on that door. I said, "Lord, give me strength." I tried to get the [bed]sheet so I could wrap myself in it and go, but I didn't have time. When he was really engrossed in beating JJ, I was gone. God gave me strength and I tore that chain off the door and I was gone.

'I couldn't get the elevator, so I started down some steps. I was down the steps and at the mezzanine at the elevator — these guys was cleaning the elevator. I looked around . . . he was coming down the steps and he had the gun in his hand. They say you look back when you're scared, but I never looked back. I didn't care if he got me in the back, I was movin' real fast.

'Down in that lobby they got some sheets and wrapped me up. JJ had left Nelson Small's brother in the car, the one that was his bodyguard – he died in New York from an overdose at a party he was at – he was sitting there so long. Small came in as I was going out. I was barefoot; this was winter-time. I was going barefoot with the sheets. He said, "What are you doing like that?" I said, "Jack is crazy; he's gone completely nuts now. He's killing JJ. You'd better see if you can save his life."'

At least in part, what lay behind Jackie's out-of-character behaviour is that someone had stolen his credit cards and run up enormous bills. Jackie was trying to determine who, and thought initially that Freda had done it. In calling JJ over, it's likely he had finally figured out, or learned, who the true culprit was. Said Freda of Jackie's entourage, 'They didn't mind dying for him, JJ and those guys. But he paid them more than they could earn. That's why I was surprised that JJ was stealing his credit cards with Cecil [Franklin, brother of singer Aretha Franklin]. Cecil was a minister of religion. [After that] I couldn't even listen to him [preach].' Freda meant by the last remark that she knew Cecil too well; his drug-taking and womanising, and now the illegal use of Jackie's credit cards.

'Cecil was hanging around with Jack, too, and other entertainers, naturally, because of his sister,' says Freda. 'He had just got out of college and was supposed to be a minister. They were all doing it . . . snorting cocaine. JJ and Cecil took all these credit cards and they rented a car and went all around the world. They bought a lot of clothes and stuff. The cocaine was messing up JJ's brain. They used to say he had a "big nose", which meant he'd snort a lot. Plus, he could smoke weed at the same time, for two hours.

A friend of Jackie's, Jimmy Smith, says of the credit card incident: 'JJ used to look after the credit cards and money. Jackie wasn't keeping up with what was going on. They just went too far with it. I know Jackie's mother saved JJ. Jackie would have killed him.'

Freda recalled what happened after the events at the hotel in connection to the fraudulent use of his credit cards, as she explained: 'He had me in the bedroom, my sister and the kids in their bedroom. JJ and them were standing at the door. Jack was really angry. Everybody was keeping anyone from going out. His mother tried to get in. He had men downstairs to prevent anyone exiting the house.

'I was working for the FBI [Jackie believed], so I hated being alone in the room with him. He was trying to make me tell him what we did with his credit cards and all this money and stuff. I didn't even know what the man was talking about.

'They tied some sheets together and they let my sister, Jacqui, down as far as she could go [to escape from the upstairs bedroom window]. Then she jumped. She went and got Rever, my sister Anne's husband, and he brought Red, the one Jacqui later married, and five brothers and one other guy came to get us out of there.

'Rever came up to the door. He had a sawed-off shotgun up his arm, which he always carried. They knocked on the door and Rever showed them the sawed-off shotgun. He got everybody out.'

Help had arrived too late to prevent Jackie inflicting a severe beating on Freda. Freda went on: 'My head was like two heads. Everything was broken in the bedroom. Jack didn't remember doing any of this. They asked him to open the door and he told them to go away, he was busy. So Rever and them kicked the bedroom door in. When he saw Rever, Jack said, "Hey, my man." He forgot all about me. That's when my mother-in-law really knew what was going on. She didn't know this was happening. But she would never have called the police, unless she thought we were really being hurt.

'We got all the kids together and Jack started crying. I went off to my mother's. He wanted me to come back. I said, "Let him come over and talk to me. Maybe he's OK now. I'm going trust him one more time." He talked like he was OK, he said he knew what had happened – that this lady had changed it [cocaine for heroin].'

Freda had sought refuge at her mother's home, but Jackie was still looking for trouble. Says Freda, 'They did get Jack together and to the house. Before he came over there, he called my mother and said, "You'd better save her life." He was really crazy. He was going [mad]. Nobody could change him. He was scary. My mother got out a gun, and she didn't use guns. The kids was scared to death, they was hiding in the closet. Jackie Jnr was trying to protect me. He was standing in front of me with a knife in his hand. I was ready to jump in this closet.

'He wanted to talk to me, he told my mother. I said, "I can't talk to him." She said, "I'll tell him," 'cause he had broke my mother's front door with his fist. She said, "Jack, don't hit the door any more or I may shoot you . . . I don't want to shoot you. If you settle down, you come on up here and talk to us and I'll stay here, too.' He did. She put her gun down beside her and she sat there. He cried and said he didn't know what the matter was. I didn't either, and I didn't know how to cope with this situation. I said, "We should stay away from each other until you can get this under control." So that's what we were doing. We were going along like that, because I was scared of him. Scared to be alone with him.

'[After our divorce] I never really left him, like when he came home, as long as someone was there, I was there. I'd go upstairs and he'd come upstairs and sleep. But I didn't sleep and I had a whole lot of people around all night. They'd just be standing around, like Rever [brother-in-law] and my sister. I was scared to go to sleep while he was there. I would be a nervous wreck at the end of ten days. You never could tell though, he had such control. He could control you and you didn't know you were being controlled. You'd think everything was fine and he'd be smiling at you and in his mind all kinds of things would be going on. He'd be planning what he was going to do. He'd be thinking, "She thinks she's smart – she's got all these people around her. She ain't going to get away with doing me like this. I'm Jackie Wilson! I can do anything I want to do." 'Cause he was raised like that; Mama would make it all right or someone would make it all right.

'He couldn't handle [the fact] that I was fighting that. I was supposed to be doing what I was supposed to do. He said, "I raised you, you don't do this. You don't defy me. I'm Jackie Wilson, your name is Freda Wilson – I made you!" Now I was supposed to be doing like I had all these years.' Freda thought facetiously, 'OK, yeah, if you say so.'

Jackie couldn't stand interference in what he considered his personal affairs. Freda gave an example: 'My doctor said, "What are you trying to do, kill her? She's been pregnant 15 times before she's even 30." He said, "That is my wife, I can do what I want and you stay out of it or you'll be in trouble. I certainly don't think you'll be her doctor any more." Things like that. One time the doctor called him long distance, saying it was an emergency, and he told the doctor off.'

Again Freda relented, returning to her home on LaSalle. 'I went back home and we left the kids with his mother,' Freda explained. Jackie felt like going on the town: 'We went down to the Brass Rail [bar], downtown. That's when he started acting different again.'

The incidents were so traumatic, Freda recalled, that: 'I had to take them [their children] all to a psychiatrist. They saw me by myself, then they saw each child alone. Then they put the story together. 'Cause those kids were really messed up. Denise was less affected than the other kids. Sandy wasn't too bad, but Jackie Jnr and Tony were. Jack was their role model. It kind of did it to them.' However, Freda recalled an amusing incident that occurred in 1965, after the credit card incident. By then she was living at the home of a boyfriend, Michael. 'You know when I was staying down in the ghetto with this dude and Gino [the dog], Jack came down there,' explained Freda. 'Jackie Jnr called me, he said, "Daddy's at the house." Jack comes down there, knocks on the door. I said, "Who is it?" "Jackie Wilson!" I opened the door and I couldn't believe my eyes. I was still a little scared.

'Jack took Gino into town. We went back towards LaSalle and stopped at every blues bar along the way. He brings Gino in, tells Gino to lie down. "Nobody messes with Gino, 'cause I'm Jackie Wilson." Within minutes every little bar was packed; word of mouth. Then everyone wanted him to sing. So he sang in every little bar. By then he wsa getting high, plus he took the bottles with him. JJ was driving, [and] Gino was still in the car. He really tried to get rid of some stress.

'We went back to 16522 LaSalle [which now belonged to Freda]. He said, "My name is Jackie Wilson and your name is Freda Wilson." It's three o'clock in the morning and he's drinking up some of that Cutty Sark. He said, "We're going to listen to some Jackie Wilson records," and he was singing with the records. Everybody was there, all the kids and everything. About ten o'clock in the morning he finally got tired and went to bed.'

Freda explained that despite the divorce, Jackie still treated her as his wife and their sexual relationship continued as normal. After he awoke, Freda said, 'He came down there and he propped himself up and said, "Fix me something to eat, woman." Michael [Freda's boyfriend] was right there, we was in the bathroom [having sex].' It is an extraordinary revelation about Jackie's nature and, to some degree, his arrogance.

As for JJ's fate, Freda says, 'Jack hated JJ; he got rid of JJ after that beating up in the room. That was really scary.' The strong friendship that had existed between Jackie and the ever-loyal JJ was severely strained. JJ later rejoined him as valet, driver and bodyguard, but the closeness was no longer there.

One of the unfathomables in Jackie's life is his half-sister, Joyce Ann Lee, 11 years his junior. By many estimates she had a vocal delivery the equal of Jackie, but apparently she was not interested in a stage career. While Jackie lived the good life in New York, his cousin, Tom Odneal, got Joyce a job as a welder with Chrysler Motors in Pontiac, just north of Detroit, where she worked for over 30 years. Joyce Lee refuses to speak to anyone on the subject of her brother. There was sibling rivalry between them; Jackie was charming and good-looking, a famous singer with the world at his feet. Joyce had the talent of a fabulous voice, but was unattractive. Guitarist Billy Davis said of their mother, Eliza Mae, 'She loved both of them, but it was a special relationship between those two [Jackie and his mother].' Freda put the matter this way: 'The relationship between the siblings can best be described as love-hate.'

Johnny Collins, also a singer, married Joyce and would later tour with Jackie, often opening the show for him. He says of his ex-wife, Joyce: 'We went to Mumford High School together. If you told me I was going to marry her, I'd die.' However, marry Joyce he did, although it didn't last. They have one daughter, Kelly. Collins continued, 'She gave her brother notes to hit. But she would never do it [sing] on her own. Joyce was self-conscious. She had a natural talent that was frightening. She had a foundation for music that would scare you. She could go from the lowest of the low, then hit the high note, and come back down, and never miss the fact there was a space in between. That can only be done on certain musical instruments. Joyce's voice was so strong she could crack glass with it; it was so strong and pure. Aretha Franklin said she would have stopped singing if Joyce had ever come up on stage with her. Cecil [brother of Aretha] would come to the house and get loaded. He knew talent. He asked Joyce what it would take to get her to sing. She said, "Kill everyone in the family." It wasn't shyness [that prevented her from becoming a performer]. She is not the prettiest woman to look at, but she had lungs. When she hit a note you could close your eyes and memorise every single nuance. She could rattle you in a chair with a note.' Collins says, 'Jackie liked Joyce, too. She didn't like him all that much.'

Collins became part of the family, living for many years in the same house as Jackie and his mother. Says Collins, 'Dysfunction, mis-function was part of the family. Jack's mother would prepare dinner, make everybody wait; make this big platter and feed him [Jackie] first. She'd feed him before she'd feed her own husband! It was disrespectful. She adored her son.' Collins harbours a lot of resentment towards the family.

He had many differences of opinion with Jackie. His comments are a combination of unstinted praise and near-loathing. He understood the expectations and the pressures that Jackie experienced and said, 'Eliza Lee was his best friend, bar none. He double-crossed everybody. He was fearful of everybody. He'd been duped by everybody, because of who he was. He was dogged by the best. He loved and admired several people and allowed several people to use him. But you never got to do it twice, if he could help it. He never knew how much money he generated.'

Eliza Mae and John Lee never actually married, even after Jack Wilson Snr had died in 1953. 'I know why they were never legally married,' said

Collins. 'My mother-in-law had no problem getting social security or anything with Johnny. But Johnny worked every day and always drove a big car.' It seems amazing that with Jackie earning large sums of money, his mother would have any need for welfare support. Johnny Lee was Joyce's father, and Collins and all others have only kind words to say of him. 'John Lee was the coolest person you ever met,' says Collins.

On Jackie's relationship with his children, Collins is scathing: 'Do you think that Jack cared about his kids? Jack loved singing. The minute they could speak he didn't know what to do with them, 'cause they were like him – they were a challenge. He didn't like challenges. If he couldn't pay for 'em and send 'em away, he didn't want them around him.'

Collins said of Jackie, 'He was down-to-earth, but he was an asshole. He was loving; he was a good-hearted person, but he was afraid 24/seven. He had been done [used] by everybody, including his ma. 'Do this for me' – he got sick of hearing that shit. Nobody put their lungs on the line but him. I watched him sing with the flu; he was sicker than a dog but he sang his ass off. Jack was a hard, stomp-down rock 'n' roll star. He kicked ass 24/seven. When he sang 'Night', he opened up a whole new world.' Collins relationship with Jackie is clearly influenced by his relationship with Joyce, yet tinged with respect and admiration.

The career and lifestyle Jackie had chosen wasn't conducive to family stability. Growing children need a father, or a father-figure. His children saw him only when he passed through Detroit. Jackie lived in New York, while constantly touring. Not unnaturally, the children began to get into trouble. Some of it was petty, some serious.

FREDA REPORTED AN INCIDENT that occurred in 1966: 'Denise and Jackie Jnr went shopping and used some of Jack's travellers' checks.' Denise, only 15 when the crime occurred, interjected, 'Jackie Jnr was only 12. They [the shops] didn't give us no problem – we were throwing $100 bills at them. I had this note I'd written [purporting to be Jackie's authority to cash his cheques].' It was an audacious crime for children, but it worked – for a while. Freda didn't explain the outcome, but said to Denise, as she related her story, 'When Jack found out, he was going to kill you.'

Denise had an amusing tale about her interest in a young musician, Truman Thomas, Jackie's keyboard player. Truman Thomas had been recruited by drummer Jimmy Smith. 'He was from Los Angeles, playing in a house band,' said Smith. 'I liked him 'cause he was a young kid and he played the hell out of that organ.' Everyone described Thomas as both talented and sweet. Smith said: 'Truman was the best organ player. He was the youngest.'

'I was only 16, right,' says Denise, 'I was still a virgin. Father caught himself being a father, which he had a hard time being, 'cause he was too hip. But, me being a girl, he was looking back every now and then. He said, "Be careful with all these band members, you might get hot and excited." He was back in his dressing-room. I had just graduated from high school and Truman was young and handsome.

'I went to Alexanders [store] and bought this dress that was right down there [sexy]. It cost me about $300 and it was all up here [short]. I was only 16, but I was trying to excite this man. My father was putting his make-up on; he was checking me out. I was sitting on the dressing-table. I went to Truman's dressing-room. My father said, "Come in here!" Sadly, the well-liked Thomas was still young when he died of a drug overdose in 1984.

Says Denise, 'My father did not believe in wooping his kids, he'd just get angry. He could be so cold. He'd look into your eyes; he'd do that to keep you off guard. He won a million fights that way. He took his fist and went pow, right on my kneecap and said, "That's cute, eh?" It hurt so bad, I thought he broke my kneecap. I couldn't even move. I said, "You're hurting me." He wouldn't even act like he was angry. He said, "I'm sorry, baby, I forgot you were a girl. I know it hurt." I could have killed him.' Freda interjected: 'He had a saying, "As bad as I am, as good as I am." If he did something that hurt you, he'd try to do something doubly good to make it right.' Denise said, 'But he immediately checked you if he didn't like something. It didn't matter if he was right or wrong, if that's how he felt emotionally – it could happen in a matter of five minutes, it could happen in a matter of five seconds. He would be on your case.'

Even with domestic problems Johnny Roberts could be useful, as Freda explained: 'Jackie Jnr had taken some barbiturates. He had bags of 'em, tons of 'em. He'd taken them at school and he passed out. I called Jack and told him. The Mafia are family-orientated people. I mean, they might have their women on the side, but they keep their family together. They believe in doing for the family: make sure the family is OK, then you mess around. They sent two Mafia lieutenants to my son. One of them I knew; Johnny Roberts. That's the one who was on the road with Jack. I said, "What you want to do with him, kill him?" They said, "We don't want to kill him, we want to chastise him."

'They took him somewhere, he didn't know where, but whatever they did they straightened him out, got him together. He couldn't get to nobody and nobody could get in [to the place where he'd been taken]. He could use the pool. He always had nice manners, but he improved that way too! He didn't know where he was. I don't know what they did, but he never did it [took drugs] again. [Jackie Jnr] said they didn't hit him or nothing. He couldn't say what they did. They may have shown him somebody who had messed up on something [such as a drug overdose victim], or some pictures or something. They have access to all sorts of things. Anyway, Jack took care of that; he would take care of things.'

All the Wilson children were growing up and experiencing problems due, at least in part, to not having Jackie around to guide them. Freda described another incident: 'Tony [their youngest son] was getting involved with things, so I let him go to Syracuse, New York, to stay with my mother. She lived on a small farm in the country. I let him go up there to get away from the environment in Detroit. She had him under control, 'cause she's very firm. I holler a lot, but it's pitiful. I say, "Oh, well then." I had a lot of help from my mother and my grandmother.

'Tony went to school there for about a month, and he met these three white boys who lived out near my mom. They used to drive to school in this little old car. They said, "We drive right past it, we can take you home, too." So one night they were coming back and the police saw them. They saw one black dude and three white dudes, so they stopped the car, patted them down, checked the car. They saw a roach [the butt of a marijuana joint] and took him to jail. All this for a piece of roach! What that signified, I don't know; New York is very hard about anything. The police said, "Where's your mama live?" Tony said, "Michigan."

'I just called Mr Wilson. Jackie was in New York. I didn't know what to do. They [the Mafia] pulled him [Tony] out of there so fast it wasn't funny. I don't know if he'd called the Mafia or not. The Mafia were always telling him, "If you love your life, take care of the family."'

Denise, concerned after hearing rumours that her father had fathered many children throughout the country, asked him about it: 'He told me when I was 13 years old,' says Denise, "If I don't come and tell you, this is your sister, this is your brother, then it ain't.'"

Freda says of her relationship with Jackie after their divorce: 'I took all my kids to Chicago, but I was scared of Jack. He didn't want me to get a divorce. He had been hallucinating when he got hooked on that stuff [cocaine/heroin]. Anyway, I said, "We're going up there to get some of our money."

'We were signing in [to the Chicago motel] and I signed "Mrs Freda Wilson". The man behind the counter said, "Oh, yeah, we've got another Wilson here, Mr Jackie Wilson" I could have fainted. Of all of the motels and hotels; I just knew he'd be downtown some place. Anyway, there he was staying at the same one! I sent the children over there to check him out, to see if he was going to do anything. Anyway, he took all of Jackie Jnr's clothes off and put his sweatshirt on him, and sent him back and told me he was coming over. I said, "Oh, my goodness, what should I do?" There's a question mark there; I was just sitting up there, I didn't know what to do.' Freda need not have worried, as she explained: 'He had this big shopping bag full of BBQ ribs, potato salad and all this stuff. He said, "Hey, baby, we're going to have a party." That was the last time he ever used a rib to kill me,' Freda joked.

According to Freda, Jackie had a saying he used when he was trying to control a family situation. 'He'd say, "I'm the bull and you're the ram." I would say, "There ain't nothing you can tell me." See now, with Jack I knew I could not control that Gemini. I used to wanna try, because if he didn't want to listen to what I wanted to say he didn't even hear me. He might turn the radio or record player up to drown me out.'

The children knew what their father expected of them whenever he arrived in town. Denise explained, "When he came home we knew what records to play – Jackie Wilson! I didn't go for that. We kept looking out the window for that limousine, [then we'd say] "OK, here he comes, hide your records." And he didn't let us have no James Brown.'

Jackie's expectations of Freda and his mother differed. Freda says, 'When Jackie was coming home, that house better be spotless. I mean, there wouldn't want to be a fingerprint on it.' Denise interjected, 'He wanted her [Freda's] house to be spotless, but at Mama's he wanted to smell food. He didn't bother her [his mother]. Bottom line; two different people, two different loves, two different purposes. He wanted both of them to be fulfilled. His children, we'd better be standing in line, at attention, looking just so cute: "Hi, Daddy, we've been listening to your records." You know what I think? It was a form of insecurity. He knew he had us on his side, but he had all these people that loved him, all these women. His records were number one, but if we didn't act like we liked his music . . . . He knew we were growing kids, especially myself, and I was going to school and had all these friends. My father was a very good friend of mine, apart from being my father. I loved him a lot. I truly believe he made music he thought my friends might like – that we could dance to. He didn't want me to feel like an outcast. Even if he'd never done anything you could dance to, he was still "the man". It was nice going to basement parties and hearing "The whispers getting louder . . ." [a line from his hit "Whispers", 1967] I was in the tenth grade.'

'Even my younger sister and his sister Joyce, they were kind of tight,' said Freda. 'Jack came home one time. We were divorced then. He gave Joyce $50 and Jacqui $50, because she lived with me and helped me take care of the kids, 'cause I was busy a lot. They were supposed to go to a dance at the Greystone Ballroom; they did go.

'Now, Joyce liked to hang out. Jacqui said she kept telling her, "We should go home." They left the dance and, when it was over, they went to an all-night movie – stayed there. Jackie was sitting there [at home] drinking and drinking, but he was not high. He said, "What time do they usually get home?" He looked at me like I'm supposed to know what time . . . they had never did that before. They'd never had $50 before to spend either! They were supposed to have got in a cab.

'Finally he says, "Get in that car, we're going to find them." I said, "Well, where we going to look?" He said, "We'll find 'em." We was driving up and down Woodward [Avenue]. Finally we came back past this all-night movie. They played all these old cowboy movies, and there'd be all these winos hanging there. Here they come, strolling out. He backed the car, jumped out. "Get in there!" They were scared then. At first Joyce was going to try and play it off. She's a Gemini too; her birthday is 6 June.

'He takes them back home, brings 'em upstairs, see. Sits 'em down. He says, "Who's the initiator?" Jacqui said, "I told her, I said we'd better come home." Joyce said [defiantly], "So?" He said, "What'd you say? 'So?'" He backhanded her. She didn't get smart no more. He said, "You got any money left?" She said, "Yeah." He said, "All right, keep that money. I'm going to let you go out tomorrow, I want to see what time you're coming home." They was home at nine o'clock.

'He always liked to protect the girls – that was his thing. Nobody better do nothing to his mama, me or any of those young ladies.' Jackie, no doubt, hoped to protect them from predatory males – those like himself!

Due to his life-long habit of not taking care of details, Jackie fell constantly behind in the reasonable, court-ordered, $50-per-week, per child, support payments. Freda was forced to take legal action and had a warrant out for his arrest issued. 'At first I didn't want to do it, but my lawyer kept saying, if we don't get him now we might never get him 'cause he ain't going to have nothing, or he might die,' Freda explained apologetically. 'The lawyer said, "You'd better file a warrant." So I did. Jack called me and said, "If you'll hold your warrant so I can come there, I will give you some of your money. Just hold it and let me make the gig."' Jackie had an engagement in his home town, but risked arrest if he didn't reach an agreement. 'So I did and my lawyer said," "I'm not your lawyer any more.' Jack's request made sense to me. He had his mother bring me down there. She did everything he told her.'

Another explanation offered by Jackie's half-sister, Joyce Lee, suggests that initially he did send regular payments to Freda, but that 'Freda blew it all. She went out and ran all the time and never took care of the kids. My ma [Eliza Mae] spoonfed those children. She always took care of them.' According to Joyce, Jackie chose to send the money to his mother instead, so that the children obtained benefit.

Denise had a great love and respect for her father, but nevertheless related an embarrassing incident involving him: 'I remember humiliations. The one I remember most involved that great shark-skin silk suit – oh, Mr Excitement, you're so tough. My father had this perfectly formed booty [backside] that the girls liked. He turned around and showed the girls his booty and he didn't wear underwear; all his ass was hanging out. It was in Atlantic City.' His pants had split wide open at the rear through the exertions of his performance.

Denise continued, 'That's where Michael Jackson, Prince and Elvis Presley got it [the stage moves] from. My father loved to sweat, 'cause when he sweated his hair would fall. The girls would go, "Oh, take my panties off." His hair was long; he thought he was hip.'

Record producer Carl Davis was born on Chicago's south side in 1934. He formerly worked with Vee Jay Records, where he produced the massive Gene Chandler hit 'Duke of Earl', which reached No One in 1962. Curtis Mayfield was assistant producer at OKeh Records and, with Mayfield doing the songwriting, they were a winning team, creating hit after hit. From June 1962, Davis worked as A&R manager for Columbia, which owned

OKeh Records. The music that came out of this team became known as 'Chicago Soul'. In 1965, Davis was forced out of OKeh Records. However, he retained a publishing company jointly with Irv Nahan, a long-time promoter and shareholder of Queens Booking Agency.

Davis explained the complex way he came to be involved with Jackie's career, through Tommy Vastola: 'Irv Nahan, he and I had a booking agency up in New York called Queens Booking Agency. I had ten per cent, some other people owned ten per cent and Irv owned 50 per cent. Irv Nahan had this group called The Drifters [originally Clyde McPhatter's group], but he had the Drifters in another booking agency called Shaw Booking Agency. Then, all of a sudden, word got out on the street that there was a "hit" out on Irv Nahan, but nobody could find out anything about it. I said, "We'll try to find out why."

'I didn't know Tommy Vastola at that time, but a friend of mine, Larry Maxwell, knew him. Maxwell called Tommy and arranged for him to meet me. We had to go to the Black Bear, or Bull or something, restaurant on 8th Avenue in New York City. We sat in their damn restaurant. I saw this big black limo pull up, and two guys came in and told us to get in the car and we drove to Brooklyn somewhere. I was scared shitless.

'We explained what it was all about. So he [Vastola] said, "I tell you what, there is a hit out on Nahan. I don't know what it's about." So he said what we needed to do was get Irv out of town until he could find out. I had an apartment in Chicago, down at Marina Towers, so we flew him into Chicago and had him hidden there. I called singers Gene Chandler and Otis Leavill. I said, "Pick Irv up at the airport." Otis had a key to my apartment: "Take him up there and you stay with him." So we did.

'I was fooling around with singer Mary Wells at that time. I had Irv hidden out at Mary's apartment. Well, about two days later we got a call from Tommy. We went to some tavern in Brooklyn. [It was] pitch dark. They took us through this back door. They had this guy sitting at the table. There were four guys in each corner, but you couldn't see them . . . you knew they were there. There was this one table in the middle with a little lamp on it and an old guy sitting there. They said, "Well, here's the deal."

'Irv Nahan had a group called The Drifters and [his partner at Shaw Booking] Milt Shaw thought Irv was going to take the group out of the booking agency and put them in Queens, which we owned. So Milt Shaw paid $10,000 for a hit on Irv Nahan. We assured this guy at the table it wasn't the case; that we weren't going to change agencies. The guy said there was three occasions when he was going to be hit.

JACKIE WILSON

'After we got that cleared up, one of them said "Who is going to give us the $10,000?". We were all looking at one another. Tommy said, "Carl, don't you manage Gene Chandler? This is what I'd like you to do. I want you to sign Gene Chandler up to Brunswick Records, and you get 20 per cent management, right? We'll give you $50,000 to sign Gene Chandler up. You get 20 per cent, which means $10,000, so we keep the $10,000 and Gene Chandler gets $40,000 for signing with Brunswick to put in his pocket. I said "OK." I figured that somewhere along the line Irv would pay me back.

'That was the reason I went to Brunswick, because we did this deal through Tommy to sign him, Gene Chandler, up with Brunswick. At that time Tommy had [owned] some part of Nat Tarnopol, or Brunswick, or whatever it was. This was 1966. That was the reason I went to Brunswick.'

In the 1950s, Larry 'Max' Maxwell. <A> Said Maxwell: 'Tommy [Vastola] and I were friends and we came up together. The old man [Godfather] was my protection, and he had Tommy protecting me. I started out shooting pictures and he made it so I could shoot pictures in all those places.

'I put Tommy and Carl [Davis] together. I was really supposed to have part of their business, but then I had my own thing going. We're good friends. Tommy was the person that helped him [Nat Tarnopol] out. After he got big, Nat turned on him. Nat did some funny things to a lot of people at that time. It was Carl and Tommy that were together, and so when Carl went over there that was like part of Tommy.' It appears that Vastola, in turn, arranged for Davis and Tarnopol to meet and for Jackie's recording career to enter its 'soul music' phase through Davis in Chicago.

Tarnopol decided that the new 'Chicago Soul' sound was the way for Jackie's career to go. At the same time, Berry Gordy's Motown Records in Detroit was also having phenomenal success around the world. By comparison, Jackie's New York releases, with their big band backing and lots of strings, were sounding downright dated.

Davis described his first meeting with Nat Tarnopol, who at the time was only vice-president of Brunswick Records but in effect ran the company on behalf of Decca: 'I met Nat Tarnopol at a DJ convention [August 1966] in New York, at a hotel.' Both men got along well and Tarnopol appointed him A&R director for Brunswick. 'He wanted me to do a production deal on Jackie Wilson; I guess his career had gone down a bit,' says Davis. 'I told him, "OK, but first I'll have to meet Jackie." I'm the type of guy that had to have a feeling for most of the act sI had. When

157

I met Jackie, we just clicked. We worked on some tunes and we finally did a couple of sides, then I had to take it back to New York and sit in a meeting with all these so-called heads of Decca, which at that time [still] owned Brunswick.'

Davis'explained his association with Tarnopol: 'I went to Brunswick because of Nat Tarnopol. I liked something about him. At Decca they didn't like him at all because he used to sit there and pick the zits on his face. They couldn't stand him. But he was nice to me and the fact was that after he'd gotten so successful with Jackie, he offered me the job of heading up the A&R department and I accepted it. When I went to New York I met Berle Adams, who was head of MCA at that time. So when I got there Nat told me, "I know what they want to do, they want to make you the A&R Director at Decca and Brunswick, but I don't want you to do that. I want you to work for me, and I'm going to sweeten the pie and give you a share of the company." So he gave me ten per cent share of his fifty per cent. Berle Adams called me and said, "Carl, I want you to head up the A&R department." I told him that no, I would stay where I was. I felt like Nat was the person who recognised the talent before I felt it and it wouldn't be right not to stick with him. Adams understood, though he didn't necessarily agree.'

As part of the inducement, Tarnopol offered Davis ten per cent of the 50 per cent of Brunswick, which Tarnopol then owned. He would later also be appointed vice- president. After Tarnopol acquired 100 per cent control of Brunswick, Davis's share would double.

Davis continued: 'Then I brought in Gene Chandler, the Artistics, Barbara Acklin and everybody. Every record was go and go, to the point where Columbia had offered, back in those days, twelve million dollars for the company, and my ten per cent would have been $1,200,000, because by that time a deal had been worked out whereby Nat had the other 50 per cent from Decca. Then when [in 1969] he got the other fifty per cent of Brunswick, he changed it over to BRC [Brunswick Record Corporation] and BRC Music.'

Up until the time Davis joined with Brunswick in 1966, Jackie's hit-making career was in decline, despite recording some fabulous albums. And, if Jackie was struggling, so was the Brunswick label. In Davis's words: 'Jackie couldn't get off the Brunswick label. When I got on the label he had stopped recording.' This statement is correct, because Jackie recorded with Brunswick for 18 years, 1957 to 1975, even after his relationship with Tarnopol had turned into deep hatred.

Davis insisted that he remain in his home city of Chicago, and Tarnopol agreed. Davis established an office and recording studio on South Michigan Avenue. Said Davis, 'I built that studio, with [sound engineer] Bruce Woodene, from the ground up. We tried all different kinds of sounds. We did reverb with slap-back echo. We'd try to find things within a song and make everyone do it. I used to do the music around the singer. [Berry] Gordy did the opposite [at Motown].'

Even as late as 1966, Jackie pretty much *was* Brunswick, but with Carl Davis coming on board the Brunswick stable would soon include some fine soul singers. Eventually it would be home to the Chi-Lites, The Artistics, The Young-Holt Unlimited, Tyrone Davis, Major Lance, Gene Chandler, Billy Butler, Hamilton Bohanan, Erma Franklin and Barbara Acklin. For a short period LaVern Baker, and even Little Richard, recorded on it.

In the 1960s, even the talented studio musicians working for Motown on million-seller records were poorly paid. Davis regularly called upon them to come over from Detroit and work on Jackie's sessions. They gladly engaged in this 'moonlighting' arrangement. 'When I was cutting Jackie I had the whole rhythm section from Motown, including the backup singers. This was only on the weekend. [Bassist extraordinaire, James] Jamerson was there,' said Davis. 'We used them a lot. Benny Benjamin started coming in. He used to be the drummer. [Arranger] Sonny Sanders used to send for them from Detroit. I used to pay them in cash, and more than the union scale. Motown's Addantes did background vocals. I did eight albums with Jackie.'

The way their first hit, 'Whispers', came to be written and recorded is a wonderful story in itself. A young Barbara Acklin was secretary to Carl Davis in the newly established Brunswick office in Chicago. She explained how she became a songwriter: 'I started songwriting when I was in high school. "Whispers" wasn't written for Jackie, it was written for The Artistics. Jackie was in Carl's office. Carl kept pushing the tape back and Jackie said, "What was that?" Carl said, "You don't want to hear this, it's not for you." Jackie said, "Let me hear that one," and he did. He liked it right away. [He said] "I want that one." Well, he did it and the rest is history. Dave Scott, who co-wrote it, was with a group. It got Jackie's career kick-started again.'

Davis, Jackie and the musicians did the rest, resulting in a hauntingly beautiful love song. The record-buying public liked it, and it reached No 11 on the Pop charts. By 1966 Jackie's career was in the doldrums, so when 'Whispers' was released, in September of that year, it steered Jackie's career rapidly back on course.

Davis, it is fair to say, was enamoured with Jackie. 'Jackie is what you'd call a professional, no matter what was required,' says Davis. 'He would dance while recording. You couldn't be around Jackie without becoming motivated. I don't know what others say about Jackie, but he was a gentleman. Everybody loved Jackie. He was a great entertainer. He's the greatest artist who ever lived.'

From a hit-making point of view, Jackie had needed a change of material and Carl Davis proved to be vital in this regard. 'I would do a demo of the song and send it to him, wherever he was. I had either Willie Henderson or Sonny Sanders do a song. We would just lay down a demo thing, send it to him and let him get a key. The writer would do the demo.' From there Jackie would work out his interpretation and send a tape back to Davis. He continued, 'All he would do is, he would call me up and ask, "Did I like the song?" 'He would get this kid who used to travel with him to work it out on the guitar and find a key.'

Eugene Record, who was born in 1940, did not form the highly successful and innovative Chi-Lites group, but left his job as taxi driver to become their lead singer in the late 1960s. Davis immediately recognised the group's talent and signed them to the expanding Brunswick label. Their biggest hit was a beautiful ballad composed by Record, 'Oh Girl', which achieved No One, a feat Jackie never attained. 'I was with Brunswick seven years. Wonderful years,' recalled Record. Along with Carl Davis, Record either produced or co-produced three of Jackie's albums: *Do Your Thing* (1969), *It's All A Part Of Love* (1970) and *You Got Me Walking* (1970). The Chi-Lites also did considerable backup at the sessions.

Record, who was physically assaulted by Johnny Roberts over a dispute regarding money he believed Tarnopol owed the Chi-Lites, nevertheless says: 'I loved Nat Tarnopol, we had no problems. He was always warm to me, he always treated me well. Whenever there was a financial thing, he always came through for me. I have no complaints. Whatever he did he did on his own; I don't know what that was. I loved the man.'

In the beginning, Davis would record the orchestra in Chicago, then fly to New York with the tapes so that they could over-dub Jackie. After some problems in New York, which will be explained later, Jackie subsequently stayed away from the city and did all the recording work in Chicago, except for his last album which was done in Detroit.

Davis went on, 'Jackie was always ready. You know that if somebody understands a story, they sing it better. Jackie was like that; he could sing anything. He could do opera and put some feeling into it.' Apart from the sheer joy of Jackie's performances, he vocalized what most people feel deep inside.

Shortly after the success of 'Whispers', Jackie had another million-seller on his hands, 'Higher and Higher', released in February 1967. It reached No Six on the Pop charts and was in the Top 100 for nine weeks. It is also the most frequently played of Jackie's records today. There was also a *Higher And Higher* album, again arranged by Sonny Sanders and produced by Carl Davis. Gerald Sims directed it. Once again, says Davis, the Motown musicians, The Funk Bros, did the backing; there was James Jamerson on electric bass, Eddie Willis and Robert White on guitars, Johnny Griffith on piano and Benny Benjamin on drums.'

Carl Davis recalled how 'Higher and Higher' first came to his attention, 'There was a young guy that used to write for Chess Records down the street and he had written "Higher and Higher". One of my writers was Gary Jackson. They all used to write for Chess. Then 'Billy' Davis and everyone jumped in when the record was a hit and claimed writer's royalties. The "Higher and Higher" tune was huge.' The 'Billy Davis' Carl Davis is referring to is Roquel 'Billy' Davis, who had co-written Jackie's early hits with Berry Gordy. At the time he was A&R manager at Chess Records, just down the road from Brunswick.

Roquel 'Billy' Davis recalls the 'Higher and Higher' fiasco in rather more detail: '"Higher and Higher" was written by Carl Smith, Reynard Miner and myself, originally. Gary Jackson got on the piece because Reynard and Carl were writers, two of my team of writers at Chess. It was to be recorded by The Dells and Gary came along and he wanted to become a writer. Reynard and Carl liked Gary and were going to make him a partner. I was a publisher, partners with the Chess boys, Chevis Publishing, which I own today. So we cut Gary in. Gary stole the song and took it to Carl Davis. Carl Smith may have been involved as well. They changed some of the lyrics. The hook was the same, so was the melody. Jackie recorded it . . . it came out. Somebody said, "Your Dells song is out." So I called Carl and said, "I've got some bad news for you. This is my song, I recorded it with The Dells." I took the Dells recording to Carl. "Well, you can tell some hanky-panky went down somewhere," Carl remarked.

'We had a meeting with Gary Jackson and Carl Smith in Carl Davis's office, and the truth came out. Carl said, "What do we do about it?" I replied, "The song was stolen, you produced it, but because of my relationship with Jackie, I'll share it with you 50/50." Carl said, "I'll talk it over with Nat." Then Nat came into the picture. We hugged, the whole thing. Nat said, "I can't give you half of my song." The past came back to me. So I said, "Screw you, I withdraw my offer." Nat had an attitude. I contacted my attorney. We ended up striking a deal and I ended up with 80 per cent of the song.'

Carl Davis went on, 'We had it to the point that if I pointed up with my finger he knew Jackie was supposed to hit that "bird note" [high C]. I would point and he'd hit the "bird note" and fly. Not many could go up and down like Jackie; he could go up and down the scale so easily. Jackie could do it great – he could hold it way up here.'

Jackie only had limited chart success during the nine-year-long Chicago period. Indeed, his Top 40 successes were limited to four songs spanning less than a two-year period. They were "Whispers (Getting Louder)" at No 11, '(Your Love Keeps Lifting Me) Higher And Higher' at No Six, 'Since You Showed Me How To Be Happy' at No 32, and 'I Get The Sweetest Feeling' at No 34. This last song, however, did much better in the United Kingdom, reaching No Six.

Jackie and Freda's second daughter, Sandra, born in 1953, was better known as Sandy. Throughout her life she suffered from severe visual impairment, but despite having full-strength glasses, she would avoid wearing them due to the cruel jibes of her Catholic school classmates. While Jackie was touring in 1969, he met a young man whom he decided was likely husband material for his 16-year-old daughter, Denise. The young man, however, took more of an interest in her younger sister, Sandra.

Reginald 'Reggie' Abrams was 18 and a singer. He explained the association with Jackie: 'I met him in Birmingham, Alabama. I knew some of the stars on his show. I met Jack, showed him my Q-card and everything.' Jack said, "Talk to me after the show." I asked him if I could put on a live audition. I've been with him ever since. I would open for Jackie.' Reggie Abrams was young, slim and good-looking. Indeed, he looked quite a lot like Jackie and his singing style was also similar. But Jackie apparently had another plan in mind.

Abrams explained his introduction to Denise by Jackie: 'The way he introduced me to Denise in Chicago, he said, "Denise, this is your husband. Reggie, this is your wife Denise." We stared at each other and said, "Wow, what's he talking about?" After the tour, I was going to go back down south, but he asked me, "Why don't you spend Christmas at my home?" He gave me the plane fare. So I did, and everything took its course. I married the baby daughter; not the one he wanted!

'I got to Detroit and caught a taxi and got to the house. I told the cabbie to wait and went to the side door. I was really skinny and had long hair, I had on make-up. Tony [Wilson, around nine years at the time] called out to his mother. "There's a faggot at the door." Grandma [Eliza Mae] came to the door and said, "That's no faggot, that's the boy from down south."'

'Jackie brought Reginald up here to live with us,' said Freda. 'Reginald thought he was going to be singing with Jack, but Jack left him home and told me to take care of him and raise him, and treat him like the rest of the kids. He brought him up here for Denise, but she was too swift for him. He said she was too fast.' Despite knowing that Jackie had never been down south as early as 1949, when Abrams was born, Freda would still maintain, 'I still think Reggie Abrams could be one of Jackie's children.'

Things didn't go quite according to Jackie's script. Sandra interested him far more and was quieter than Denise. She soon became pregnant and the family knew that Jackie would be very angry. 'Me and Sandy got together,' Abrams explained. 'We was running around the house and I thought I was going to get hit because Jack had said, "Don't mess with my baby daughter. You and Denise can do anything you want, but leave my baby daughter alone!" I tried, though.'

Sandra was 14 or 15 at the time. 'I had Freda walking around saying "Jack's going to do this to you",' Abrams went on. 'Everybody was worried about Jack . . . I was worried about Jack! I said, "How am I going to break this?" So when he called on the phone from New York, I thought, "Might as well got it over with." I said, "Jack, I'm going to say it real fast. Sandy is pregnant, and that's the bad news. The good news is I'm going to marry her." He said, "OK." I gave the phone back to Freda and said, "You all was worried about Jack, I was worried about Jack, but he ain't going to do nothing." But Sandy told me later that he ran his fist through the wall when he heard about it.'

Abrams says that after their marriage, 'We stayed on LaSalle [at Freda's house].' In November 1969, the first of their three children was born. He was named Reginald Jnr and would grow up to become a rap singer.

Abrams continued, 'When Jack had everyone come up on stage at Phelp's Lounge [in Detroit], he wanted to introduce his family and stuff. Grandma [Eliza Mae] gets up on stage when he starts singing "Doggin'Around". Grandma would say, "You all better stop doggin' my Jack around." Joyce got up with him on stage and did "Danny Boy". They tore the house down.'

Jackie, despite the fame and adulation, never forgot his roots. Reggie gave an example: 'His wino friends in Highland Park; he'd go in the store, buy a case of wine, and sit down there and drink it with them. One time when I was with him, Jackie sent the chauffeur in for a box of wine and sat out in the car with the winos drinking with them; over by Phelps Lounge.'

As for Jackie's habits, Abrams relates: 'When I was there, he wasn't on drugs . . . he was drinking. He'd change his liquor every now and then. He used to like Scotch and later on he switched to Smirnoff vodka, you know – 100 proof.' Jackie wouldn't drink from a pre-opened bottle: 'So I had to stand there in front of him and break the seal. If the bottle was opened, he wouldn't touch it. He'd say, "Go back and get me another one and bring it here, and I'll open my own liquor." He didn't trust anybody to open his liquor. He wouldn't let nobody mess with his drink, because he told me somebody once put something in it.'

Denise was very different from her more introverted sister. She was intelligent and hardheaded, like her father. It was a major disappointment to Denise when, in July 1967, Jackie couldn't find a break in his gruelling schedule to attend her debutante's ball. One family friend later said of Denise, 'Denise is an interesting situation. She had a real father fixation and her perception of her dad was not totally normal. It was out of kilter. She loved her daddy, there's no doubt about it, but she was kind of messed up.'

On 3 and 4 January 1968, there came another high point in Jackie's long career. Nat Tarnopol arranged for him to record *The Manufacturers Of Soul* album in Los Angeles, with the 23-piece Count Basie Orchestra. Jackie made the mistake of announcing on a coast-to-coast TV show, 'I'm in Hollywood to record an album with Count Basie.' The album was produced by Teddy Reig, who had this to say: 'Needless to say, their [Jackie's and Basie's] friends and fans flocked to the studio en masse. They were all there; finger-poppers, head-shakers, coffee and soda drinkers, and other kinds of drinkers.' The eleven tracks were laid down in a total of nine-and-a-half hours. The album was only a moderate success, but Jackie's mastery is evident on every track.

Once he was famous Elvis Presley only went out in public on rare occasions, but in 1966 Jackie was performing at The Trip Nightclub in Hollywood and Elvis wanted to see him perform. The Trip is a small club seating only a few hundred, but James Brown and The Rolling Stones also showed up. Simon Rutberg witnessed Jackie's performance: 'Elvis and James Brown were there. He'd been nervous, but once Jackie was on, man, you'd think he was born to it. You couldn't get him off! He did a shop-stopper; it was non-stop and moving. He was cooking. The thing Elvis does with his wrist [with arm extended and hanging his hand limply]; he took from Jackie. Elvis was really crazy about Jackie. I saw what I saw; Elvis went nuts. I'm putting it very mildly.'

IN THE DEFINITIVE BIOGRAPHY on Elvis Presley, *Last Train To Memphis: The Rise Of Elvis Presley*, author Peter Guralnick describes Jackie as 'one of Elvis's favourite entertainers', further explaining the meeting between the two backstage at The Trip: 'In between sets he [Elvis] finally got the opportunity to meet Jackie and express his unreserved admiration for Wilson's talent. With all he had going for him, Elvis said, he could see no reason why Jackie shouldn't be the number one singer in the word.' It was a wonderful tribute which Jackie would have appreciated.

Jackie talked of the Elvis visit in his radio interview with DJ Norman N Nite: 'Elvis did me a nice favour once. I was in Hollywood, California, playing a club called The Trip and we were having a little difficulty getting people to come out at that particular time. So he came out twice for me and, well, you couldn't get in. They said if Elvis goes, well . . .hey, let's go.'

Jackie's drummer Jimmy Smith recalls: 'Elvis came to the club in a white suit and a white Rolls Royce. I said, "That man's got style, ain't he?" When Jackie went on stage he wasn't nervous. Jackie would be anxious — so would I — but when he hit that stage, he was like a robot. Once you head out there, you're in the home straight. Elvis came into the dressing-room after the show. I used to mark [copy] Elvis; the thing he did with his legs.

Jackie said to Elvis, "You've got to see a black Elvis." They had me doing it. Elvis was a nice guy.'

Sonny West, friend and bodyguard to Elvis, was also present. He recalled, 'Jackie went out to MGM studios. Elvis invited him out to the movie set to see him after he visited Jackie at the Trip Nightclub. Elvis didn't go out much, but he went out there to see Jackie because he'd always liked him. They used to compare Jackie to Elvis, called him 'the black Elvis'. Elvis really liked Jackie and thought he was a terrific showman. He admired Jackie's showmanship.' Jackie took up the offer, visiting Elvis at MGM, where they had photos taken like two old friends. Elvis signed the photo for Jackie, writing 'Jackie, you have a friend forever, Elvis.' Jackie carried the photo everywhere thereafter; it was a treasure.

That night Jackie was singing, and Brown joined him on stage, where they performed a duet. Brown was performing across town, so the next night Jackie showed up and they performed to 10,000 fans. 'James Brown and Jackie were friendly,' recalls Rutberg. 'Brown loves Jackie Wilson. Whenever he was in town and Jackie was performing, Brown would be there.'

'There are two artists; I don't think any two men on this planet ever had the charisma of Elvis Presley and Jackie Wilson,' said singer Hank Ballard. 'The two of them remind me of each other; the charisma. Jackie'd just walk on stage and the house would come down. Jackie would walk out with a cigarette in his hand, do a spin, and the house would come down. Elvis would go out there and shake his ass and legs like he had the rickets. When you've born with that sort of charisma, you're born with success.'

In April 1967, trouble found Jackie once more. The incident showed that blacks had still not achieved the liberty they had fought so hard for. The *Detroit Courier* newspaper reported the story this way: "'CAUGHT NUDE WITH WHITE GIRL IN COLUMBIA, S.C [South Carolina]." Police in this far-south city arrested Jackie Wilson and a member of his band here last week and charged them with having been in the nude at a motel with two white women.' Jackie, who was 32, was touring with BB King at the time. The other band member arrested was his drummer and friend Jimmy Smith, aged 28. The two white women involved were 24 and 25, very much adults, yet they were charged with 'immoral' and 'disorderly' conduct. Their bonds were set at $200 each. Jimmy Smith said of the arrest: 'When the police came in, Jackie was sitting in a chair with his hat and clothes on. He was not nude; he had got up and put his clothes on. It was a messed event. We had to pay our way out of it.'

As ridiculous as these South Carolina 'moral conduct' charges may seem today, at the time they were considered dynamite for his revived career. It could mean no radio airplay, or that promoters might not book him so readily. And so it was arranged for Jackie to marry his long-time girlfriend, Harlean Harris. Jimmy Smith says the wedding was very hastily arranged: 'I believe it was to do with South Carolina. It busted up a whole lot of stuff. It made a lot of trouble.' It was Tarnopol who thought the plan up, according to some who were around at the time. Harlean was mother of Jackie's son, John Dominic ('Petey'), who'd been born in 1963.

Jackie and Harlean were married in June 1967, at a private civil ceremony performed by a New York Civil Court judge, Amos Bowman, in his chambers. Present was bridesmaid Mrs Johnny Brantely, August Sims as Jackie's aide, Nat Tarnopol and Jimmy Smith as best man. The press photo of the wedding shows everyone looking very solemn, Jackie with his eyes downcast.

Soon after their marriage, a serious rift led to Jackie moving out of their luxury penthouse apartment. For Jackie, this meant a slide into a dangerously depressive period and an even more serious drug-taking stage. He may well have lost the desire to live. Exactly why the couple separated is a matter of conjecture. Some close to the two say Jackie found Harlean in a compromising situation with Tarnopol. Although Jackie had untold affairs with women, both married and single, he was devastated that his friend and manager was having an affair with his wife. Joyce McRae claims singer Sam Moore, now her husband, was with Jackie when he discovered Tarnopol in bed with Harlean. The effect on Jackie's mental well-being was devastating, due to the initial friendship and respect he had for Tarnopol. Jackie had finally determined that Tarnopol was not paying him his due and, to rub salt into the wound, now believed his friend was having an affair with his wife. It was the final straw. Jimmy Smith believes the affair did take place, saying simply, 'They was; Nat swore to God he wasn't doing it, but I always believed he was doing it.' August Sims, too, was as close as one got to Tarnopol and he maintains the story is factual.

Billy Davis had been a neighbour and friend of Jackie's since their teenaged years. In 1968 he joined with Jackie as his touring guitar player. Davis and 'Pop' Watley, Jackie's driver, helped Jackie move from the apartment he had shared with Harlean. Jackie moved into the 'flop house' Alvin Hotel on 52nd Street, near Broadway. Said Davis, 'He took only his clothes, portable stereo, his comic book collection [which was mainly of the

JACKIE WILSON

Captain Marvel series], and his record collection [all his own recordings].
He couldn't live with Harlean, but he always loved her – it was just over.'

This was a miserable period for Jackie. Although only 34, the best of his
hit-making days were over. The last hit of his career, 'I Get The Sweetest
Feeling', was released in August 1968. The album of the same name was
released in October, featuring a painting of Jackie with a beautiful woman
leaning with her elbows on his back. That woman is Harlean.

Quite likely, Jackie had given up the fight. Billy Davis observed
something that made him realise how serious Jackie's position was. In a
Goldmine magazine article of 1 November 1991 on Jackie's life, by Robert
Pruter, Davis reported: 'One night I came back to his apartment in the
Alvin Hotel and Jackie was as white as a ghost. At first he wouldn't say
anything but after talking till four in the morning Jackie told me what
happened. His main concern was with his mother, and he made me swear
never to tell anyone lest his mother found out. You know it might have
happened more than once.' Davis went on, 'Jackie had a number of
companies who wanted to record him over the years, but he never went
to them because of fear.' Jackie apparently admitted that he'd been held
out of a high-rise window by Tarnopol's henchmen. Of course, no
witnesses to this supposed incident ever came forward, but the question
remains, why had Jackie remained on the Brunswick label for 18 years
despite the obvious fact that, in later years, he and Tarnopol hated each
other?

The exact year that the incident was said to have occurred varies
between 1964 and 1968. According to some close to Jackie at the time, it
was done at Tarnopol's behest to ensure Jackie re-signed to Brunswick.
Without doubt, Jackie was controlled or, more bluntly, he was owned!
Robert Pruter's thoroughly researched book, *Chicago Soul*, states:

> Joe McEwen, a well-respected writer on black music and an A&R
> man at CBS Records, said of Brunswick that it had a "dubious
> reputation". He was being kind. Brunswick had been the subject of
> a lot of nasty stories over the years, many of which related to
> presumed links with the Mob. [Eugene] Record testified at the
> Brunswick trial that he was roughed up by an associate of Tarnopol
> when he demanded an advance for re-signing with the label. I asked
> Record why a company would treat its artists that way, and he
> replied, 'Hey, it wasn't the company. It was the people who were
> maybe connected with the company but who weren't involved in

168

recording per se. In other words, they were outside people that was on the company side.' When I pointedly asked if these 'outside people' were gangsters, Record silently nodded affirmatively, fully cognisant that the tape recorder was on.

Sonny Woods, for many years a member of the Detroit-based Midnighters vocal group, told a tale that at best should be classified as hearsay, but it indicated how artists viewed Brunswick. According to Woods, when Jackie Wilson refused to re-sign with Brunswick, Tarnopol and his associates hung the singer by his feet outside the window of a high-rise hotel until he agreed to put his name on the dotted line.

Public relations man Harry Respess had known Jackie from his teenage years, but was especially close to JJ. Respess is sure that the incident actually happened and gave this frightening version: 'Johnny Jones [JJ] was there. They called me right after this happened. They wanted him to resign with Brunswick, but he didn't want to 'cause Brunswick wasn't putting the money into promotion that he thought was required to get him a hit record. So the big boys just grabbed him and held him out the window. They way I understand it is that if he didn't sign, they'd [Nat's associates] drop him. They let one hand free, so he could sign while hanging out the window.' There were a number of contracts between Jackie and Tarnopol. The first contracted him to record for Decca's Brunswick label; the second concerned Jackie's resigning to Tarnopol's Brunswick in 1968; and the third related to Jackie's management. These contracts could not be located.

Another incident of intimidation is said to have occurred around the same time. Says Billy Davis, 'He told me about all that night, after it happened [being hung out of the window]. I knew something was wrong. When we went on tour we stayed in a suite together; that's when he told me. He was also tied up in a basement one time. Jackie told me that. There were rats down there. It was in a dark basement, he said, and he shuddered. With him it wasn't really the money. This was because of a contract with Nat. Freda also told me about it. It would have been during the mid-60s. It was before the marriage [to Harlean]. He just wanted to sing.'

While denying knowledge of the window incident, Davis did say, 'Nat Tarnopol didn't want to pay Jackie for 'Higher and Higher', so Jackie didn't want to record any more. He was pissed that everything he did would go to Nat. But Nat would say, "He owes me." It was such a battle going between Jackie and Nat, that I don't think Nat put in any sort of effort on his behalf after that. But that was hard, because Jackie was the best he had. After 'Higher and Higher', Jackie never went to New York. If he called and asked Nat for money, he'd be told "No". It was an uneasy feeling at that time. Nat didn't promote Jackie.'

Jackie was always a very proud, macho individual. He tried to convey the impression that he was in control, totally self-confident. His long-time friend Billy Davis knew better, as he related to Robert Pruter in his excellent 1991 *Goldmine* article on Jackie, 'When I came to live with him [in 1968], he looked terrible. He would lie around the apartment for weeks and weeks, drinking heavily and not doing anything but reading his comic books. He had thousands of comic books stacked in his apartment, mainly Marvel, *Conan the Barbarian*, things like that. I eventually persuaded him to go out on tour again and stop his drinking, but he never complained that he never achieved great success. You could tell, though, that it had affected him.'

Tommy Hunt, who knew Jackie well, was a singer of immense talent himself. Hunt rates Jackie amongst the best: 'I would put him up there with Sinatra, Nat King Cole, all of them. He used to tear the Apollo up. When he walked out, the girls were falling in the aisles. He was an excellent singer, the control he had over his voice was amazing. He could control his voice . . . that's what he was trying to teach me. He had control like nobody I ever heard. He could have been up there with Elvis Presley. I don't know why they rave about James Brown so much when Jackie was "the man". Not only a singer, but an actor. I mean, when he went down on his knees you could see the girls' knickers dropping.'

Hunt could also see that all was not as it should be. In his words: 'Jackie was scared, he was scared to death, and that probably contributed to his drug taking as well. He was trying to run away from the reality of it all. I know he was under pressure, he'd always tried to laugh it off. He was a bigger star than me, so he looked at me as, "This is my little friend, Tommy," or "A little star trying to make it.' He kind of protected me, but I know that under all that strength he was trying to show me there was a little boy trying to get out. He was the macho type, but I could see through it, because the guy would call and start crying about his life and how people were cutting him to pieces and hurting him, stealing from him, lying behind his back and trying to be his friend to his face only for the money. I said, "Listen Jackie, you've got to know how to control that, only you can control it, but taking drugs ain't going to do it, because the more drugs

you take the further you are going to lose yourself in that hole you're in."'
Hunt went on: 'Jackie thought he was God. The fans make you feel that
way. But you've got to look at reality. There's a "you" that can do that
thing on stage and also a "you" that needs a real life.'

Jackie had developed deep paranoia. He'd been used and abused by so
many people, didn't know who to trust. JJ was his long-time friend from
Highland Park, the Shaker Gang and his Ever Ready Gospel Group, yet
Jackie had fired him. Hunt recalled, 'I know Jackie and JJ were very close,
they went way back. But Jackie would have his little tantrums and he'd sack
everybody, and then turn around and say, "I ain't got no friends." Then
he'd want them back again.'

Hunt confirmed another behavioural quirk, 'Jackie'd lock himself in the
toilet. He was looking for that space to be alone, but he knew damn well
he couldn't be. Jackie was crazy but I loved him, God bless him. I
remember nights when he threw chairs out of the hotel windows. He'd get
mad at the world and I'd say, "Why'd you throw a chair out the window?
Make yourself feel better?"'

Lead singer of The Four Tops, Levi Stubbs, had known Jackie from the
amateur nights at Detroit's Paradise Theater. Stubbs commented on his
friend Jackie, 'It's hard to say anything negative about Jackie except he was
just a "street person". Jackie did more things for people than you would
ever imagine. I can remember on various occasions in the northend [of
Detroit] where we were raised, when he was in town, he would load up
the trunk with heaps of wine, drive around the area and give it to the
winos. That's what they wanted, and they loved him. People loved him; he
was on their level. He'd help people with their careers at the drop of a
hat. In this business, performers, especially years ago, would tend to be
thought of as faggots; not fully a man, a gay. Jackie Wilson would be the
wrong guy to say that to. He could give a punch, pal. I tell you one thing,
whoever it was he had an altercation with, when it was over they didn't
want it to happen again!'

Singer Chuck Jackson believes that Jackie most of all wanted to 'get over
the hump'. 'You see, Jackie Wilson was not an R&B singer; Jackie Wilson
could sing, period! 'Night' – that's where he should have been. That's
where it was. He could do rhythm songs, but here's a guy who could truly
sing. I'm telling you he was a singer.'

After his separation from Harlean Jackie became very morose, seemingly
losing all reason for living. Billy Davis recalls, 'All the stars that had looked
up to him, they didn't come around. He was stuck up in the Alvin Hotel

and he was getting boozed up 24 hours a day. He just seemed out of it. I could see something bad happening. I lived there more than I did in my own place in the Bronx. I'd just hang in there, but all these other guys weren't there. The ones that came around later, or with something to say, they don't know what he was going through. It was like he didn't have anyone.

'He was coming out of a fairly depressive spell at that particular time. I knew I was responsible for helping to pull him through, 'cause everybody had deserted him. This was a man who had one of the greatest voices in the world and who had been feted by the world and now . . . he'd just be in moods when he laid around getting high, fucked up for weeks. He would just smoke weed [marijuana] all day long. He would drink and he wouldn't put on clothes for weeks at a time, just get in the room, get knocked out and lie down until he woke up and got enough strength to roll another joint. He kept that up constantly. I never saw him act that way before.' Jackie, always a big eater, needed activity to burn off the fat. Lying around, he became overweight and this became noticeable as his face fattened.

Davis provided his opinion on what Chuck Jackson meant by Jackie wanting to get 'over the hump': 'What he means is he wanted to get to where he used to be. He wanted to reach the stardom – he never talked about it, but I knew he knew he deserved better. He knew he was down in the dumps, but he never complained about it. I would sit there and watch that, and it would depress me to the point where I came out of my apartment in the Bronx, but I stayed there more than I did in my own place. With the guitar, me and Alonzo [Tucker], writing tunes and pulling him into it; "Say, how do you like this?" And after a while he'd look forward to that. We kept it up for weeks. In the beginning we'd pull him in, but he would leave. Sometimes we were there from nine o'clock at night to six, seven or eight o'clock in the morning. So he would stay so long and then he'd be gone. He wasn't there every day like I was. It looked like Alonzo had given up on him too. He just didn't have any enthusiasm. But when he saw me having him there singing, it kind of got him, he kinda came on in. Alonzo had the attitude, if he ain't going to do nothing, I ain't going to. He'd never said it, but that was his attitude. He [Alonzo] just looked like he felt he was over the hill.'

The effort to bring Jackie back on track began to have an effect, as Davis recalled: 'We had tapes full of new songs. He started to get back into wanting to tour again.' Davis had another ploy to pick up his spirits. 'After the down times in 1968, we'd go and park some place and I'd deliberately get people to ask for autographs. People wouldn't believe Jackie was in that area.' Jackie couldn't help but respond when the fans came around, and Davis knew it. Gradually, Jackie began to be his old self and the touring began again.

Jimmy Smith, Jackie's close friend and drummer for around ten years, has a different explanation for why Jackie was so depressed: 'I believe he couldn't see himself the way he had started living then.' His career was in definite decline and the alcohol and drugs were not just needed for recreational purposes. Smith went on, 'Harlean had been with him through all the good times. I believe he really needed her.'

Billy Davis had been guitarist with Hank Ballard And The Midnighters. He joined Jackie as one of his three travelling band members in 1968. Davis talked enthusiastically of the period he toured with Jackie: 'Some of the dates were the "Chitterlin' Circuit" [the black circuit]. We did some good sets such as Miami Beach, but we also played some small circuit gigs. Then we'd have some big ones. In Fresno, California, they had to get the fire department hoses to spray the women to get them off him.'

Davis recalled another incident that indicates the level of pressure Jackie was experiencing. 'We was on tour and Sims was mad at him for something, so he threatened to hit Jackie. Jackie was sitting with his shirt off, putting his make up on. Sims drew back and threatened to hit him. I said, "Damn! What's the matter with you?" I'd never seen Jackie back off like that before. I confronted Sims. Jackie stopped me and said "Billy, stop! You don't understand." I knew it was something serious and Jackie didn't want me to get involved.' It's true Sims was a big man, weighing around 230 pounds, but Jackie was a 'real scraper', in Davis's words. 'He had a punch like a heavyweight.' No, it was a lot more than that. Sims was Robert's henchman, put there to keep an eye on Jackie. Billy Davis also recalled another possible cause of conflict: 'I know he lost a lot on investments. Tarnopol put Jackie onto these investments . . . he lost as much as $100,000 in one investment.'

On 22 March 1969, barely one year and nine months after their highly publicised marriage, it was reported that Harlean and Jackie had agreed to separate and had signed an agreement to that effect. Herbert Lippman, Tarnopol's friend and Jackie's lawyer, made the announcement. It ended by stating, 'She's due to fly to Mexico soon to secure her freedom.' Their son, John 'Petey' Dominick, was five years of age.

Freda's explanation concerning the divorce is blunt: 'Harlean was only with him for a year. After she found out she couldn't go shopping when she wanted to, she left. He was married to Harlean, but they only stayed married a few months. He found out all she wanted was his money. Afterwards, she found he didn't have the kind of money she thought he had, because he owed the income tax so much. Then she went to court. He just assumed she was getting a divorce.'

Soon it became difficult for Jackie to visit New York, with Harlean pursuing him through the courts for unpaid alimony. Former Brunswick producer Carl Davis explained: 'The problem between Jackie and Harlean was women. I kept out of their private lives. She was very rough – vindictive. For a time, every time he got to New York they [the police] would lock him up. How Harlean knew he was coming in was through Nat, because Nat would know I'd scheduled the session 'over-dub'. Then, all of a sudden, he would get out of the cab on the way to the studio and the police would jump upon him and take him to jail. He would get out on bond. He used to get sick of that and we'd do it all [the recording sessions] in Chicago after that.'

Travelling over long distances with the same small group created tensions, which these high-spirited young men had to find ways of alleviating. Said Smith, 'I rode in the limo [with Jackie]. I took shots at the signs. We was lucky nobody got seriously hurt. One time the limo got caught in a flood in Atlanta. Another time I threw a fire extinguisher up against the wall of a hotel and it blew up. We tore out some toilets and basins.'

Racial segregation was strictly enforced throughout the south, but Smith didn't feel that this was the cause of Jackie's pent-up anger: 'Segregation didn't really bother us. The atmosphere Jackie was in was really above it. Only one time we really got into it and JR [Johnny Roberts] cleared that up real quick! We went into a place down there in Alabama and this woman talked about burying us in hot chilli. Jackie always carried those [Mob] guys with him. Johnny Roberts cleared it up. It didn't take him ten minutes! He was good at that. Johnny was a heck of a guy. He represented 'the people'. I got along all right with Johnny Roberts. He was like a godfather to me.' Of Tommy Vastola, Smith says, 'He was a real nice guy.' However, Smith conceded that Jackie was 'owned' by 'the people', a euphemism for the Mob. Said Smith, 'They made the man, so they figured they owned him. They did own him!'

At one time Smith, who was nine years her junior, had a liaison with LaVern Baker. Jackie took umbrage at the affair, as Smith described: 'Jackie beat the hell out of LaVern one time in New Orleans, at a black motel. She always liked young guys and Jackie was the type that didn't care what you were doing. Jackie and I were pretty tight. He thought she was taking advantage of me, but I was kind of going for what she was doing with me. He knocked that woman down the steps.'

Life on the road with Jackie involved partying all night and not waking before two in the afternoon. Their sexual activities were totally uninhibited and Smith conceded that women introduced their daughters to them, offering sexual favors. 'They were trying to capitalise; we had mothers and daughters, too,' says Smith. There were other kinky things, as well. 'The Jewel Box Revue was a bunch of men [transvestite dancers]. We wouldn't get involved, but they would demonstrate for us,' explained Smith.

No matter how long he had been a stage performer, Jackie always approached it as a true professional. 'He'd warm up in the bathroom,' Smith related. 'He'd scrape his tongue with a knife; get that stuff off his tongue. The whole time I was with him, I only heard him miss high C twice. He could hit his high C easy.' This is the counter-tenor range for male opera performers and sounds exactly like a female voice, an extraordinary feat. Jackie's trick was that he could do it so effortlessly. 'That guy could sing like hell,' Smith recalled, 'the way his range was and the way he could carry a lyric.' Before hitting the stage, Jackie had one more ritual. 'He'd warm his throat with some whiskey,' says Smith.

Incredibly, Jackie never rehearsed prior to a performance, although he always tuned up his voice by running up and down the scales, often while in the bathtub. Daughter Denise explained, 'Jack never rehearsed with his people; he never rehearsed. He was honest but arrogant at the same time. "I can sing with no music, 'cause I'm Jackie Wilson!"'

In 1966 Jackie recorded the single release 'Be My Love', which Mario Lanza had previously recorded. The song required him to make full use of his vocal chords in the operatic fashion. Said Smith, 'He recorded that song in the morning. Later, his throat looked like cantaloupes.' Smith recalls it was usual for Jackie to record around three or four o'clock in the morning, when he was at his most sober.

Smith also recalled, 'They said he would never perform again after he got shot. Every time he got sick we'd race him to the hospital, because we thought the bullet might have moved. They said the jumping around on stage would kill him. In Birmingham, Alabama, they showed us the X-ray. The meat had gathered around it. There was nothing could make it move in.'

Smith doesn't see Jackie's penchant for 'scrapping' at the drop of a hat anything more than high spiritedness. 'Jack was a boxer,' says Smith. 'He would tell me how he used to fight and stuff [as a teenager]. He could fight; I've been in scraps with him! His whole thing on stage was shadow boxing.' With regard to the fights that were a part of it all, including with his road crew: 'We loved it, we'd be on stage and the audience would be fighting. Either Jack or myself would jump off the stage and help them. I saw him slug cops a whole lot of times; he didn't care.' One time an invitation to a social barbecue led to some pretty serious trouble, recalled Smith: 'There's a DJ down there called Buddy Beau; he had a barbecue going on. He had two – one for the hoodlums and one for the classy people. He sent the limo to pick us up. Me, Jackie, Billy Johnson and [Clarence 'Pop'] Watley. He took us to the hoodlums place.

'Jackie was kissing and going on and we were doing our thing. They had a great big old hog on the table and they wanted Jackie to eat. Jackie said, "Just fix the food", so he could take it with him and eat it. They said "No", so Jack told Watley to go in and fix him some meat. A guy stopped Watley, so Jackie went in there and snatched the whole hog up. And, man, we got to it! We were fighting like hell up there in that place. I had the briefcase – I jumped up on the bed and was trying to hold on to it – it had the money in it.

'If Sims had been there there would have been some shooting, because he wasn't going to stand up there and have a fist fight like us. We went downstairs and Jackie struck up another fight with those guys. One guy pulled out a pistol and started shooting. That's the only thing that stopped us. He just shot up in the air.' Nevertheless, it all ended amicably. 'They came to the dance that night and we bought 'em beer and stuff. Every time we went to Florida, they bragged about how they wooped our ass. It was fun.'

After years of touring with Jackie, Smith began to take stock of himself. His body was a mess and he had great difficulty sleeping. Says Smith, 'I'd run myself into the ground. I'd have to get people to drive me around just to get some sleep. It got so bad. With music, if you don't enjoy it, it's no good to you. If I didn't go [out on stage], Jack wouldn't go. I feel I wouldn't have lasted another six months. I was never really hired, I was just doing him a favour.' The favour lasted for ten years! 'I liked to be jolly . . . him and I, together. We had plenty of fun. If I would just tell half of the stuff!'

Sadly for his fans worldwide, Jackie seldom travelled to other countries. But he did travel to Mexico City, a trip he enjoyed. Smith explained that visit: 'We got over; we was over there for two weeks at one of the biggest clubs. When we got ready to leave, Jackie said he wasn't going to go in there [immigration office] and do nothing! You've got to go through all the procedures to get out of the country. You know, they locked us up. The folks said, "You've got to live with our rules."' The rules won out, as they invariably do. Smith says, "We went to jail everywhere we went, for a whole lot of different things." The run-in with the Mexican authorities made them late back to New York for a one-month engagement at the Apollo Theater.

LESS KNOWN WAS Jackie's involvement with Hubert Humphrey's 1968 campaign for the presidency of the United States. 'We did some campaigning for Hubert Humphrey,' says Smith. 'We did some commercials. Jackie did some speeches. In New York we went around with Humphrey, campaigning. Jackie got up and made some speeches and stuff and Nat Tarnopol said, "My man's going to be in politics one day."' Unfortunately, as the world knows, Richard Nixon won.

Typically, Jackie drank too much and abused cocaine and other substances, while constantly touring. The bond between Jackie and his mother was always strong, but when unwell his need for her was strongest. Billy Davis remembers: 'We were at the Saxony Hotel on Miami Beach. We got the doctor, who examined him and told him he needed rest. He'd come off stage and collapsed. We'd be on stage about one to one- and-a-half hours and I'd tell him he ought to slow down. He was fatigued. He called Mama and said, "I think I got sugar [diabetes] – it runs in the family." He was like a child in a sense. Had a lot of little kid ways. Jack's mother and he were extremely close.' Eliza Mae was also a chronic diabetic.

Jimmy Smith got to know Eliza Mae, recalling one conversation with her: 'That lady told me if it ever came to where she had to lay down her life for Jackie, she'd do it. He couldn't have gone on without her. That woman loved Jackie.' The conversation was prophetic. Jackie loved his mother's cooking and she loved preparing his favourite foods. His needs always came before those of other members of the family. Says Smith, 'That woman could cook up some pork chops, boy! We'd leave [to go on tour] about two o'clock in the morning. She'd cook, say, around 30 or 40 pork chops. She would cook 'em with barbecue sauce and mustard and, man, we'd be eating down the road, throwing bones out the window.' In a discussion with Jackie's eldest daughter Denise, she explained: 'She [Eliza Mae] treated him like two people. One of them was Sonny and one of them was Jackie. When Jack was in control, cool. But she didn't like Jack messing around with Sonny. He used to call her up on the phone and say, "Mommy, this is Sonny, you tell Jack to leave me alone. He's making me do this. He's making me act like this." She would patronise him. She would keep certain things from him and make him weaker; weaker to understand certain truths in life.' Freda interjected, 'He didn't never want me to tell his mother when the kids were in trouble.'

The problem was that Jackie's mother, Eliza Mae, had two offspring and his half-sister, Joyce Ann, would often be compared unfavourably with her famous brother. Freda made the comment: 'When your mother compares one child to another, that causes a problem. You don't mean it to cause trouble, but it does.' As a close relative put it, 'Joyce Ann is funny. She was envious of Jackie. Eliza Mae gave her love to Jackie.' Former Shaker Gang member and friend, Harry Respess, also knew Joyce. 'Joyce didn't hate Jackie, they were quite close,' says Respess. 'She loved him. She was dark and unattractive, homely. Jackie loved her. He spent quite a bit of money getting her recorded. Jackie adored her and she adored Jackie, she really did. Close to idolisation.' But the other element in their relationship was envy.

On 10 June 1967, a day after Jackie's 33rd birthday, his step-father John 'Johnny' Lee died. He had been a heavy smoker and had suffered for many years from emphysema. It seems rather pointless, but Eliza Mae initially didn't want Jackie to be told, most likely because she did not want to him upset. 'Jack did finally find out and he was angry,' said Freda. 'He went to see him in the hospital just before he died.'

A sad example of Jackie's effect on women occurred in November 1969. Jackie was appearing at a club in Cincinnati, Ohio. A white, 21-year-old ex-'bunny', Karen Lynn Calloway, who worked at the club, somehow struck up a friendship with Jackie's entourage. She was married with two children at the time. Shortly after, her jealous husband shot and killed her.

The statement made to the court on behalf of Dennis Calloway, her husband, claimed that his wife had become infatuated with Jackie and when he confronted her one of his bodyguards snapped, 'Butt out, man, Jackie doesn't like anyone messing with his women.' Calloway is said to have replied, 'That's my wife and we have two children. I'm not afraid of being hurt.' On another occasion, Calloway's statement to the court said, he came across his wife and one of her woman friends 'in a car full of Negro men'. Jimmy Smith explained the incident: 'She wasn't involved with nobody. She'd come over to our parties and just sit there on a chair. The girl wasn't in Jackie's room, she was in mine. She was so sweet; I was trying to get to her.'

During the confrontation, the husband claimed that Jackie offered him an evening at the club with all expenses paid. Calloway refused the offer and, it is said, was threatened by his bodyguards. The upshot was that Dennis Calloway shot his wife six times as she ran out of the house a few weeks later. The court ordered Jackie to be a material witness at the trial. Jackie explained the true situation to the courts. Incredibly, the husband was not sentenced to a jail term.

Tony Drake was a young, talented singer whose manager, Leonard ('Lenny') Lewis, introduced him to another no-nonsense manager, Johnny Roberts, Jackie's well-connected personal manager. Roberts quickly realised that Drake had the 'right stuff' and said, 'Well, OK, kid. If you do the right thing, you'll make out fine. We're going to send you to Chicago and you're going to record with Jackie Wilson.' Drake relates the next two fascinating weeks of his life, after he'd arrived at Brunswick's Chicago offices: 'One day, I overheard someone say that Jackie Wilson was coming in to record. I noticed that everyone was so excited, like Christmas was coming. A few days later Jackie arrived. I heard somebody say, "He's on his way up!" Then Jackie walked in. His entourage consisted of a valet and bodyguard type named JJ, a blonde, and a couple of guys I never saw again. When Jackie walked in he greeted the receptionist by falling on his knees, holding her hands and kissing her all over her legs.' A friendship between Jackie and Drake ensued.

'Jackie would take us out at night. We went to visit [singer] Bobby Womack who was staying in a hotel across town, where he was performing. Bobby was also very nice. After everyone left the hotel, Jackie took the rest of us to visit his aunt [Belle Williams]. The yard was filled with people and his aunt came running towards the car, saying, "Come here, Sonny, and give me a kiss." They gave us a half-pint of liquor. We just drunk the liquor right out of the bottle and the people in the house were dancing, talking and drinking and more, and the neighbours kept coming over. Neighbours came from all around and it was a party. That's when I noticed that Jackie could not dance with anybody else, yet he was an unbelievable dancer on stage. As great a dancer as Jackie was on stage, at a house party he couldn't dance at all. He was a lousy dancer. But he slid onto the stage – I've never seen anything like it.

'Jackie had borrowed a pair of my cufflinks. A lady asked him for them and he gave them to her immediately. She kissed him, in fact every woman there kissed him. Jackie stopped and called someone on the phone and in about one hour a high-class lady arrived. Jackie embraced her and kissed her passionately, while the blonde looked on angrily but never said a word. Jackie flirted with every woman that was there and they all loved it.

'On the 23rd of February [1970], I recorded my two songs for Brunswick. Jackie and I arrived late in the car with my lady and the others. I mentioned it to Jackie and he said, "Don't worry, I own the company."'

Although Jackie was not charting in the Top 100 during the 1970s, he was still a popular performer and was still recording for Brunswick. Harry 'Dale' Respess knew Jackie from their teenage years, when they were both involved in the feared Shaker Gang. Respess had gone to school with Berry Gordy, the founder of Motown Records. Over the years Respess kept in contact with Jackie and was especially friendly with JJ. Speaking of Jackie, the performer, he says, 'Wherever he went he'd bring the house down. Incomparable . . . nothing around like it today. Jackie would make me cry. He got screwed royally by Nat [Tarnopol].'

Respess had moved to Chicago, where he was involved in PR for local nightclubs. In the late 1960s, Jackie was down on his luck and, through JJ, they sometimes sought assistance from Respess. 'Johnny [JJ] was the one I was close to,' relates Respess. 'He'd come to me and ask for a couple of hundred bucks from time to time. I'd always help if I could. I got most back . . . some slipped through the cracks, of course. JJ wasn't a quiet guy; he was kind of flamboyant. He played up his association with Jackie. Lots of jewellery and fancy clothes, lots of fancy cars. He wasn't real clever; an everyday kind of guy. A 'wannabe', I'd call him. But he was Jackie's confidant. He took care of his everything.

'Toward the end of his career Jackie was losing it,' says Respess. 'He was out of touch. His clothing was sort of dated, and he couldn't get into the groove of the youngsters. His career went down because he didn't want to change. He really tried to change; he changed his style of dress and started to look a little younger. But he was lost in a time warp for a while. Me and Johnny convinced him to change and he did. He was uncomfortable with it at first. I booked him into the Whiskey A Go-Go for ten nights and he was overwhelming. That was either 1968 or 1969.'

Respess also was witness to the crazy side of Jackie when he was 'loaded'. 'He could handle himself quite well [as a boxer]. He prided himself on that. He was average size, well-built. He'd alway have a gang with him, of course; safety in numbers. Jackie ripped up the Essex Hotel on Michigan Avenue,' says Respess. 'Ripped the sinks off the walls and a toilet – he destroyed that hotel. He'd go into fits of rage sometimes. He was a little monster then. He went berserk, so they barred him. He couldn't go back there to live. He was quite a guy when he was under the influence of coke. He had pent-up rage. He liked people, but was paranoid about Harlean.

'I took him to the Red Lion in Stagger, Illinois; this was basically an all-white community,' Respess went on. 'They knew of Jackie, but had never seen him live. So when I took him there, for $1,500 a night, it was standing room only. They loved him. JJ had just wrecked the Cadillac. He was rather short of money at the time and he did the show to get money to get his Cadillac out of the workshop.

'Jackie was kind of a proud guy. This was 1969. He was down on his luck and he'd hide out from people. He wasn't gregarious and a show-off like he used to be. He was a little ashamed. JJ had been re-hired again, as Jackie and he were such close friends. So I got him these couple of gigs real quick so he could get his car out and he could be himself again. I loved him to pieces. JJ was right there. He babysat him.'

Respess described another little event which indicated Jackie's extravagance and his sense of fun: 'In 1967 we had a party and Jackie put a diamond ring in a cake. Everyone got a slice of the cake and they took their forks and started mashing it up. A girl down the street got the ring.'

In 1970, Nat Tarnopol made a major decision that would seem to provide major benefits for himself, but it is entirely possible that it also had a nasty downside for both Jackie and Nat. Tarnopol's son, Paul, gave his version of the Brunswick takeover: 'What happened was, in 1970, my dad was auditing MCA [which had taken over Decca] and they owned half of Brunswick. Until 1970 my father would make the records, they'd sell the records and report to my father. My father found they were stealing tons of money. He was getting ready to sue MCA and, as they were a public company, they couldn't afford that kind of law suit, so they settled by giving him the other half of Brunswick.' Remarkably, Tarnopol now became its sole owner.

Dick Jacobs gave (11 January 1988) his version of what occurred to *Musician* magazine: 'Due to the strength of Jackie's records, Nat Tarnopol decided that he wanted to own all or nothing of Brunswick Records. Despite the fact that he did own 50 per cent of the company and was doing quite well financially, his rapport with Marty Salkin [of MCA] was at a low ebb and it was continually one fight after another. So Nat went to Milt Rackmil and Leonard Schneider [Decca top executives] who were both still around and told them in his own words, "You name a figure and I'll holler buy or sell." At this time, however, neither Rackmil nor Schneider could make a decision and they informed Nat that he would have to go to Los Angeles and broach the matter to Lew Wasserman [MCA's chief executive] himself. Nat thought he would be able to handle Wasserman, but he knew little of Wasserman's ability as a businessman. It was like going into a den of wolves, with Wasserman the chief of them.

'Nat went and presented his story to the head honcho. Wasserman was so disgusted with Nat's attitude that he took an immediate dislike to him and, after the meeting, called New York and told them that he didn't give a shit how many records Jackie Wilson sold, he wanted Nat and Brunswick out. A deal was struck and Nat Tarnopol walked away with the Brunswick trademark, all his masters, and the whole thing came to him for nothing more than a handful of beans.'

The article went on: 'So Nat left the MCA fold, taking his Brunswick properties with him . . . Artist-wise, Nat took with him Jackie Wilson, The Chi-Lites and Tyrone Davis . . . he had by this time made a good connection with Carl Davis, who had produced Jackie's record of 'Higher and Higher' and Nat bought into Davis's studio in Chicago and switched his recording activities out there. After some minor successes, and some legal problems, Nat leased all his masters to CBS and for all intents, that was the end of Brunswick.'

Around the same time, Jimmy Smith and Jackie's friend, Launa Toledo, agree that Jackie finally decided that Nat Tarnopol was not giving him his fair share of his earnings. After a huge falling out, Jackie decided he would be his own manager. Of course, he was still bound to the Brunswick label and could do nothing about that.

Smith says of Tarnopol: 'He was a wheeler and dealer; he looked out for Nat Tarnopol. Jack felt the sun rose and set with Nat.' Said Smith. 'He woke up about two years before I left [in 1972]. He stopped Nat taking bookings for him. He started doing his bookings on his own then.' Smith explained what the 'final straw' had been for Jackie: 'What really pissed Jack off was in 1969 he wanted a new car. You see, all Jack had to do was say he wanted a new car and the car would be at the office. This time, Jackie wanted this limousine and Nat wouldn't get it. Nat was a schemer, man. Jack had to go out on tour and take the money and get him a car. That's when Jackie started waking up on Nat. He [Jackie] ended up with the Sedan de Ville [bottom-of-the-range model of Cadillacs]. He was really upset.'

Jackie Wilson never won the 'Father Of The Year' award. His career kept him constantly on the move, so he couldn't maintain a strong relationship with his children. This caused him extreme anguish on receiving news that his oldest son, Jack (Jackie Jnr), had been shot dead on the night of Monday, 28 September 1970. Jack, known to the family as Sonny or Little Sonny, was 16. The report in the Michigan Chronicle newspaper states:

Jackie Wilson Jr, son of popular rhythm and blues singer Jackie Wilson, was shot and killed by an unknown person, or persons, Monday night as he stood on the porch of a friend's home.

According to a report, the 16-year-old youth, who lived at 16522 LaSalle, had rung the door bell at the residence of Richard Holmes, 16625 Prairie and, just as Holmes opened the door, several shots were fired from the street. Wilson suffered a shotgun injury to the upper left back and side, and Holmes was shot in the right forearm.

The shooting occurred at approximately 10:25 p.m. The two men were rushed to Detroit General Hospital (Central Branch) by police officers who answered a radio run to the scene. Wilson was pronounced dead on arrival at 10:40 p.m. Holmes, 26, was reported tobe in a serious condition.

Wilson, according to a statement from a witness, was concerned about a dispute he had had earlier with a young woman friend who was visiting at Holmes's residence that evening. He reportedly telephoned Holmes and discussed the argument with him. After affirmation of their friendship, the telephone conversation ended and, a short time later, Holmes answered his door bell and Wilson was on the porch.

Three spent 12-gauge shotgun shells, a 12-gauge Spanish-made double barrel shotgun, two 12-gauge unspent rifle slug shells, taken from Holmes's flat, were being held as evidence at the Detroit Police Dept. Homicide Bureau.

Only weeks earlier, Jackie had taken Jack Jnr on tour with him to Mexico, where he worked for two weeks at one of Mexico City's biggest clubs.

The shooting was the result of a dispute between Jack Jnr and a near neighbour, Richard Holmes, ten years his senior. Jack Jnr took another man, Robert Jackson, 34, with him to confront Holmes at his house. Holmes apparently expected trouble and came to the door with a revolver. In the panic that ensued Jack Jnr backed into the shotgun, causing Jackson to fire off three heavy-duty rifle slugs. Holmes was seriously hurt in the forearm, but Jack Jnr was caught in the line of fire and killed.

At the time of the shooting, Jackie's former wife, Freda, lived in Toledo, Ohio. She explained how she was informed of her son's shooting: 'Jack called me from Chicago. He was drunk and out of it. He was so hurt when he called me. He said, "Your son is dead, your son is dead!" I said, "What do you mean 'My son is dead?'" "Jackie Jnr." I said, "He is not." He said, "Yes, he is." He was crying. I said, "You're just drunk. Oh, man, you're out of it," and hung up the phone.

'He must have called his mother. She [Eliza Mae] called me and said, "He's at the hospital," and then I hung up. A few minutes later my mother calls and said, "I think you'd better get to Detroit." She said, "Jackie Jnr . . ."Then I knew he really was dead, 'cause something hit me. I said, "Oh, wow."' A possible reason Freda didn't catch on to the reality of the situation was that at the time she too was a serious drinker.

Freda continued: 'I didn't have no money. I didn't have no ID, which you were supposed to have to get the money. I went down to the bus station. I explained to the manager. He could see by my condition that I must be telling the truth and he gave me a ticket. I was like a piece of ice. They told me to go to Detroit. I didn't, I went straight from Toledo to the morgue. When I got off that bus, I knew he wasn't there. My mind said, "He's dead," but my heart didn't want to say so. I went to the morgue; that was to prove myself wrong. When I got there they wouldn't let me see him, so I knew he was there. I said, "I'm part of it." They wouldn't let me see him, though, until my family got there. I called my sisters and they came down. They wheeled him out there and took that sheet off his head. My sister said I pulled the whole railing out. I didn't remember anything. His face was all puffed up. The shotgun blast in the back blew him all up. He had a ring with so many rubies and diamonds; they had trouble getting that ring off. Next thing I remember I was at 16522 La Salle – that's where we lived.' Denise, who was 19 and five months pregnant, had the grim task of officially identifying the body of her brother.

Although only 16 when he died, Jackie Jnr already had fathered a daughter. 'Jackie Jnr's girlfriend, Ladar, had a baby to him when she was 14 and he was 15,' said Freda.

In an interview with Susan Morse of the *Detroit Free Press* (11 January 1976), Denise said: 'My father wasn't an unhappy man until my brother's death. He blamed himself for that . . . He admitted to me he didn't consider himself a father to any of us. It was the first time he admitted to any of us that he was wrapped up in what he was doing . . . The things that Jackie Wilson Jnr did were all for "noticement". He was saying: "Notice me, damn it, I'm your namesake."'

The tragedy devastated Jackie, but, true to form, he didn't go to the funeral. Said Freda, 'Jack was a Gemini. They are all sensitive. His father tried to prevent him from being hurt. When Jackie Jnr was shot, he never went down to see him. He couldn't stand funerals. I directed it. He stayed at the house. He had a photographer take pictures of Jack Snr [his father, who had died in 1953] and a photographer from *Jet* magazine take [pictures of] Jackie Jnr in the casket.'

Close friend Launa Toledo recalled, 'Jackie didn't go to Jackie Jnr's funeral. He said, "Baby, I brought him into the world; I will not stand by and see them put him into the ground."' Jackie Jnr rests at Lincoln Memorial Park Cemetery, to the north of Detroit, the cemetery where Jackie's father is also buried.

Without doubt, the killing traumatised Jackie. It caused him to reflect on his lifestyle and, for a time, he completely quit his drinking. His brother-in-law, Johnny Collins, said: 'This was a man who could out-drink anyone. He stopped drinking – for a period.' Lynn Crochet, who would later become Jackie's commonlaw wife, says, 'When Jackie Jnr was shot it nearly destroyed Jackie. Jackie kind of put him [Jackie Jnr] on the path he was going on and he regretted it. It changed his whole life. It put him down and I think maybe brought him back up. I really feel he was on the way back when this happened; grew up.' Said Lynn, 'I saw him cry on numerous occasions. Usually it was about Jackie Jnr.'

Lynn maintains that the loss of Jack Jnr shattered Jackie emotionally. She explained a strange event that resulted: 'Jackie was a very emotional person. He had a little boy in him, definitely. He was into the occult also: Jackie told me his son, Jackie Jnr, talked to him through me. I don't know, I don't remember it. It happened in Houston, Texas. He believed in the hereafter and the dead being able to communicate with the living. '

The tragedy pushed Freda even more towards solace from alcohol but, naturally, this only made things worse. Eliza Mae Lee, Jackie's mother, looked after Freda and the children. Freda had converted from Baptist to Roman Catholic, so the children attended good Catholic schools in the Detroit area. She explained that the church provided her with support throughout this and further tragedies that would befall her over the years.

In1970 Jackie, aged 36, was firmly in the grip of alcohol and cocaine dependence, although he could still knock an audience out with his scintillating performances. In October that year he was performing at the Black Knight Club in Metairie, outside New Orleans, where Lennie 'Lynn' Crochet was working as head cocktail waitress. Aged 26, she was a native of Beaumont, Texas. Lynn explained how she came to know Jackie, 'I was dating the owner of the club, where I worked, who was also married at the time. I told him to hire Jackie, and I was like Jackie's bodyguard when he got to New Orleans, to make sure he got to the club on time. He was drinking really heavy at the time and doing drugs and shit. Jackie and I became real good friends and Ed [Delduga, the Black Knight owner] got jealous and fired me because of Jackie. 'Cause I was doing what Ed asked me, and Jackie and I just became good friends. There was nothing going on — just real good friends, 'cause Jackie Jnr had died. But Ed fired me, so that's when Jackie hired me as his road manager. Jackie fired his road manager {August] Sims and let him go back to New York.

'Ed Delduga was heavyweight . . . he got very angry and I wasn't allowed in the club. When Jackie went to New Orleans, the [Jackie's] bodyguard stayed with me. There was a contract out on my life and Jackie kept buying it off. It was pretty heavy. I didn't know about it at the time, I found out a year later: then I got kind of scared.'

A romance blossomed and on 27 March 1971 Jackie and Lennie 'Lynn' (nee Belle) Crochet were married in a civil ceremony at the Whiskey A Go-Go Nightclub in Los Angeles. The marriage was never formally registered, most likely because Jackie realised that to do so could have left him open to the criminal charge of bigamy.

Jackie's second cousin, Horace Spain, witnessed the wedding. He worked with Jackie for eight or nine months in 1971 as his driver. Years later, he made a court deposition stating that Jackie told the marriage celebrant not to file the marriage documents. Effectively, then, it was not a legally constituted marriage. JJ was no longer part of the road team, while Jimmy Smith, August Sims and Johnny Roberts, surprisingly, were also absent.

Lynn realised that Jackie had a major addiction problem: 'What people don't realise is that when Jackie was drinking, he was paranoid because they had abused him. He'd remember that when he was drunk. He wouldn't have trusted anybody back then. I remember when he would go and buy oil cloth and put it all over the room. It was to protect his stuff, so if it moved he'd know it. It was bad.'

Lynn continued, 'Jackie was a damn instigator; the old shithead. I've seen him pull a gun on a guy to get [him] on his hands and knees and act like a dog.' Lynn confessed, 'Jackie slapped me a couple of times, but as far as being real abusive to me goes, he was not. He would slap me 'cause, as I say, I'm a very forceful woman. I'm three-quarters Cherokee and I don't stand any shit when I'm drinking – just like him. I get very arrogant when I'm drunk. I can tell you stories of evil things he did, but at that time he was still on the drink. When the drinking stopped it was another Jackie and that is the person everyone should remember. He did his dirt, but it was the time; the era he grew up in.'

'I know we had a safety deposit box in Chicago and it did have some money in it,' recalled Lynn. 'It was either one or two weeks before Thor was born [March 1972]. Jackie sent me to Chicago to get some money out and send it to him. He always led me to believe he had boxes in New York with money, jewels, and documents, but he could not tell me where they were at. I have wondered, for all these years, but they [the boxes] weren't in a conventional place. They were in a jewellery store or something.'

At the time of the divorce from Freda in 1964, she been granted the house on LaSalle. Jackie purchased another home in Detroit for his mother, on Strathmoor. It was there that Jackie and Lynn lived whenever they were in Detroit. 'We had lived with Mama, off and on, for five years,' said Lynn. 'We'd go to Detroit to see her and the grandkids, and we moved my mom and two boys [by a previous marriage] up there; they had a separate house.'

Lynn thought highly of Jackie's mother: 'She was a wonderful lady. Mama kept her act together. She played the numbers and she did all right. She was strong and determined, but not so much with Jackie as with Joyce Ann. 'Cause Jackie was her baby.' Says Lynn, 'We were the perfect family. Three years without arguing. He didn't have anything except Diet Pepsi and Viceroy cigarettes, for over three years. He'd have a pack, pack-and-a-half a day.'

Lynn confirmed Jackie's oral hygiene practices to be unusual, but thorough. 'He did something that I found very strange. He used to take a butter knife and scrape his tongue. He'd sit in the tub, do his [musical] scales and take that knife and scrape his tongue. He would warm up. I got so I hated the damn scales. Sitting in the bathroom for an hour! Sometimes he'd take honey and hot tea [to soothe his throat]. He would sit in the bathroom for an hour and cough; clearing his throat. Get all the phlegm out of his voice. I would give him a massage every night and do his hair before he went on stage. I considered it his job; he was getting ready for his job.'

In 1972, August Sims had been Jackie's road manager for around nine years. Although he answered to Johnny Roberts, he evidently loved Jackie. By messing with a mobster's woman, Sims believed that Jackie could have got them all killed. Said Sims, 'In Jackie's bedroom, in New Orleans, at the Purple Orchid – that's when the guy wanted to kill all of us. Jackie fucked with that jive-ass white woman at Down's Lounge; Lynn. I had to straighten him [the man with the gun] out. I said, "Why don't you shoot her, shit? We ain't had nothing to do with that junk." That guy came to me next day and he said, "Hey, Aug, we ain't going to ride you no more."' According to one version, this incident caused Sims to quit as road manager. Lynn, on the other hand, is certain that Jackie got rid of Sims at her behest.

At first, the drug taking continued. Lynn says: 'Jackie, Jimmy Smith and the bodyguard, Henry, got into it. They was always getting into it. Jackie let people rob him, but when I was around it didn't happen. I made him get rid of the excess baggage. I didn't want all those hoodlums around our children.'

August Sims remembers it differently, claiming that after being on the road all those years he was just tired of it. As well, he was tired of seeing Jackie being ripped off. In 1972 Sims asked to remain in Brunswick Records' New York office. Says Sims of his role: 'I took Jackie off Johnny

Roberts' ass up at the Rennie [Renaissance Theater, New York] on 66th Street one day. Jackie jumped into him. I had to take Jackie off his ass. He didn't give Jackie his money. I said to Roberts, "He deserves it. He played the gig. Give him all his money." Johnny said, "We won't have any." I said, "I don't care if we don't have none ourselves, give it to him." I knew where he was coming from anyway. I said, "I don't need to be bothered with this garbage anyway. . ." I'll wind up killing... ' Sims didn't expand on the final comment, but he truly was fond of Jackie.

As road manager, Lynn was tough with the roadies and musicians and, consequently, not too popular. She recalls, 'When he was drinking he had cousin Horace [Spain] driving [and brother-in-law] Johnny Collins doing backup singing. I said, "Why should you pay this man, and then you're paying your mom and they are living in the house for free? You're taking care of them twice." He got rid of all of 'em. Once he sobered up he saw it himself and it wasn't hard. The band had given me a nickname: 'HNIC'– Head Nigger In Charge – because I took care of all the business.'

It was unusual for Harlean to travel with Jackie for any period of time while they were married. However, with Lynn the converse was the case. 'Everywhere he went, me and Thor [their son] went. He never went anywhere without us. Maybe a one-nighter, or when he went to do the "Midnight Special" concert in California. He went out there and got on drugs real heavy. I had to stay home the last six weeks I was pregnant with Thor [early in 1972]. He spent all the damn money he made.' Lynn observed Jackie's addictions with concern. 'His only drug use was snorting and he smoked a little weed. My thing, when Jackie met me, was speed. I'm no saint; Jackie had a lot of pressure. I never saw Jackie do drugs, he would go in the bathroom and do it.'

In September 1972, Jackie and Lynn travelled together on his first visit to the United Kingdom, where he was hugely popular, playing to ballrooms and clubs. Jackie was 38 and hadn't had a hit since 'I Get The Sweetest Feeling' in August 1968. However, British audiences are very loyal to the rock 'n' roll pioneers so Jackie had no difficulty packing them in.

In the early 1970s, by which time Jackie had fully woken up to the fact that Tarnopol didn't have his best interests at heart, Lynn reports: 'Jackie went to Johnny Roberts to take the management away from Nat. All ties had been broken with Nat Tarnopol. He was never going to record for him again. Johnny was a mean little bastard, and I loved him to death. I respected him and always will, till I die. Jackie would come home and tell me, this is the way it is; Jackie always told me to do what Johnny told me, and I did. Once Jackie sobered up, he took care of business and had most of his discussions with Johnny Roberts. Jackie found out there were lean times when he had to live from hand to mouth, and it wasn't that easy.'

It had taken a long time for Jackie to partially break free from Tarnopol, although he was still bound to him through the Brunswick label. Lynn explained, 'They were all in it together, then Tommy [Vastola] and JR [Johnny Roberts] turned on Nat. That's why Nat went down the tubes. Jackie never did tell me what they did, but he said, "Nat is out of there."'

Carl Davis, former Brunswick producer and vice-president, explained Jackie's management move this way: 'What was happening was, at one point, the booking agency that was booking Jackie would require 50 per cent of the money sent into the agency [Queens]. The agency would pay the management money out of that, and then Jackie would go out and perform and get the other 50 per cent. Then, at the end of the month, the agency was supposed to settle up and give Jackie the difference between what he paid the management and what was left of the 50 per cent. In most managements the fee is 20 per cent. He'd pick up his fee in cash. Then he told the agency, "Don't book me; I'll book myself." He was probably getting less than he should, but he was getting it all.

'Then they sent Sims out there to collect their share and Jackie fired Tarnopol. It got to the point that Nat Tarnopol said, "If you don't pay me management money, I'll not give your record royalties." And Jackie said, "Fine, I'm not going to record," and he stopped recording. Nat Tarnopol really treated Jackie like shit. Nat changed – when I first met him he was an honourable guy.'

In September 1970, Tommy Vastola ran into some trouble of his own and was sentenced to prison. The conviction was for conspiracy to extort $12,000 from two operators of an illegal dice game. In court, Vastola and his accomplice were described as 'reputed Mafia soldiers'. While Vastola was inside, Johnny Roberts took advantage of his absence and started taking a bigger slice of the pie, which, in this case, was Jackie. Someone very close to the action put it like this: 'While Tommy was away they started stealing from each other, and money that was supposed to go to Vastola for his portion, for whatever Jackie was doing, they were spending and saying Jackie was making less. It was a big mess and the good thing about Tommy, he will tell you, is that he don't kill nobody because of money. He kills them out of principle. So the fact that they were stealing money from him just pissed him off.' Roberts was now in deep trouble with people above Vastola. He wasn't safe in New York or New Jersey and ended up moving to Palm Springs, California, where Vastola apparently arranged some kind of truce on his behalf. Said the informed source, 'That's who probably saved Johnny from showing up in a barrel.'

Lynn Crochet firmly believes there were plans to put Jackie back where he'd been at the height of his career: 'Johnny Roberts and them were fixing to put him back on top. Nat had lost interest. He wasn't giving him the right kind of music, the right arrangements. They weren't keeping him up-to-date. They were holding him back. It wasn't Carl [Davis], it was that damn Nat Tarnopol, 'cause I would hear Carl and Nat on the phone during the sessions. And Nat would tell Carl what to do.'

Although Jackie was long divorced from Freda, he still treated her as if she were still his wife. Their eldest daughter, Denise, related a story that is partly amusing and partly cruel: 'One time he brought his girlfriend [Lynn Crochet], left her sitting in the car. He went in the house. My mother was living with her boyfriend and my father told him, "Sit down and shut up!" He takes her in the bathroom. They were in there kissing and slobberin'.

'Then he told [his son] Tony, "Go out to the car and tell Lynn what I and your mother are doing. I want to see how she reacts." Tony's the kind of person that if you tell him to say one thing, he's going to add some fool thing – make it really juicy. Lynn came into the house. She got mad. She was saying, "I don't appreciate that. What the hell's going on? What do you think this is?" She looked at my mother, "What do you think you are doing? You're not married to him any more." He said to his girlfriend, "Sit down and talk to my mother, or something." He looked at my mom, especially after he gave her one of those "old time kisses from way back when". Anyway, Mom gets all "geeked" up by Dad's "slarms". He loves to instigate stuff, particularly against women. My father liked to see women fight over him anyway. He didn't say anything. He was going to let my mother control the situation. Of course, he had no idea she was going to control it this way. My dad looked at my mother, "You hear this? You going to let this woman speak to you in your house, about your husband? I mean, what's wrong with you, oh, God." She [Freda] was high. She had a little firewater in her a little Indian-water. Man, she beat that little lady so bad. He [Jackie] said, "Get her, Pee Wee [Freda's pet name]." Dad was cracking up.

'My mother even moved to stop him doing things like this; she moved to Toledo [in Ohio]. So that when he came home he wouldn't see her.' Freda interjected, 'He told me I did a good job. And my [boy]friend

[Michael] was sitting over there. He said later, "What the hell? I don't really understand this. Tell me what's going on?" After this, Jack said, "I guess I'll have to take the poor child to the hospital."'

Although Freda never learned to drive a car, she saved her money and bought one. Said Freda, 'After we were divorced I bought a Cadillac Coupe de Ville. Jack said, "Whose car?" I said, "Mine!" He said, "Oh, so that's what you're doing with the money I sent you." I said, "Well, it was my money." I waited long enough till I could buy a Cadillac. He left his girlfriend on the porch gazing. He said, "Give me the keys, I'm driving our Cadillac." We left; it was on Sunday. He said, "Can't you get any Scotch?" I said, "We can get anything you want. You want some?" He said, "Yes." We went up to Archie's store. He said, "I'm Jackie Wilson" – he was already high – 'and I want to know, what kind of liquor do you have?" Archie said, "Anything you want." The police knew it, but Archie was paying 'em off. Jackie got some stuff.' The law forbade selling alcohol on Sundays. Freda went on, 'He always said, "That's my wife." He didn't care what nobody else said.'

In the summer of 1971, rock 'n' roller Jerry Lee Lewis invited Jackie to appear on the pilot of his planned regular TV musical program, entitled *The Jerry Lee Lewis Show*. Lynn recalled how this came about: 'Jerry came to see us in Nashville or Memphis. He asked Jackie if he would do it, but I don't think Jackie really believed him, because he was drunk. I think it was a pilot.' Anyhow, Lewis was serious and the pilot was taped. The largely country music-oriented program never went to air in the USA. Jackie did four songs, mainly in the country vein, and his voice was majestic.

In March 1972, Lynn gave birth to a baby boy, who would be named Thor Lathan Kenneth. Thor took his name from Jackie's favorite comic book hero. At the time, Jackie was working in Los Angeles and was as nervous as expectant fathers usually are. When the phone call came through from the Detroit hospital announcing the good news, Jackie was with a platonic friend, Trina 'Cookie' Johnson, a young dancer with James Brown's Brownies dancing group. Johnson says, 'He was doing a show in Los Angeles, on Western Avenue. I had to knock some vodka out of his hands; I had to knock several things out of his hand that night. I was one of the few people who could do that. He was nervous 'cause he was waiting for the baby to be born.'

Thor became the apple of Jackie's eye. Quite likely, at the age of 37, he was at last mature enough to appreciate the simple pleasure of being a

JACKIE WILSON

Jackie and boxer Floyd Patterson in 1961 or 1962.

Jackie and stripper girlfriend, Angel Lee, backstage at the Palms Café in New York in 1971 or 1972.

The Everly Brothers with Jackie and vocalist Clyde McPhatter (far right) in the late 1950s.

Jackie with friend Little Richard backstage in Florida, 1971.

Jackie's first wife Freda at her home with author Tony Douglas in June 1994.

Jackie and Freda's home on LaSalle Blvd, Detroit, which was confiscated by the IRS.

Jackie's eventual gravesite at Wayne, Michigan. Initially he was buried nearby in a pauper's grave.

The house that is listed on Jackie's birth certificate. Lyman Street, Detroit.

Jackie's first wife, Freda Wilson, on her first visit to Jackie's gravesite
in July 1987.

Jackie on a Universal Attractions studio promo pic in the early 1960s.

Jackie with Elvis at the MGM Studios in 1966. Elvis signed pic – 'Jackie, you got you a friend for life. Elvis Presley.'

father. Says Lynn, 'Jackie came back to Detroit when Thor was 11 days old and took us to Boston. We flew from Detroit to Boston and he performed on stage with him in his arms and introduced him to the world. That's when Thor made his first personal appearance.'

In 1972 Jimmy Smith, Jackie's friend and drummer of ten years, decided he'd had enough and left. He felt that had he stayed on another six months, he'd have been dead from alcohol abuse. Smith admitted himself for alcohol rehabilitation and claims that to this day he has not taken another drink. Smith maintains he wasn't paid a set wage during his ten years as Jackie's touring drummer and recalls that Jackie owed him tens of thousands of dollars, but he has no hard feelings. Smith was replaced by a 17-year-old named Johnny Fox, better known by the unlikely nickname of 'Peanuts'. Fox became known for his drug taking and love of the party life and, as such, wasn't much help in getting Jackie straight. Fox and the young guitarist at that time, Larry Blassengane, were no better than Jackie concerning abuse of alcohol and cocaine. Fox wouldn't confirm Collins assertion that Jackie had hit Blassengane in the head, perhaps causing him a permanent injury. He just said, 'Jackie hit a lot of people around the head for a lot of reasons.'

There were wild times. Fox remembers the first time he saw Jackie's temper erupt into physical violence. It was at a hotel they were staying at: 'We took it over. That's where Jackie pulled the manager of the hotel over the counter and kicked his butt for turning the phones off. That's the first time I ever saw him really box. You couldn't knock him down. So he was a little hotheaded, but who isn't? But if things were that bad, he didn't need no help from people who were supposedly taking care of business.'

August Sims was still travelling with them in early 1972 and, to some degree, was part of the 'fun'. At the same time, Fox says, 'We never knew where Sims stood. He was boisterous, but at the same time he would always mind Jackie. You see, Sims was working for Johnny [Roberts]. Roberts was the don. He was a no-good son-of-a-bitch.'

When Fox joined Jackie's band, Jackie had only recently dumped Nat Tarnopol as his personal manager, employing Tommy Vastola and Johnny Roberts to replace him. Says Fox: 'I met Nat Tarnopol one time. Nat had the money, and Jack was on the road. There was bad blood between Nat and Jack. It's ironic that Jackie felt so deeply disturbed by Nat that he would jump into the fire.' By which he means Vastola and Roberts. They were under the watchful eyes of the Mob: 'There was a code of silence. We'd come into places and see a couple of guys sitting there.

Unemotionally we knew who they were. It didn't play very well with us. It was very dangerous, and intriguing.'

Even though the period was after Jackie's halcyon days, he always remained the consummate professional and would tune up prior to going on stage. Fox recalled: 'Jackie would always say, "Mi, mi, mi" – he was tuning up. It could drive you mad, too. He'd do it in the washroom. I said, "Boy, you don't sound so good as you did in the washroom, do you Jack?" He'd say, "Oh well, Peanuts, how we going to be tonight? We going to kick ass. All right, you're my man, let's go." He would get to his job. If he sneezed, I had him. If he "falled', I had him; I hit him. Jackie was my best friend. We'd been with the best, so what the fuck?'

For Jackie, the show had to go on regardless of what mayhem may have ben happening around him. Explains Fox: 'Jackie was shot at a few times. I remember one time in the south, something broke out. Guns were fired, tables turned over. There was Jackie, still singing. When it all cleared off, Jackie got on the stage and said, "Well, ladies and gentlemen, there's always a little difference of opinion around here. As the song goes, 'baby workout . . .'"' and he'd go on singing as though everything was quite normal. I thought, "Shit, let's get the fuck out of here before we get killed."'

While living at the house Jackie had purchased for his mother, Lynn and the family shared the home with Jackie's half-sister, Joyce. The relationship between Lynn and Joyce was strained. According to Lynn, 'Joyce hated her brother. She'll give you a front that she loved him to death, but it's wrong. She was jealous of him.' Because of Joyce, Lynn also fell foul of Jackie, as Lynn explained: 'She had gotten pregnant and she needed an abortion, but she wouldn't ask Jackie for the money. She came to me for it and I gave her the money. Jackie wouldn't have approved, he was very old-fashioned. It was amazing. He fumed at me for it. I said it was her choice, her body. She already had [a daughter] Kelly.'

Joyce's husband Johnny Collins was present when the ill will between Lynn and Joyce came to a head. 'Lynn confronted Joyce about something stupid and drew her hand back,' says Collins. 'Joyce hit her so fast her eye was closed before she could get her hand forward. Joyce said, "Don't you ever do that; don't you ever come at me that way." Lynn ran up the stairs holding her crotch. Everyone said, "She hit you in the eye, why are you holding your crotch?" She answered, "I'm trying not to pee." That's how hard she hit her! The first time she ever got her ass whipped. The biggest black eye you ever saw in your life.'

Elvis had gone out of his way to see Jackie perform. Now Jackie and Lynn returned the compliment, travelling to Las Vegas to see Elvis perform. After the show Elvis invited Jackie and Lynn up to his penthouse. Lynn says, probably unfairly, "Jackie was the only black man Elvis liked. It seemed to me Elvis tried to copy Jackie. We went over to see Elvis at his penthouse. Jackie, Elvis and I spent a whole night together. They sat there and sang gospel songs all night. Elvis's back-up singers were there."' Johnny Collins, remembered the evening well: 'They sang gospel and talked crazy to each other all night long. Then Jack ordered a breakfast like no two horses have ever seen. He could wreck a table!'

Jackie and Lynn developed a personal relationship with Sonny West who, along with his cousin Red West, worked for many years with Elvis as part of the so-called 'Memphis Mafia'. Red West said of the relationship between Jackie and Elvis, 'They admired each other and had a friendship.' Sonny West was one of Elvis's bodyguards but was also a close friend, and spoke fondly of his association with Jackie: 'He told me when I met him, "You know what? That's my name, Sonny." I said, "Really?" That's what his mom and family called him. He told me, "You'd better be cool because you're my namesake." Sonny West was there when Jackie visited Elvis at the penthouse: 'I was there at the Penthouse in Las Vegas when Jackie visited. Elvis did impromptu gospel songs all the time with entertainers that came up there.'

West then arranged complimentary tickets for Lynn and Jackie to see Elvis perform in Memphis. While Elvis was making his enormous comeback in Las Vegas to sell-out audiences, Jackie was playing the Flamingo Hotel Lounge, which seated only around 500 people. Elvis saw Jackie perform again later that month.

Sonny West related a very interesting incident involving Jackie's manager, Johnny Roberts: 'We were appearing in Las Vegas and came backstage [to see Jackie], up to the suite and everything. A few days later – I think Jackie was playing in the Lounge at the Flamingo at the time – his manager called me and said he'd like to speak with me privately, but didn't want to talk on the phone. I said, "Sure." I went down there and met him at the lounge at the Flamingo during the day. He told me about someone putting down Elvis; being high on drugs and being like a pincushion. He said there was a masseur that used to work at the Hilton, but now works at the MGM Grand or Tropicana. His name was Bill. Elvis, when he was getting that inhalation therapy, would have the masseur massage him and also break up that stuff in his lungs so he could excrete it. I think the massage was $50 and Elvis would tip another $50. It was a few months later that Bill was saying these bad things about Elvis. Roberts said, "Do you want me to do anything about this guy?" I had all kind of visions in my mind about what might happen. So I said, "No, let me try something first."

'I called this guy [the masseur] where he was working and said, "I've just got one thing to say to you, you run your mouth any more about Elvis Presley: you know what you've been saying; do it any more and you're not going to be able to talk to anybody." He said, "Who is it, who is it?" I hung up. I told Jackie's manager what I had done. He said, "You son-of-a-gun." I said, "Could you have your guy put an ear to it and see if anything's happening?" And he said, "I sure could." The guy went over three or four times a week. A few days later he called me and told me that everything seemed to be fine. "Yeah," he said, "My guy tried to strike up a conversation about Elvis . . . he had nothing to say."'

West added, quite simply, 'I believe Jackie could have been a lot bigger than he was, had he been able to get a label like RCA did with Elvis, to promote him and let him play the big venues. Jackie had the Mob behind him, that's why he worked the clubs so much. I always felt he could have been bigger than he was if he hadn't spent so much time in the clubs. I think Jackie could have been a big main show sensation in Vegas. When those guys [the Mob] tell you something, you have to do what they say. There's no stopping them. Even when they can say they are businessmen, they are very vicious and vindictive. You can be tough and still be afraid of them. It's ironic, but that's the way it was founded [the USA], to be free and all that – do what you want to do. These sons-of-guns took it seriously and kill people. It's not right.'

Lynn credits herself with getting Jackie to quit alcohol abuse. After a lifetime of indulgence, this would not have been easy. Lynn 'I got him off the booze. I gave him a choice: either it was me and his son, or it was nothing; his choice. He dried himself out. I want him remembered as the good person he was, not for the bad stuff that everyone saw.'

For a few years, in the late 1960s and early 1970s, Jackie's brother-in-law, Johnny Collins, travelled with Jackie. Their relationship was often turbulent and occasionally led to blows, but he has admiration for Jackie and, as an in-law, was privy to the family machinations. Collins was ambivalent about Jackie; while there was enormous admiration, it is also clear that there were some aspects of Jackie with which he was less enamoured. Says Collins: 'There were so many people who loved him and so many people who hated him at the same time — who wanted to control him.

'HE TOOK SHIT from everybody and survived it over and over again. He got stomped down and he came back up singing. He got beat up and he came back singing. He got whipped and he came back singing. He got sued and he came back singing. He never quit singing. He was true to his profession. That's a "master-blaster". He never quit singing and when it hurt him, he sang. I watched them beat his ass and they told him, "You have to go out there and if you don't, I'll kill you." They had me outside in handcuffs. They'd kicked my face in. He sang like an angel . . . bloody as hell. He cracked notes. It was as clear as a bell, with no anger, no hurt and no pain. He did it. He said to me, "You must separate yourself from your job." I watched him sing with cracked ribs, a cracked jaw, with a gun to the back of his head, 'cause he was supposed to sing at a party for this little girl whose daddy was the law. There were two ways they did it. There were band members and Jack with guns to their heads. Jack said, "Shoot me." They answered, "What about these kids, we'll shoot them too." Jack said, "That ain't fair." They said, "We ain't about fair."

'One time they busted his ribs and he went out and did two shows. He left Louisiana and went into Texas and he was with a woman who was not of colour. The local police beat him up. He got stomped. He went on stage bloody. The police chief wanted to degrade Jack because there were two women in the audience who adored him. Do you know what it was like for a white man to find out his daughter, wife, sister, was totally in awe of a black man in the south? They were still lynching then. You have to sing to these bitches. The Klan will "take care" of them. The chief of police said, "I don't care what else you do, make sure he walks out on stage and shows those other niggers who are upstairs." They were separated [whites in a segregated area]. He had to walk out on stage with the blood on his shirt. They said, "I don't care what else he does but he does the full show." And he did. Jack announced, "I want to thank the assholes that kissed me tonight," and they were out in the audience. He said thank you after they beat him up! He said, "You made me know I could do it, even though I was tired."'

Collins says Jackie's performance was flawless, despite the pain he was experiencing: 'Nobody ever cried for him when they beat him almost to the point of death and he went out on stage and sang that night. He went right downstairs where the paramedics were waiting and they took him to the hospital, 'cause he was bleeding internally. The Texans said, "Well, the nigger deserved it."

'We went to a club where they had cut off the electricity, because they were trying to harass the black club owner. They put candles on the top floor. We sang in darkness with only a drummer. We did two shows. Sold out! They brought corn whisky. These people had no money, they just wanted to see him. He sang for the lowest of the low and the highest of the high; and just as hard. He was down-to-earth. Everybody loved him. There were times when our clothes got stolen. He said, "When you walk out, walk out like this is the new style." The minute he snatched his jacket off, the show was off – off the map!'

Jackie would rarely be without a supply of Jack Daniels whisky, or vodka, as Collins relates: "He would have a briefcase full of 20 to 30 vodka bottles. I've been drinking vodka since I knew him – I hate him for that. I can outdrink the average ten guys.'

Collins spoke unflatteringly of Jackie's eating habits. 'He ate like an animal. He hated to have people around him when he ate, other than his children and his wife. It was disgusting for him. Oh man, the sounds, man! It was like a razor. You wouldn't believe it was a human being eating. He was just down-to-earth, he was country. He was relaxed and you didn't bother him then. With Jack it was like, "I've got this job to do, I'll do it, I replenish my nourishment and I'm through" 'that was it. He didn't bother anybody. You could love him for that. This was a human being and he was not pretentious. "Don't be around me when I do this if you are going to be disgusted by somebody enjoying themself . . . it was so good I'll lick my fingers' – that's the way he was and people loved him for it. He wasn't ever going to change.'

'Jack didn't eat in public, he'd take it back to his suite,' recalled Collins. 'He was mad 'cause I didn't want to eat in the room.' During some of his drinking binges, Jackie would vent a lot of anger on those hotel rooms. 'We caused $1,200 damage to a hotel room. We weren't invited back. It happened; we tore it up.'

Collins, who was a martial arts exponent, had difficulty with Johnny Roberts. Explains Collins: 'I used to open for Jack, and then I sang [duet] afterwards with him. You know who Johnny Roberts was? He was a Mafia bastard, a Mafia chieftain. Jack was supposed to go on stage, but he got sick. I said, "Jack, take a few minutes and drink some water." Johnny Roberts said, "Who the fuck do you think you are to tell him anything?" He said, 'Who are you to walk up to me and say anything" 'He hit Jack in front of me and he took a swing at me; I body-slammed him, snatched the gun from his belt and threw him in the trunk of the car. I cracked two of his ribs and I slammed the trunk on him. When I jumped on Johnny Roberts, you know, I knew who he was – I didn't give a shit. Jack said, "You are out of your mind, nobody ever challenged him." Jackie'd been ripped off, raped, beaten, and the first person he ever saw stand up to Roberts was me. Roberts said, "I want him dead by tomorrow morning."'

Collins was now in serious trouble: 'They tied me up and took me out of town. They told me, "How far can you run in two days?" I had two days. I said, "Guess what? I'm going to Detroit.' When I got back there I had one thumb. They set fire to my car; they thought I was in it. I was stabbed in the stomach and the back.' Brazenly, Collins returned to his home in Detroit rather than try to hide. 'Jackie walked into his house and I handed him his coffee,' recalled Collins. 'I said, "Honey, how's your coffee? If it's about killing let's do it. If its about dying, we gotta do that anyhow. It's not about a thing. It's about a process. You don't take from me and you don't threaten me and mine and make it happen that way." Johnny Roberts was Mafioso, straight up. Everybody knew that. He said, "No nigger ever put his hands on me that I didn't kill." I said, "Guess what? I don't give a fuck about you, and if you come after my family I'll tear your head off and your family's, too. There won't be a member of your family left to fight over." I don't back off and I don't quit.'

Remarkably, Collins claimed there was another time he challenged Roberts and lived to tell the tale. This suggests that he went back out with Jackie on the road. The incident revolved around Launa Toledo, a fan and friend of Jackie's, whose house Jackie often visited whilst in California. Says

Collins: 'Launa told Johnny Roberts, "Kiss my ass." He drew his hand back and I put a gun to his head. He said, "You got away with it twice."' Johnny Roberts was well known to Launa and, despite his reputation, she wasn't afraid to speak her mind to him. She believes he was necessary to Jackie's career: 'It was safer to have him, that's why Jack did it. Better to be safe than sorry.' Launa once asked Roberts how many bodies he'd put in the river that week. He answered, 'The barge hasn't come in yet, so I don't know.'

Collins knew the Mob owned Jackie, just as they owned Sammy Davis Jnr and other entertainers. 'Jackie was on three percentages,' says Collins. 'On the table, above the table and below the table. There were gigs we did where he was paid cash. He immediately sent Nat his money, or handed it to Johnny Roberts . . . always in cash. You booked to do two shows, you did five. They [the Mob] would take a big percentage. They didn't give a shit about talent. They used calculators that never stopped counting. They would not allow you to threaten; they would pull up the root. If you weren't protected, you were used. There was no middleground.'

Still, as part of the Wilson family, Collins did very well and Jackie's typical largesse is exemplified by one gift he received. 'Jack got a watch from Nat Tarnopol, a Braume and Mercer; platinum with diamonds. Jack gave that to me for a wedding present, plus a suede sweater-jacket worth $350,' Collins recalled.

Collins's stories about Jackie could not always be verified and seem nothing short of extraordinary. He says: 'I had $63,000, carried it all over the country in my clothes for him. He told me, take it here, take it there. I didn't do anything wrong. We were in Metairie, Louisiana, in the head of [Ku Klux] Klan country. We were in the Hilton; he hid the money in the curtains. We went on to Atlanta and I had to go back to Louisiana and undo the seams to carry the money back myself.' Large sums of money being transported around with Jackie wasn't usual.

Collins went on: 'I belong to three families; Wilson, Collins and Lee. Who raised him, who stood by, took care of him? I took three bullets for him – he was shot at seven times. You loved him simply because he was not fearful. He would say, 'I can do this." He would be shit-faced drunk or hurting. They would have beaten him.'

Collins confirmed Jackie's great fear of flying and a possible explanation for it: 'Jackie hated to fly. He'd take bottles of vodka with him. If you got him on a plane, you'd done something. Put him in a slingshot and shoot him, but if you'd take him a plane, oh man, you'd a problem coming. He had just talked to Buddy Holly [in 1959. Holly had asked him if he'd do the short tour with him. That would have been super-major money. He'd said yes. The next call he got told him Buddy Holly was dead.'

Despite Collins's love-hate relationship with Jackie, he had deep respect for Jackie's talent and tenacity. Collins gave details of frightening incidents that he says happened to Jackie. Even allowing for a certain amount of exaggeration, they paint a remarkable picture: 'He never passed a show-up. "Mr Excitement" was his nickname. He was a true entertainer, because what he had to give to the public was his personification. Not what he was personified as, but what he owed. If you paid $3 for a $10 ticket, he gave you as much show for that price as if it had been $100. He did that.' Collins went on, 'Jackie loved himself. He was an asshole; the most prestigious asshole I ever met. He was an unusual individual. You want to know the truth? He got hurt so bad that when his paranoia took over it ruined everything for everybody. You could not eat before him. You could not drink water before him. You could not drink liquor before him. He would buy 20 bottles of liquor in a case and pour out ten of them. He would randomly say, "You drink some of this." And people who didn't drink vodka would suddenly be drinking vodka . . . whatever his drink of choice was. Is that normal?

Collins still harbours resentment towards Jackie and especially Lynn for dumping him in 1972. He says, 'You know what Jack liked to do? Fuck; that's it – if it was a pretty girl. He thought he was above everybody. He was a country boy who liked to do two things; sing and fuck!' Perhaps Collins should have said 'three things', because he added, 'I'm telling you. He could out-drink the average two or three sons-of-a-bitches that called themselves drinkers. It was never about drugs. He wasn't into that scene, he was an outcast. The first time they hooked him up with cocaine it was a trick. They hooked him up with these chicks and it was like his dick wouldn't go down. He said, 'Wow, you mean I can fuck forever?" He said, "I can handle this." It wasn't true. Jack had several massive nosebleeds behind Nat. He beat it [drugs] for years and years, and then he got it pushed to him through the company. He didn't do it on his own, 'cause he wasn't into it.'

Lynn's explanation for the decision to dump Collins was: 'He was on the road with us in 1972. He's nothing but mouth. He has a vivid imagination. I can see Jackie slapping the shit out of Johnny Collins, because he didn't respect him at all. Jackie was paying Collins for backup singing and still supporting his fucking wife. Collins wasn't giving Joyce Ann nothing. I said to Jackie, "This really sucks, you're supporting him and his family." I said, "It's time that he went," and he fired him.'

In the 1970s Brunswick had moved from the Brill Building on Broadway to 888 7th Avenue, nearby. Tarnopol employed Joel 'Joey' Bonner as Brunswick's promotions man. He arranged to take Jackie around the country doing personal appearances, particularly on TV and radio. However, Jackie had a 'bad boy' reputation, often not showing up for interviews. Bonner needed to improve Jackie's image with a view to getting more radio airplay. Bonner explained: 'When I went over there to work with Jackie he wasn't radio-friendly. He was notorious . . . he wouldn't do [media] spots. Nat was afraid that if he made appointments Jackie wouldn't show up. A lot of radio stations wouldn't play him. I said, "Listen, Jackie, first of all your image sucks out there – it's terrible. We've got to go on the road two weeks and say 'hello' to radio. Now if you don't like to do it, just tell me and I can get out of it." He said, "Joey, if I give my word to do something, I'll do it." He did interviews and he cut what they call radio ID spots, things like that; and he was beautiful. I was lucky, no question about that. In those days the jocks [DJs] would talk to one another and the word got around. Radio was really friendly to him again; that was in the 1970s.'

Bonner described the brilliance of Jackie: 'Jackie was big. He was a master of the stage. He could dance! A lot of entertainers learnt from him. In that era nobody could touch him on stage – he was dynamite. He knew how to work the stage. He was magic on his feet, and it was all instinct with him. I remember one time in Atlanta, he was so drunk we had to put him in the tub . . . we bathed him and he was still drunk. We put his clothes on him and got him to the gig and we just threw him on stage. It took him about a minute-and-a-half to realise where he was, then the instinct took over and he put on a hell of a show. He knew how to work the audience. He wore great suits and silk shirts, and when they got wet they'd cling to his body. The sweat would roll off him. He was exhausted when he got off. He was the baddest son-of-a-bitch on stage.

'One night we were in Louisville. Jackie and Little Willie John performed together at a club after the show, and it was one helluva night. Willie could stand there flat-footed and hit 'em [difficult notes]. Jackie, you could see him getting ready to hit the notes. Basically not even Sam Cooke could hold a candle to Jackie, performance-wise.'

But on the subject of the control that Jackie was under and the people who made up his entourage, Bonner is less sanguine: '[Valet] Frazier was big into drugs; cocaine and the like. They made Jackie get rid of JJ and Frazier. JJ sort of disappeared; they chased him away. Jackie had all these vultures around him; he was surrounded by vultures. That was his big problem in life. Those that he didn't hand out to stole from him. They weren't friends, they were all vultures. His valet, Frazier, he was basking in his glory. They would order suits and Jackie would paying for them. They all looked like dynamite and they were all blowing his money. But Jackie was that kind of guy. Jackie was in the pitfall of all entertainers. They all think its never going to end. The problem is, it ends; it ends for all of them.'

Bonner continues: 'Sims did the best he could; he was basically a pawn. August has done a lot of things I don't think were right. I don't think he had Jackie's interests deep in his heart. He just became an extension of what they were, in my opinion.' Nevertheless, Bonner concedes that Jackie wasn't easy to manage: 'I've seen Jackie blow many a date and, if he did show up, he'd show up late. Frazier and JJ, they couldn't do anything to control him; they couldn't make him get up. Jackie was that kind of person. Bad luck – he self-destructed. And bad luck about those around him. It was like, everybody was going to get what they were going to get. Jackie was just irresponsible and, in my opinion, Jackie was one of the nicest people – to me. If there was trouble he found it, or it found him. That's the way Jackie lived his life. He was just that kind of person. He had no conception of; the rent's due, telephone bill's due, this or that is due . . . and the people around him made sure he didn't know! I blame them more than him, because he wasn't bright as far as money goes or anything like that. It was just a sad, sad situation. The wrong people were behind him. His biggest mistake was signing everything over to Nat.'

Bonner was well aware of Jackie's chronic drug use: 'He was using everything; back then he was doing cocaine. He had an apartment on 57th Street, the same place where he got shot [Dorchester Apartments]. This was the early 1970s. I was there and they all came in with coke. Everybody was into it and I remember Jackie said, "Joey, you never fucked with it, don't fuck with it now." And I didn't. When somebody asked me, he said, "He doesn't fuck with it, leave him alone!" In those days it was the in thing. After he got shot [in 1961] the drugs got much bigger. He always drank, ridiculously; breakfast, lunch, dinner. There was always alcohol around.'

The power Jackie exerted over his fans amazed Bonner: 'Jackie had a way with women, and with people. I remember one night at the Regal

Theater in Chicago. After he did the show there was a line of people there for autographs. There must have been 100 or 200 people. He signed those autographs and kissed every girl. I mean, *kissed*. Sometimes I've seen JJ and Frazier get nasty to his fans; and he'd get angry with them: "They're my fans, don't fuck with 'em." He was a strange dude. There's no question; he had a magnetism. With me he was a perfect gentleman. Overly polite. He was just a nice guy.'

On and off since 1960, when they first met, girlfriend Lynn Ciccone kept in contact with Jackie. She'd often flown out to wherever he happened to be, spending two to four days with him. In the 1970s her husband was dying of cancer so Lynn was in need of money. During that period Jackie wasn't well off, but despite that she says: 'Jackie gave me $2,800. He continually kept in touch with me; he knew where I worked, that's how we kept in touch.' To this day, Lynn treasures her time with Jackie and thinks of him daily.

A dedicated fan who became a close friend of Jackie's around 1965 was Launa Toledo, from California. She also became a friend and confidant of Harlean. Launa says of Jackie, 'Jack was one of the warmest people to me. He was like a big brother. If I had a problem, I could tell Jack. Even if I had marital problems, I'd tell him and he'd go talk to [husband] Rudy; he settled many fights between us.'

One summer's evening, Jackie decided to hold an impromptu party at Launa's house. Launa explained: 'I remember coming home one day and seeing a big truck in front of the house. I said, "What the hell is that truck doing there?" I walked in and there was Jack and the entire band, including instruments. I said, "What are you doing?" Jackie said, "We are going to have a party." He gave me $500 and said, "Go and get some stuff, and make a pile of spaghetti, too." I went and bought everything. He opened up all the windows, then went to all the neighbours and invited them onto the front lawn. He was unbelievable. The mayor even came. At the party, Jackie performed for everyone.'

Jackie did other crazy things too, said Launa: 'He'd lie out on the patio in the back. I once asked, "What the hell are you doing?" He said, "Getting some sun." "Why?" He said, 'You know, right now black is beautiful, and I'm beige." I said, "You're weird."

'To drive in the car with him was the most frightening thing in the world. Oh, my God, he would go up the wrong side of the street. If they weren't going fast enough for him he'd go over to the next lane, straight into oncoming traffic. If he wanted to drive on the sidewalk, he would. He was the world's worst driver. I'd say, "You're not driving my car." He'd reply, "I'll buy you a new one if I wreck it." Then he'd get on the bikes with my girls to go to the store. Jackie would sit for hours and play with my daughter. She'd had five major eye surgeries; a birth defect.'

While in California, Jackie preferred to stay at Launa's house rather than a hotel, because nobody would bother him, but most of all because he would be amongst close friends and he enjoyed Launa's home cooking. 'He would check into a hotel,' explained Launa. 'His name would be there, but he'd be with us. He'd say "They can call there all day long, for all I care, they're never going to get me."'

Launa spoke of one crazy escapade: 'He came out one night; he had on black pants and a black shirt. I said, "What are you doing?" "We are going out to steal a dog." "What are you talking about?" He replied, 'The guy down the street beats on his German Shepherd all the time. I tried to buy the dog from him but he wouldn't sell it, so we're going to steal it." I said, "Jack, you can't do it. If you get caught, it's going to make every headline in the business." He told me, "I can," and he did. Jackie called [promoter and artists' manager] Walt Cohen and told him, "Get a kennel cage and get it over to Launa's. I want you to ship this dog to Detroit to my mother." And that's what he did. He stole the dog! They got over a six-foot fence to get the dog. That's Jackie for you. Couldn't stand for something to get hurt. He never forgot where he came from. He was good to everybody – that's unless you crossed him! If so, he usually called up JR [Johnny Roberts] and had him handle it.'

Jackie's wit was always sharp, as Launa attests: 'He used to say, 'There's only one thing faster than a nigger." I said, "What's that?" He said, "A scared nigger!" It was all right for him to say it but nobody else could. He was a crack-up. He liked to tell jokes, but he couldn't. He would start to tell you a joke, and he'd think about it and start laughing. He laughed so hard that when he told you the punchline you couldn't understand it. He was a funny man.'

Sometimes Jackie and Launa went to the market or shop, which brought him into contact with the public. 'It drove him up the wall if people walked up to him and said, "Aren't you, uh, Johnny Mathis?"' says Launa. 'He say, "No, Jackie Wilson!" One time I went to the flea market. He didn't want to go. He said, "People will jump all over me." I told him, "It's so busy, nobody will notice." So we went and got all the way through. Then a guy spotted him and people started walking over to him. He was his usual amiable self. He said later, "I'm kinda glad it happened, for a while I thought nobody recognised me."'

At times, Launa would become exasperated with Jackie. She relates one such incident: 'He and my husband would go out and I'd tell them they had to get in by a certain time. This one night I locked them out. They came home and went into the patio around the back. I could hear they were both drunk, trying to get in. There was a doggie door. Jackie was trying to get in the doggie door, to get into the house! They were singing, "Don't you step on my blue suede shoes." I thought the neighbours might call the cops. Jackie said, "I've got a key here, it might work." That's how drunk he was. I jerked the door open and they both fell into the hallway. I was mad and went to bed. Rudy went to sleep on the couch. Later I heard a bunch of noise, so I went down to the kitchen. There was Jackie with a frying pan and flour from asshole to breakfast time. Oh my God! He was wearing a shocking iridescent-blue outfit, he had flour in his hair and his face and he was flouring pork chops, trying to fry them. He looked like a ghost. He said,''I'm starving, nobody feeds me." He would do things like that; he was a crazy person.

'He didn't like to eat in restaurants. We'd go out and he wouldn't order anything. He would order just before we were leaving and he'd take it 'to go'. I said, "Why do you do that?" He said, "Haven't you noticed? Look at people when they eat, it's so ugly! People putting stuff in their mouth and chomping on it; it's an ugly thing." He said, "Invariably someone will come in and stare at you and it turns my stomach. I'll just take it home and eat it." If he was playing in Oakland, he'd send his chauffeur to my house at three o'clock in the morning to get whatever he wanted me to cook. Usually, in a day or two, he was at the house. He'd say, "I can't take the hotel any longer."

'Another thing he'd do is call me, say from Chicago, and it would be three in the morning, my time, six where he was, and he'd say: "I'll be there at such and such a time, can you have some Yankee pot roast ready for me with potatoes and carrots or ham hock, Lima beans and corn bread? And potato salad." I'd say, "OK, Jack." I'd go out and get it. '

Much to Launa's chagrin, Jackie loved nothing better than to accompany her when she bought her groceries. She explains, "I'd go to the grocery store and he'd say, 'I'll come." I hated it. I said, "Don't do me any favours," and he'd say, "I'm going." Then we'd get to the grocery store, which was horrendous because he'd never go to the grocery store when he wasn't hungry. Invariably, he'd be hungry. Anything in that store looked good to him. He would throw things in that basket and we'd get home and I wouldn't have any room to store the stuff. '

Launa, a keen judge of the human voice, says: 'Jack could outdo just about anybody, if he decided to. He probably had one of the most tremendous talents of this century. He had a vocal range unequalled by anybody. Once my mother asked him, "Jackie, why didn't you go into opera; you seem to love it so?" He replied, "Mama, did you ever see any black Pagliacis? They just didn't let us black boys in the Met [Metropolitan Opera House]. I had to do what made money." I said, "You don't mind plagiarising some great guy's [operas]." He said, "Well, nobody listens to them [meaning the original operas]; they can't understand them, for God's sake." He used to warm up in our bathroom – luckily, we had two of them.

Launa recalled other amusing incidents: 'The funniest time was when the chauffeur forgot to put his wardrobe bag in. We got to the club and he didn't have pants to put on. Jackie had a muscular chest and so he took the same size of shirt as my husband. He turned to Rudy and said, "Rudy, take off your pants." He said, "I won't." Jackie said, "Take off your pants, damn it! I have to go on in five minutes." He put Rudy's pants on and they fell off of him; he had a tiny waist and absolutely no rear end. He turned to me and said, "Take off your pants." I replied, "Jackie!" He repeated, "You've got black pants on . . . take 'em off." He wore my black pants on stage; I was about a size seven then.'

Launa could see that the people that people who surrounded Jackie were taking advantage of him. 'Jack knew people were ripping him off,' says Launa. 'The hangers-on took Jackie for everything and anything they could. It was amazing what they would do. I'd tell him, "Hey, Jack, these guys are robbing you blind." He'd say, "Oh well, that's all right, kid. Don't worry." I told him, "You're the one that's working for it." Jackie was an amazing person. He made life great for everybody, except himself. There wasn't a mean or unkind bone in his body. At least not to me; I never saw one.'

In 1973, a young songwriter and singer, Jeffree Perry, wrote an entire album on his own for his long-time idol, Jackie. Even though Jackie was years beyond his gigantic hit-making days, the resulting *Beautiful Day* album truly is beautiful. It came about through a chance encounter, as Perry explained: 'I was in Detroit at the time, working for Invictus Records with my brother Greg. My uncle Robert Bateman's group, the Satintones, was the first group to ever record on Motown. My uncle used to do a thing with Sonny Sanders. Sonny was doing the charts [arrangements] for Motown and Jackie. He did 'Whispers' and 'Higher and Higher'.

'Sonny ran into my uncle Robert and said, 'Have you got anything [songs] for Jackie Wilson?" I was in the studio cutting some things myself. Originally some of the songs Jackie did on *Beautiful Day* I was going to record myself, as the artist. Meanwhile, Sonny came over to Detroit and got with Robert. We had just cut this song, 'It's All Over'. Sonny took the demo tape to Chicago. Brunswick producer Carl Davis and Sonny got a hold of it and I think the next day they cut it, because they were crazy about it.' It was later released on Jackie's *Beautiful Day* album in March 1973.

Perry continued: 'So one weekend, about a month later, I decided to go to Chicago about some other things. I decided to check out what was going on in Brunswick. I met Carl Davis and all the crew that were down there. It was an exciting time. And they said, "Hey man, we want you to start working with us," so I did. Carl wanted me to do a whole album with Jackie, which was a first; it had never happened before, and we did it. We used Sonny Sanders, got all the Motown musicians; in my opinion, the best musicians that were ever assembled in the world were the Motown musicians. I thought it wasn't promoted properly. Jackie was trying to break away from Nat Tarnopol and this album was going to be the one to do it.'

Perry was unstinting in his praise of Jackie: 'In terms of what I thought of Jackie Wilson; in my opinion there were two people who revolutionised R&B, pop, soul, like no other performers and they were Jackie Wilson and Sam Cooke. I've never seen such a performer to this day . . . Jackie was a natural. He could just make up a step, right, and entertain on the spot. In my opinion, Jackie was the greatest performer that I've ever seen on stage. I also think that in terms of the singing voice, Jackie was one of the greatest singers. He was somewhat miscast, though, because he had an operatic voice; he could sing opera. Jackie didn't have to have a microphone. The wonderful thing about Jackie – he was a high tenor – is he never had a bad performance; he never sang off-key. Out of all the times I saw Jackie, I never heard him go flat or miss a note when he went after it. That's unique!

'Jackie was city-slick and hip, he was cool and could talk, he was articulate, he could dress, he was pretty, he was good-looking, he was intelligent, he was sophisticated. Jackie epitomised what it meant to be a recording artist. Jackie was entertainment, 24 hours a day. Even when he wasn't on the stage, he was on the stage. And he was a regular person.

That's the truth. I've never met a person who was more compassionate. He was an artist's artist. And Jackie was a person . . . I don't like to use the expression "ahead of your time", 'cause I don't believe in that.

'He was a star and knew he was a star, and wanted to be treated as such. He fought about it. In my opinion, it's by design that Jackie did not receive the type of popularity he should have. If it hadn't been for Jackie Wilson there wouldn't be a Motown. You see, Jackie was a star in Detroit before he knew Berry Gordy. Jackie was the first major star from Detroit. Jackie was a hero to Smokey Robinson, David Ruffin, all those people. Jackie would come into a room and no matter who was doing what, everybody took their hats off to Jackie Wilson — he was just a star. Jackie was what I would call the star-of-star's star. He was always impeccable in the way he dressed. He was always sharp, and I loved him.'

Perry also had some interesting observations concerning Nat Tarnolol: 'I enjoyed Nat, we didn't have too much of a problem. But he had a love-hate relationship with Jackie. He loved Jackie because he was the greatest performer, entertainer and singer in the world, but he was insanely jealous and envious of him at the same time. That's what I saw.'

'Even Elvis Presley, he used to come to Jackie Wilson's shows,' Perry recalled, 'and every time he saw him he gave him a watch or ring. He wanted Jackie to know he loved him. Elvis caught a lot of flak for being a soul singer; singing black music. Elvis is the main person who made black music popular. He took a lot of moves from Jackie; he wanted to be Jackie Wilson on stage. He didn't quite have the movements, nobody did, but he was said to be "the white Jackie Wilson".' Perry's final words are typical of musicians who knew the greatness of Jackie: 'I listened to Jackie today. I think it's a shame that many people do not know his contribution to the record world.'

Generally, the greatest of Jackie's songs relied on a soaring buildup and crescendo. Jackie relied on the thrilling technique of the unexpected. He was a master at the technique, being seemingly able to take his voice in any direction at any point in the song.

Beautiful Day was the second last album that Jackie recorded. In 1974 he recorded his 28th, and, though he didn't know it, his last album. Entitled *Nobody But You*, it again was a beautiful and unique, contemporary recording. It was released in early 1976, but was so poorly distributed that the people closely involved in its making believed it had never been released. By 1974 Jackie, aged 40, had lived a fast life and smoked a million cigarettes. Nevertheless, as Lynn Crochet says, 'His voice was in perfect shape on *Nobody But You.*' The studio recording that Jackie did for the album used a method known as 'tracking', meaning his voice was laid down over a previously completed music backing.

Lynn Crochet was one of those who believed that the album wasn't released. 'I was at the last two recording sessions,' says Lynn. 'They would lay the tracks and we would go to Chicago and he would do the vocals. It didn't matter to him [whether it was live or not] at that point in his life.' By this time, Jackie and Tarnopol were not on talking terms and it's amazing that it was ever recorded at all. Says Lynn, 'Everyone hated Nat – it amazes me he got so far. It got so bad there in the end that he wouldn't even take Jackie's calls. Jackie had to talk to him through Johnny Roberts.' Carl Davis commented, '*Nobody But You* was recorded in Detroit. Jackie and Nat had fallen out. It wasn't properly promoted.' The arranger for the album, Motown arranger David Van de Pitte, was also a talented horn player. He, too, believed the album was never released.

Lynn was fed up with Jackie's addictions. He'd quit and all would be well for a time, and then he would relapse. Says Lynn, 'I cared about Jackie. The thing was, he was killing himself with the booze and all the bullshit and I wanted it stopped.' She decided to leave him after one angry incident: 'The reason I left him was he pulled a gun on me and shot it out the back door. You don't do that kind of shit to me. He'd came back from California after doing [the TV show] *Midnight Special*, and he was all messed up. I rang Eliza [Jackie's mother] from Atlanta and told her, " Tell him my mother [who was, at that time, still living in Detroit] had a heart attack and I have to get up there.' That's how I got out of the house.

'The next day he was on a flight to Detroit to get me. And I wasn't going back. I said, "It's either me or the booze." So he dried out for six weeks in my mama's house. He got me off the speed and I got him off the booze.' Lynn continued, 'I'm not saying Jackie was a saint, I'm just saying that the last five years of his life were nothing like his heyday. When I got with Jackie he wasn't making that much money. He was making $5,500 a week. He had to take care of expenses. He went from there to $10,000 a week. He cleaned up his act . . . we were fixing to go on tour. We were going to Vegas for six weeks, then Hawaii, Australia, back up to Germany and England and back to the States.'

Around late 1974, Jackie, Lynn and the family moved to Marietta, Georgia where they bought a new home. Says Lynn, 'The reason we moved to Marietta in the first place was to get Thor and my boys away from that environment [referring to the drug taking and the bad company].' As well as two-year-old Thor, Lynn's two adolescent boys, Arty and Randy, lived with them.

Jackie only earned so long as he was performing and this wasn't every day of the week. Still, it was pretty good money, with the average American earning only around $150 a week. The tax return lodged by Jackie in 1969 provides an interesting insight into his earnings. His gross earnings were reported as $106,696.93, with Federal tax of $63,745.37 — leaving net earnings of a reasonable $42,951.56. On the same return he listed three dependents: Eliza Lee, his mother, Harlean and their son, John. In Jackie's 1970 tax return, listed under 'other business expenses', are some examples of his professional expenses: Outside labour $63,950, hotels $18,732, costumes and clothing $6,518, auto expenses $5,206 and travel $3,870. A very expensive business, the entertainment business! By 1971, Jackie's earnings had crashed. His gross earning was $27,074.41, with a tax bill of $6,642.79, leaving $20,431.62 net.

'Jackie bought several acres of land in the country for when he retired,' explained Lynn. 'He planned to have some dog kennels up there and build a house. We were going to start a kennel and raise Maleneoas. We bought the property. I lost it when Jackie got sick; I had to use the money.'

Meanwhile, Jackie still had financial problems. The Internal Revenue Service had a lien over his earnings from Brunswick for unpaid taxes. Lynn says, 'Jackie still had IRS problems in the 1970s. He would go to his accountant [Isidore Silverman] in Detroit, who took care of it. He was a pal of Nat's. Everyone on the payroll was a friend of Nat's.' As if that weren't enough, Freda took her own legal action for unpaid maintenance payments. Freda explained her situation and the action she took: 'All that time I filed [with the court] he was supposed to be paying me all the money. At the time Tony [Jackie's youngest child with Freda] was going to Chrysler Mechanics' School. I got a judgement; he owed me $50,000. I gave them Jack's entire itinerary . . . Tony knew it. My lawyer said they wouldn't put him in jail. Tony told us his daddy's address in Atlanta, because he'd been down there. Lynn cursed him out because he was going to wear his daddy's ring and one of his chains and go out somewhere. Lynn called him a bastard. She said, "You put them back here, now!" She hit him. He said, "I'm going to tell my daddy." When Jack came back to the house, he said, "Lynn, did you slap him?" And she knew he was mad. She was in there crying. He said, "I don't care about no chain!" Tony was mad when he came back and told us.' At the time Tony stayed with Jackie and Lynn, he was 17. Lynn had difficulty getting along with him.

Freda continued: 'Jack had been sick and he never sent the money. That's why he was so far behind. He was supposed to give me $10,000. I didn't want no support, because I could work. But I needed the money to pay for uniforms and the kids' tuition . . . it kept going up. Jack kept telling me he didn't have it. I kept hearing about Lynn buying houses and this and that. Jackie Jnr [had accidentally] set our house [on LaSalle] on fire, in the attic; everything burnt real bad. I didn't have that kind of money. So the court sent some detectives down. When they went down there, Jack jumped out the window. He never really broke with the family. Never. When he came to town, he would find me wherever I was.' Freda was financially down to such an extent that she couldn't make mortgage payments on the LaSalle home and it was repossessed. She moved into the YWCA, while Jackie's mother took care of the children at the home Jackie had purchased on Strathmoor, north of Detroit.

Freda went on, 'Lynn [Crochet] called me at the "Y" [YWCA]. She said, "Honey, I don't appreciate you sending the police to my house." I said, "Who's this?" She said, "Lynn Wilson." I said, "This is Freda Wilson you're talking to, and as long as my husband owes me money, I can send them anywhere."'

Surprisingly, Jackie rarely played records at home, but when he did he generally played his own. However, Lynn says there were a number of other artists he greatly admired: 'He admired Sam Cooke, Otis Redding. He met Otis. He and Sam Cooke were best friends. He and Elvis were friends. Jackie and my sister went to Elvis's last concert and Elvis came out and said he was "the white Jackie Wilson".'

Lynn's sister, Linda Cannon, shared the Marietta home with Jackie and the family. According to Linda, in the 1970s Jackie was the perfect family man: 'If more men in this world were like him, this world would be a better place.' According to Linda, his appetite was enormous: 'Lynn cooked for that man all the time. She'd cook five, six, seven, eight things at a time. He would have two or three meats at one meal; a roast, ham, sweet potatoes, five to six pies, cakes. That was enough for an army, let alone one person. He said one time, "Cook me a cake." I said, "You couldn't be hungry after all you ate." He said, "Yes, I am." I fixed him a cake. He said, "Lynn's never cooked for me." I said, "I hope you don't go to hell for lying. Shame on you." He would never gain an ounce.'

When Thor was only three-and-a-half years old, Jackie took him on tour to Pueuto Rico. 'Thor performed with his dad. He was a born ham, stealing the show from his dad,' says Lynn. 'One time in Florida I had him in a short white suit and red socks. He told his dad, "I'm not getting down on my knees so my mama will whip my butt." They had a routine where they'd go down on their knees.'

While Thor was on tour with Jackie, Lynn was well into her second pregnancy to Jackie. In August 1975, the last of Jackie's children was born. 'I called to tell Jackie about the birth of Li-nie, but the doctor had called before me and he knew what he had,' says Lynn. Lynn and Jackie named her Li-nie Shawn. The name Li-nie is Cherokee for 'little one', while Shawn is Irish for Jack; Little One Jack.

But in 1975, the world was beginning to forget that Jackie Wilson had ever existed, though Jackie was still on the road exciting his audiences and making enough to feed his family, with a little left over for the Internal Revenue Service.

The last time ex-guitarist Billy Davis saw Jackie was early in July 1975. Jackie performed at Detroit's Masonic Temple, just before he left to tour in England and Germany. Davis, who had put on a fair bit of weight over the years, remarked to Jackie how well he looked: 'He told me he was strictly clean, that he was totally off [drugs]. Didn't drink or anything. It was amazing how good he looked. Hadn't looked that good in 15 years.'

Freda, too, went to see Jackie perform at the Masonic Temple. She recounted, 'The last time he was in Detroit at the Masonic Temple, I said, "Come on Sandy [their daughter Sandra]. We are going down there to see your father." He owed us all a fortune. He owed each one of them $50,000. He was singing "Higher and Higher" and he saw us coming. He smiled and reached down and pulled Sandy onto the stage. He was reaching for me, so I went to the back and sat on the table there. He kept singing on the stage with her. He said, "Ladies and gentlemen, this is my daughter, Miss Sandra Wilson."'

In 1975 Jackie went with Lynn on their second visit to the United Kingdom. Says Lynn, 'I was expecting Li-nic – that was 1975. That was England, and we went to Germany first: he performed the US air bases there. You should have seen the way they reacted towards him over there. They were tearing his clothes off and everything. I said, "They aren't suppose to act like this" – that was 20 years ago. It was a trip.'

In the last half of September 1975, Jackie was special guest on the coast-to-coast *Merv Griffin Show*. Nobody, least of all Jackie, knew that this would be the last TV appearance the great performer would ever make.

14. IT'S ALL OVER

Dick Clark assisted Jackie in achieving fame through his popular and infuential nationwide TV program *American Bandstand.* Clark spoke fondly of Jackie: 'He was an extraordinary performer; I've always said he was the most exhilarating performer I ever saw. He caused a phenomenal reaction amongst female fans. It was good for him and bad for him. It nearly killed him along the way. He lived the part of a superstar, he bought lots of jewellery, had lots of women, spent money that he didn't have sometimes.' When Clark put together a nostalgic rock 'n' roll revival tour, Jackie was his obvious choice to head the bill. As Clark retold it: 'The "Good Ol' Rock 'n' Roll Revue" tours were a series of engagements. We started off with them in 1973, in Las Vegas, and took the concept to the Latin Casino at Cherry Hill [New Jersey].

RECALLS CLARK, 'Jackie was a huge star with the black audience and a moderate star amongst the white audience, who were into rock 'n' roll at the time. He hadn't reached the gigantic levels of being an idol that he should have – I can't imagine why.

'When we did those shows at the Hilton and the Thunderbird in Las Vegas, Elvis Presley came in again to see him, because I guess he'd seen him before. Jackie was an influential man; people copied his every move. Later on, Prince and Michael Jackson admitted they'd studied Jackie. Anybody that wanted to put on a show looked at him; he was the consummate performer. Later on in life he became a giant star and we just saw each other on a professional basis.'

In 1975, it was seven years since Jackie's last hit. However, he could still hold a note as well as ever and audiences loved him. Prior to the New Jersey engagement Jackie had headed the bill for six weeks, doing the same show at the Thunderbird in Las Vegas. His contract for his one-week engagement at Cherry Hill was care of Queens Booking Corp. and he earned $7,500 for the week, for two performances a day.

Jackie seems to have shaken off his bad habits. Clark spoke of his professionalism: 'I had no difficulty getting Jackie up on time. By then he was completely straightened out; clean of any addictions he'd been into. He still smoked like a fiend, however. He was always on time, had two or three standing ovations a night, and we used to grind those shows out two or three a night in Las Vegas like clockwork. Jackie's act was four to five numbers. There was no fan hysteria or lots of noise, screaming and yelling; this was a casino audience.'

In September 1975, Jackie rejoined the tour at Atlanta, where he'd been with his family. On the ill-fated tour with Jackie were Freddie Cannon, Cornell Gunter And The Coasters, and Dion DeMucci. Coincidentally, Terry Gray, who produced for The Coasters group, was flying from Florida to New Jersey for the show's opening the next day. Lynn Crochet had to stay in Atlanta because daughter Li-nie had been born the previous month, on 10 August. Gray had known Jackie since 1965, when they first met in Las Vegas, so he asked the stewardess if they could sit together. Jackie conversed happily along the way and Gray recalled, 'He was very up. He talked of his wife and kids. We got in [to Philadelphia] late at night.'

The next evening, 29 September 1975 was opening night of the show, so, after rehearsals, they met for dinner. Jackie, Gray noted, was a different man from years before; he wasn't drinking and seemed normal in every way. However, Gray remembered, 'The night of the show he ate a steak and it didn't settle well. He also had vegetables. He wasn't feeling too good; he talked about eating and going on stage.' Jackie had developed a headache and said he was going to lie down for a while, prior to the show. Eating prior to a performance was not Jackie's normal regime.

On the opening night, Jackie was well into his last routine, his signature tune 'Lonely Teardrops'. Dick Clark continued: 'As soon as I saw him fall I knew that I'd never seen him do that before. He fell backwards, hit his head on the stage and was in the throes of going into the coma. It looked like part of the act, but he never got up. The irony of it was that just before Jackie was singing 'My heart is crying, crying,' and doing the splits and so forth. It is probably the worst memory of my experience in the entertainment business.' Promoter Walt Cohen was in the audience. He said, 'I heard his head crack on that floor.' Clark continued, 'Cornell Gunter of The Coasters tried to give him mouth-to-mouth, but it didn't help. None of us knew CPR [cardiac, pulmonary resuscitation]; this is probably some of my guilt coming forward.' Clark called for the curtains to be drawn.

The most detailed report on the tragedy was carried in the 6 November 1975 issue of *Rolling Stone* magazine, by Lou Gaul. In it he reported:

Jackie Wilson was performing an energetic version of his biggest hit, 'Lonely Teardrops', when he grasped his chest, sunk to his knee and fell to the floor. The audience clapped and the orchestra continued playing for about 30 seconds, thinking the fall, which occurred as Wilson sang the words 'my heart' was part of the act. Horribly, it was an all-too-real heart attack that has left him in a coma . . . and in 'very critical' condition.'

It's highly exceptional for an athletic, 41-year-old man to have a heart attack, particularly mid-performance, on stage. More extraordinary that he was doing 'Lonely Teardrops', while singing the lyric, 'My heart is crying, crying', so reminiscent of a Greek tragedy.

The *Rolling Stone* article went on:

Thinking that the singer had fainted, Clark rushed to his side. Unable to revive him Clark called into the audience for a doctor. He then began sobbing and asked the audience to 'offer prayers' for Wilson.

As others tore at Wilson's leather jumpsuit and began to massage his heart, Cornell Gunter, flamboyant lead singer for the Coasters, administered mouth-to-mouth resuscitation. 'I looked down at Jackie and said, "If you're okay, blink." He blinked twice, and then his eyes rolled up in his head and all I saw was white.'

Clark recalls: 'I remember the terrible night in Jersey we removed all of his jewellery because they thought they'd never see it again. I've got no idea where it ended up.' It is indeed a mystery. Jackie had a $20 gold piece around his neck, a gold bar, a watch, a gold bracelet and a diamond ring. It is said Johnny Roberts was the last to be seen with it.

Jackie, the superb vocalist and performer, in the prime of his life, was struck down. The question was, would Jackie survive, or was it the end? With such a medical trauma the crucial thing, when the patient's heart stops beating, or breathing stops, is the amount of time taken to restore those functions. After only a few minutes, oxygen starvation leads to permanent brain damage. In an exceptional stroke of good fortune, the ambulance quickly arrived, as *Rolling Stone* magazine reported:

An ambulance that had stopped at a nearby hotel for an unrelated illness rushed Wilson two miles to Cherry Hill Medical Center, where a team of six doctors worked on him for 25 minutes before obtaining any vital signs. 'He came in here with no pulse, heartbeat or breathing,' an emergency room doctor said. Although a team of three doctors stayed with him throughout the night, he lapsed into a coma.

Here, events become clouded. One strongly held theory is that Jackie's head had struck the stage and he suffered a severe concussion as a result. Possibly he had fainted or had a minor heart attack, causing him to collapse? Cherry Hill Medical Center was modern and well-equipped. Bud Lauer, the medic who attended Jackie, was part of the highly trained two-man ambulance crew. He was very familiar with heart attack victims and he is certain that Jackie wasn't one. His belief is that Jackie was a head trauma patient. In other words, Jackie's unconscious state was due to a head concussion. Lauer maintains that Jackie was breathing and doing well enough, but, to his amazement, when they arrived at the hospital Jackie was immediately given defibrillation (electric shock heart therapy), which encourages the heart to regain a normal rhythm. Indeed, the hospital records show that Jackie was given defibrillation nine times that night.

The report in *Rolling Stone* magazine quotes 'an emergency room doctor' as saying: 'He came in here with no pulse, heartbeat or breathing.' Unless Jackie's prognosis changed within a minute or two, the statement was in sharp conflict with that of the ambulance medic. Bud Lauer's recollections of that fateful night are very clear and troubling: 'The call was for a heart attack. I don't know how long it took to respond to the Latin Casino. There was no traffic going on the route to it; I do not recollect any traffic . . . I don't recall delays.'

Lauer continued, 'When we arrived at the Latin Casino, there was a nurse on stage. She was doing CPR; she was doing compressions and providing ventilation – mouth-to-mouth. I don't recall a [oxygen] tank being there when I arrived. Everyone was excited and emotional. There was no medical person on duty at the concert, but it was fortunate that the nurse was in the audience. Our response time was two to three minutes. Dick Clark was on stage most of the time. But no evidence of anything [having caused the collapse]. I checked to make sure the tongue wasn't dropped back. Someone advised her [the nurse] to step aside, that the emergency squad was there. You can't [shouldn't] transfer or do a two-man rescue. When you start [CPR] you are not supposed to stop; you should not stop [chest] compressions.

'Right at that time I checked his pulse; I had a strong pulse. She [the nurse] was away from him. He was not breathing; I did mouth-to-mouth. He continued not to breath on his own. The pulse became weaker. He was on his back; I don't know if he had been on his back. I didn't notice any blood, but in checking the victim, his eyes etcetera, I was told he had a heart attack. In doing that you don't check for broken bones. We had no idea whether he collapsed, or fell forwards or backwards. He had a pulse, which is important; so there's no need to do CPR. In fact you should not do CPR, if someone has a pulse; you go against the heart. You could damage it. We did not do compressions on Jackie. He was getting blood; he was not blue around the mouth. All I know is he was not breathing – he was unconscious. He was not blue; he did not have loss of oxygen, because I was breathing for him. I was doing mouth-to-mouth on him on the stage, on the way to the ambulance, inside the ambulance – until I got the demand flow, which is an oxygen-forced unit in the ambulance [a respirator].

'When you do mouth [-to-mouth] the patient only gets about 16 per cent oxygen. With [the] demand flow [respirator] he gets full oxygen. He did moan; he moaned, and moaned again. He breathed twice or three times. We had to help him breath. He wasn't able to speak or open his eyes. His chest cavity was expanding and contracting. He was getting oxygen; he was not at all blue. We [in the ambulance] were moving quite well; it was hard to stand up. He had a pulse all the way to the hospital, but he wasn't breathing on his own. We had to ventilate him all the way there.'

So far, things would seem to have been going well for Jackie, although at the hospital situation was soon to change dramatically. Says Lauer, 'I am not a doctor; there is a lot of things that could cause a person to stop breathing. It could be an aneurism [a local dilation of a blood vessel, usually an artery] in the brain that causes that particular motor skill to stop.' More accurately, the aneurism causes that part of the brain to either malfunction or to stop functioning at all. Lauer continues, 'But in heart attack, stopping breathing is common; your heart stops. The heart could stop beating, slow down, or fibrillate [to quiver, causing irregular contractions of the ventricles in both rhythm and force].' Medical experts suggest that with fibrillation the heart will continue to pump blood, though not effectively, around the body. This would lead to reduced oxygen to the brain and, if this was to occur for a sufficient period of time, brain damage would result.

Lauer continued, 'I lost [responsibility for] him at the time we opened the back door of the ambulance. He was not blue. It wouldn't be my position to claim that he was, or was not, D.O.A. [dead on arrival]. He was not in cardiac arrest [cessation of the heartbeat]. [Even] in fibrillation the blood is still moving. I checked his eyes; they were equal and reactive, they were not constrictive [indicating he didn't suffer a stroke].'

As to the possibility that Jackie could have been poisoned or drugged, Lauer had no way of ascertaining this: 'It was not possible to know. At the time there was no paramedics; EMT [emergency medical treatment] was just coming in. All we did was ventilate him. His colour was good; his fingernails were fine [not blue, which would have indicated his blood was not getting enough oxygen]. He was getting the blood when he should get it; he just wasn't breathing. In my opinion, this would not indicate a heart attack. I don't know why you would not breath, but the heart would [still] pump. At that time and today I believe he did not have a heart attack. He had respiratory failure, caused by whatever. Could be a head injury or a drug.'

Lauer is equally certain that Jackie's condition was not as a result of a stroke, as some have surmised: 'It's very strange, the whole thing. His eyes were fine, even; which would indicate no brain aneurism or stroke, anything like that. His pupils were equal [in size]. They weren't constricted – they weren't big. The stroke shows up in the eyes. One responds, the other doesn't. The man, in my opinion, did not have a coronary [heart attack] or a stroke. Something happened to cause him to stop breathing, period. He had a pulse . . . the blood was flowing. His nails were fine.'

When Jackie arrived at the hospital, the responsibility for his welfare became that of the hospital facility. As Lauer says, 'What happened inside the hospital I can't say.' In fact, what happened at the hospital was that Jackie was given an electro-cardiac thump immediately after he was admitted. This treatment calls for an electric shock to be administered to the patient's chest to enable the heart to beat in its normal rhythm. If Lauer is correct in asserting that he had a strong pulse from Jackie, then this would be an entirely inappropriate course of action. The likely result would be to cause the beating heart to fibrillate.

A likely cause of Jackie's collapse may have been an embolus (a substance in the blood stream which causes a blockage in a blood vessel). This would generally cause temporary loss of consciousness, due to either heart or brain malfunction. In the case of an embolism (obstruction of a blood vessel) being so critical as to lead to the bursting of a blood vessel in the brain, this condition is referred to most commonly as a stroke.

Lauer was surprised that the first thing which had been done was the administration of an electric pre-cardiac thump, even though he had not been debriefed as to Jackie's symptoms: 'Normally they would ask what was wrong, or else an examination would be made prior to [the electric pre-cardiac thump being administered]. At that time they would ask "what happened?"' According to Lauer, the correct time for a pre-cardiac thump to be administered is 'normally at the first instance of arrest. I saw them administering a lot of medication – injections into the ribcage.' As medical emergency staff attest, a lot can happen to a critical patient between the ambulance and the emergency room, so, to be fair to the medical staff, it must be said that Jackie could well have suffered a further cardiac arrest on admittance to the hospital.

Although no longer responsible for Jackie, Lauer did stay around for a while in the emergency room: 'I walked in the emergency room after a few minutes. There were 20 to 25 people in there. I remember them cutting his leather suit and fringe. Dick Clark was in the hospital emergency room. He was very concerned and was standing there at the foot of the bed in the examination room. Cornell [Gunter] was out in the hall.'

The official Cherry Hill Medical Center report, dated 15 December 1975, states the following:

> Jackie Wilson was admitted to Cherry Hills Hospital on 29 September 1975 in a comatose state. He presented with ventricular fibrillation [incoordinate quivering of the heart muscle]. Immediate cardiopulmonary [heart, lung] resuscitation was started with external ventilation, with the insertion of an endotracheal [by way of the throat or the mouth] tube. He was defibrillated six times in the Emergency Room and three times in the Coronary Care Unit. His status was so critical that he required intracardiac Epinephrine [to restore the heart's rhythm] as well as Vaspressors [to counter his shock state and to control blood pressure] for support of a shock state.
>
> Subsequent EKGs [sic – most likely ECGs; electrocardiograph, a machine for recording the potential of electrical currents that traverse the heart muscle and initiate contraction] showed evidence of acute myocardial infarction. It was my feeling that an acute myocardial infarction precipitated ventricular fibrillation, causing the cardiopulmonary arrest leading to a shock state with reduced cerebral profusion [sic – possibly perfusion, the passage of liquid through a tissue or organ], followed by cerebral oedema [swelling]

and compression of vital centers leading to an initial comatose state.

Neurological consultation by Dr. Leonber's group, first seen by Dr. Vanna: his feeling was brainstem damage and he made the comment that in view of the history of cerebral anoxia with the resultant edemas [oedemas] and brainstem, damage is likely.

Jackie Wilson also developed an initial shock lung state requiring a volume respirator and intensive pulmonary therapy. While in the hospital, he required a tracheostomy and developed pulmonary infection as well, treated with antibiotics. I was able to wean Jackie Wilson off the respirator. At this time I was having difficulty closing off his tracheostomy because of a great deal of retained secretions.

Except for his initial frequent episodes of ventricular fibrillation, his rhythm remained stable with an arrythmic medication.

As I mentioned earlier, he was initially in a deep coma. Now he does blink and moves his eyes spontaneously but no response to visual or auditory stimuli is present. He does tend to withdraw in response to noxious stimuli. There is no sign of the presence of higher neurological functions. He seems to be functioning at a brainstem level. The patient is not capable of talking or understanding verbal or written language.'

They were saying, in effect, that Jackie's brain had swelled to the point of inducing coma.

Soon after admittance, mobster and Jackie's personal manager, Johnny Roberts, quickly arrived at the hospital and took charge. Launa Toledo, a friend of Jackie's, knew Roberts well. She says, 'The doctor said to Roberts, "I'm afraid he's gone." JR held a gun to his head and said, "You'd better hope he isn't, or you're going with him."' It was not possible to confirm this story, though those who knew Roberts say it is true to form.

Toledo also recalls discussing death with Jackie on one of the many occasions he visited her California home: 'Jackie used to say, "Baby, you can't kill a nigger unless he wants to die." And he said, "There's only one of two ways I'm going to go; either on the stage, or in bed having a good time."'

Although August Sims was on the payroll of mobsters, having been initially employed by Johnny Roberts, he had genuine affection for Jackie. Sims joined Jackie on the road in 1963, remaining there until 1972. He was not present at Cherry Hill the night of the collapse. Sims, though, is highly suspicious about Jackie's heart attack, firmly believing it was induced. Says

Sims, 'Johnny and Tommy Vastola, you could count on them two doing something for money, 'cause them motherfuckers are hungry.'

Tarnopol and six other Brunswick executives had been indicted only three months earlier on charges that included taking kickbacks from record retailers, wire fraud and cheating the Internal Revenue Service. Jackie would have been called to testify against Tarnopol, whom he now loathed. Sims commented that Brunswick faced a torrid time: 'Yeah, with the Mob, Brunswick had a lot of shit in there and they [the federal authorities] were looking down [interested in] on his [Tarnopol's] ass, too. Nat didn't do much because he was scared to go across the street. 'Cause they were looking down on him [legal actions against him] and he was part of the Mob.'

Asked whether Jackie had been victim of a murder attempt, Sims was more circumspect: 'I think so; I figure he might have been, unless they gave him too much cocaine.' Sims thinks it more likely that Jackie had been drugged in order to give him a fright; to bring him back under control. 'I think so, and it bac-fired on their ass – it killed the kid,' Sims concluded.

Sims was quick to visit Jackie in the hospital and describes the meeting: 'I went to see him at the hospital. He was in a coma and he knew me. We [had] always squeezed hands to see who could squeeze harder. We did that; when he squeezed my hand, I said, "That son-of-a-bitch knows who I am." I felt sorry for him, boy. I thought, "August, you should have stayed out there." If I'd have stayed a couple of years, he'd still be living. 'Cause I wouldn't let that son-of-a-bitch [Roberts] do nothing to him.'

Recalling the time he'd seen Roberts taking all of Jackie's earnings, prompting Jackie to assault Roberts, Sims said, 'Boy; from then on I knew where he was coming from. 'Cause on the road he [Roberts] liked to sleep with me, 'cause he figured I'd protect him . . . son-of-a-bitch.'

Naturally Dick Clark's rock 'n' roll revue had to continue. Coincidently it was Jackie's close friend, Chuck Jackson, who was selected as his replacement.

Some time after the heart attack, Carl Davis had occasion to phone Tarnopol. The conversation shocked him: 'The thing I remember is Tarnopol. I called him one time; I was trying to get $20,000 for something, and he said, "Listen, Jackie's in the hospital, I've got this one-million-dollar policy. Don't worry about it, because as soon as he dies our pockets will have the mumps." I said "What? I don't want it that bad!"' The insurance policy for one million dollars, supposedly held by Tarnopol, was payable on Jackie's death. However, it is entirely appropriate for a record label to hold such a policy. In any case, Tarnopol never collected, as the policy lapsed prior to Jackie's death.

Regarding medical insurance, Dick Clark remarked on a fortunate occurrence: 'The terribly irony is that of all the thousand shows I'd put on, this was the first that I took out Workmen's Compensation. We used to do upwards of 150 concerts a year and I don't know why [the policy was taken out]. And that was the only funds there were to pay for his hospitalisation. I can't imagine what [how much] they were, but it wasn't nearly enough.'

Jackie's commonlaw wife, Lynn Crochet, was at home in Atlanta with their seven-week-old daughter Li-Nie. On receiving the news of Jackie's collapse she was obviously shocked, and all the more so because of a recent medical report. Lynn explained: 'Jackie had a physical here in Atlanta three months before Li-Nie was born [or approximately five months before the heart attack] and the doctor who did the physical was a personal friend; my own doctor. He had saved Jackie's life when he was an intern in New Orleans, because Jackie had walking pneumonia, and he said he hadn't seen him in better shape in ten years. Jackie was in perfect health. He looked tired before he went, that was all.'

Lynn was very suspicious about Jackie's collapse. 'He was supposed to testify before the Grand Jury ten days after he got sick, against Nat Tarnopol,' recalled Lynn. 'That's why he got sick. To the day I die I will always say that Nat Tarnopol gave him something to make him sick so that Jackie couldn't testify. And when I got there to Cherry Hill, I asked them if they had run any tests for drugs and they told me, "No". It was too late. I have since found out it could have been done and it would have told [that there was something toxic in his system]. You stop and you look at it. Cornell Gunter was there the night he died. Why did Cornell suddenly get killed? We had just talked to Cornell and he thought there was something wrong 'cause he'd given Jackie CPR. All of a sudden he gets killed.' Gunter was murdered in an mugging on a Las Vegas street.

News of Jackie's collapse reached former wife Freda, then living at the YWCA in Detroit. Says Freda, 'They called me at four o'clock in the morning. They said, "It's your mother-in-law." I answered the phone and she [Eliza Mae] was crying; and she didn't cry. She said, "Our boy is nearly dead." I said, "Who, Tony?" She said, "No, Big Sonny." I said, "How did you know?" She said she got this telegram; she didn't have the phone. It was probably from Nat or the Mafia, but it could have been from anyone. It said, "If you want to see your son alive, be on the next plane out of

Detroit." She had only been on the plane with me when he got shot [in February 1961] prior to that.

'She went to New Jersey alone. I hated to see her go by herself. She didn't wear nothing that much, but when she'd go to see Jack she'd dress up. I didn't want to get Harlean mad [by going too]. She [Eliza Mae] couldn't have taken her insulin. I cried after she left; I was trying stay brave for her. She was staying brave for everyone. Joyce went up there later.'

Jackie's friend, guitarist Billy Davis, drove Eliza Mae out to Detroit airport for her flight to New York. In Davis's words: 'I took her to the airport and she expected [Jackie to be in] for a few days. He'd just been overworking. We didn't know just how bad it was . . . I told her to tell him hurry up and get up so I could go back out on the road with him. So we had the attitude that he just needed some rest and he'd be up again. Then she got there and saw how he was.' The days following Jackie's collapse afforded a bleak prognosis. Jackie was deeply comatose. He was on full life support, on the 'critical list'. Lynn Crochet knew and got along well with Eliza Mae, having lived with her on and off for nearly five years. Lynn and Eliza Mae stayed at the home of Jackie's then driver, Billy Wilson (no relation) in nearby Philadelphia. Eliza Mae slept on the couch during her stay. After only a few days at the house, one morning she became gravely ill. Billy Wilson and Lynn rushed her to the hospital. Says Lynn: 'They brought her there with no medication. I had Dr Fisher, Jackie's doctor, refill the prescription for her and she was taking the medication, but she still went into a diabetic coma and died.' Lynn believes the trauma of seeing her 'baby' in a critical condition had killed her. She died, aged 71, on 16 October 1975. She had visited her beloved son only once or twice.

Billy Davis was informed of the death by Joyce Lee. He stated, 'Eliza Mae died all of a sudden. She was in great health, it seemed, but when she went up there and saw him . . . She was a very strong woman, character-wise. She had a beautiful smile on her face all the time. Eliza Mae had a smile that could melt an iceberg; I'd tell her that all the time. A very strong woman. That's where Jackie got a lot of his charm from. She was one of the sweetest ladies you could ever meet. She could be dead tired and when you walked in you'd get the smile of welcome. Jackie was her life; he could do no wrong.'

Jackie's daughter Denise explained: 'My grandmother loved my father. He was her heart, her soul, her life. That's why she's not here; she gave him her last ounce of everything, so he could survive as long as he did. I'm not saying my grandmother was prejudiced, but no woman was really good enough for him. And then she finally accepted my mother.'

Within weeks of hearing of Jackie's collapse, Eliza Mae's death gave Freda another shock: 'I went back to the 'Y'. When Joyce called me, she was crying, "Mama's gone." She went into a diabetic coma; she could not talk or tell them anything. She knew she was going to die. She knew she was not coming back. That's probably why she raised Joyce to be strong and independent. But Jack was dependant, on me and her – we handled everything.' To her eternal regret, Freda never went to New Jersey to visit Jackie. She recalls, 'Sandy wanted me to take her; I wish I had. She wanted to go so bad. Maybe in her mind she knew something was going to happen to her.' Sandy would die before her father.

The mutual love Jackie and his mother had for one another transcended normal family love. They were both dependent on one another. Billy Davis believes that 'If she had gone before he did he wouldn't have been able to make it. It was such a close thing between them, when she went to see him in that condition, knowing he wasn't going to get up, she couldn't take it.' Davis makes a very strong point here; Jackie and his mother were so close, needed each other so much, that had their positions been reversed and she was the one in the coma, Jackie wouldn't have been able to go on. Joyce Ann Lee knew this bond existed and was envious of it. Nevertheless, she did travel across to New Jersey, visiting Jackie in July 1976.

Gil Askey, who'd worked with Jackie early in his career, saw the love between mother and son as well: 'No wonder she died after his first visit,' said Askey. 'You should have seen her the night at Toledo when all these people ran up on stage, "Oh, my baby." She was in hysterics. She loved him, he was her heart.' Another early friend of Jackie's, Harry Respess, remembered the incredible bond between Jackie and his mother: 'I remember once at the Greystone [Ballroom in Detroit] he was performing there and his mother was in the crowd. They were trying to put her out. She was trying to get backstage and they didn't know who she was. Someone said a cop had hit his mother, and he went berserk: "Nobody hits my mother." He loved Ma; he'd have killed-a-brick for her. He stopped right in the middle of a song; he came down off the stage like a madman. He fought his way through the crowd in plain view of everybody. He was knocking cops all over the place. Man, he was punching 'em out, fighting like a wild tiger to get to her. It took a few cops to subdue him and they finally arrested him. That was a real stroke.'

After Eliza Mae's death, Joyce lived in the house Jackie had bought for his mother on Strathmoor in Detroit. 'When Mama died they never litigated her estate,' complains Lynn Crochet. 'Joyce Ann just took over the house and kicked out the three grandkids [the children of Sandra and Reggie Abrams] and had them put in an orphanage,' Lynn explains bitterly, 'She didn't have that right, because the house was in Mama's name and the grandchildren lived there. It was Jackie's house and he was still alive. Jackie's children and the grandchildren should have got the benefit from it.' Even Freda, who doesn't usually criticise, says, 'Joyce Ann had all that money; the money from my mother-in-law was supposed to be divided.'

There was a further unusual twist when the arrangements to transport Eliza Mae's body back to Detroit for burial went awry. Somehow her body was wrongly transported to a medical facility, being lost for a time. 'His mother was his life,' says Launa Toledo. 'Lynn [Crochet] called me up, crying. She said, "She couldn't find her way when she was alive. What chance has she got now?" They'd put her on a milk run; to a medical university or something. They finally found her.'

For a short time, Lynn visited Jackie in Cherry Hill. She says, 'In the first instance there was no way I would believe he did not recognise me. He would blink "yes" and "no" to me. We had it documented, but the doctors wouldn't believe me. They wouldn't come in at night when he wasn't awake and aware.<A>' Lynn soon returned to Atlanta, where she was soon to run into financial problems, having to take care of the two young children along with her two boys by a previous marriage. She believes that because she did not attend Eliza Mae's funeral, the rest of Jackie's family turned against her.

Before Lynn returned to Atlanta she'd contacted a one-time girlfriend of Jackie's, Joyce McRae, asking if she would go across to New Jersey and see Jackie. It may have been that Lynn spoke to McRae and she offered to come over. McRae went and, in no time, through her strong personality, took over Jackie's affairs. Harlean in particular, and other family members, saw her involvement strictly as a desire to take control of Jackie's meagre estate.

On Clark's 'Good Ol'Rock 'n' Roll Revue' revival tour Jackie earned $7,500 per week, but from now on, for Lynn and the children, there'd be nothing. Jackie had left a legal nightmare that raged for 20 years. The biggest problem Jackie's heart attack caused for those around him was, who was to be his legal guardian? Who would take care of the finances and who would pay the medical expenses? Sure, he'd married Lynn Crochet in 1971, but, by not divorcing Harlean, it left a large question mark. It would soon be put to a legal test.

JACKIE WILSON

'The first year I worked very hard to get him transferred to Rio Rancho in California; to get him rehabilitated,' explained Lynn, 'I felt that even if he never sang again, he could get rehabilitated. Dick Clark's insurance was paying for everything. They were even willing to buy a house and put him in it, and a van to transfer him back and forth. INA [insurance] was going to do all this and Harlean stopped it. He could have been transferred to California, but Harlean wouldn't let him. And I fault the State of New Jersey courts for what happened.'

After almost four months totally comatose, in January 1976 Jackie emerged from his coma and was taken off life support. However, he remained semi-comatose, being totally immobile and unable to communicate.

Despite Jackie having lived with Lynn as husband and wife for close to five years, Harlean, Jackie's second wife, came forward saying that she was still his legal wife and would take care of his welfare. Cherry Hill Medical Center were anxious to know precisely who Jackie's legal guardian was; who was responsible for the medical bills, and who could make the medical decisions on Jackie's behalf. A well-researched article by Bill Pollak in New York's *Village Voice* (14 August 1978) explains the increasing dilemma that was developing:

> In order to settle the dispute and get its bills paid, Cherry Hill Medical Center asked the court to intervene. In March 1976, a month and a half after Jackie came out of his coma, Judge Vincent DiMartino of Camden County Court placed his affairs in the hands of an impartial third party. He named Edward N. Adourian Jr., a Camden lawyer, as Jackie's legal guardian.

Incredibly, lawyer Edward Adourian hadn't heard of Jackie Wilson until that day. It seems he just happened to be in the court building and Judge DiMartino chose him as a good neutral party. He said, 'To tell the truth, I'd never heard of Jackie Wilson — I'm into classical music — until the judge called me.' The choice proved fortunate, as Adourian was thorough and dedicated.

The *Village Voice* article continued:

> A month before Adourian was named guardian in February 1976, a jury in Newark had convicted Tarnopol of one count of conspiracy and 22 counts of mail fraud. Three other Brunswick executives

were also convicted. In April, Judge Frederick Lacey sentenced Tarnopol to three years in prison and ordered him to pay a fine of $10,000. Tarnopol immediately announced that he would appeal the conviction.

Adourian knew what the Brunswick convictions meant to Wilson's financial problems. After Brunswick refused to allow Adourian to see the company books, he filed a suit in Camden federal court asking for a full accounting of Wilson's earnings at Brunswick. The suit charged breach of contract and claimed that Brunswick had failed to pay and account for over one million dollars in royalties due to Wilson. Somewhere between this one million dollars and the $150,000 that Brunswick claims Jackie owes them lies the true figure of how much is owed to whom.

Adourian, in his attorney's thoroughness, recounted the events as he saw them: 'He was in the Cherry Hill Medical Center and, my recollection is, sometime in February [1976] . . . nobody was paying his bills.

'There was a petition by two women [Harlean Harris and Lynn Crochet]. I was walking down the court hallway one day and the judge didn't know what to do. He saw me and said, "Well, make him guardian." I was appointed guardian of his person and property. The first thing I had to was get some financial backing for him. So me and my partner David Schicobie – he was working in workers' compensation at that time – we conceived the idea that when Jackie had his heart attack he was in his employment. He was working for Dick Clark, who had a revival of rock and roll; something like that. And Jackie was singing for this Dick Clark group at the time he had his heart attack. Dave [Schicobie] and I went up to see Dick Clark and we convinced him that Jackie was not an independent contractor, but an employee. In other words, he had direction over what he sang and what he did. We established an employee status for Jackie.

'The insurance company which was, I think, Pacific Insurance Company, owned by the Insurance Company of North America [now Sigma]. They assumed responsibility, so all his medical bills were paid; he would get temporary disability. We could pay his medical bills and maintenance and also we could get monthly temporary disability payments; not very much. We were lucky that Clark had taken out insurance there, it paid his medical bills. His hospital bill was $100,000 and various other medical bills. They were all paid off. The insurance company paid for him at Morris Hall, even though they didn't have to.'

JACKIE WILSON

Nevertheless, on 11 March 1976, barely six months after Jackie's collapse, the Cherry Hill Medical Center took civil action in the Court of New Jersey against 'Jackie Wilson, Lennie Belle Wilson [Lynn Crochet] and Harlean Wilson' over non-payment of medical bills amounting to $83,327.25. Back in 1976, these medical expenses represented an enormous amount for a single individual. The *Village Voice* article further disclosed:

> Adourian also went to court and won an insurance settlement from the Insurance Company of North America [INA]. The company was ordered to pay $120,000 in hospital bills, provide $119 a week in disability allowance and continue to cover Wilson under workman's compensation. But since workman's compensation limits coverage to therapy that will return the insured to his former occupation and on the strength of doctors' opinions that Wilson would never sing again, INA has been reluctant to authorize therapy for him.

Since it is not unknown for similarly brain damaged people to emerge from such an unconscious condition, every opportunity should have been made available to Jackie. But there was a further disappointment, as the *Village Voice* article explained:

> Adourian later found out that Wilson should have been covered by Blue Cross/Blue Shield though his union's pension and welfare plan from the beginning. Under Section 34 of the AFTRA (American Federation of Television and Radio Artists) Pension and Welfare Clause, which also includes all recording contracts, an artist is eligible for Blue Cross/Blue Shield if he earns $1,000 a year or more. Wilson had been working on an album, *Nobody But You*, for three months before his collapse, and had put in over 24 hours in the studio. Since the rate for studio time is $81.50 an hour, Wilson should have easily met AFTRA's requirement.
>
> But instead of reporting Wilson's 1975 studio earnings, Brunswick reported to AFTRA that, since Wilson owed the $150,000 against advances on royalties, they did not pay Wilson in 1975. As a result, when Cherry Hill Medical Center contracted AFTRA, it was told that Wilson was ineligible for Blue Cross/Blue Shield. But, according to Adourian, the point was that Jackie recorded and performed, and regardless of his purported indebtedness to Brunswick, the record

229

company should have contributed to Wilson's pension and welfare fund for time spent in the studio.

Unfortunately, Adourian did not discover this scam until after he had already won the settlement from INA. And once a workman's compensation case has been established, Blue Cross/Blue Shield is not required to undertake insurance payments. However, if Blue Cross/Blue Shield had been paying Wilson's bills from the beginning, Adourian and other friends of Wilson's would not have had to fight to get therapy authorised.'

All in all, it amounted to tragic misfortune for Jackie and the rest of his family.

Once the insurance was established, Adourian says, 'The next thing we had to do was determine what his medical status was and whether he was capable of rehabilitation. We had to have the neurologist that treated him at Cherry Hill Hospital and his electro-encephalograms and everything else. We were told by the medical people that he was not a candidate for rehabilitation but was in what they call 'a chronic vegetative state'. We also had a computer activated sensor test. In other words, they would bombard him with visual and auditory sensation and they would record that and it would go through a computer. They were trying to find, when they put light in his eyes and sound in his ear, whether there was any integrated neurological response from that. The conclusion was that there wasn't. Anyway, we did it [rehabilitation] just to be on the safe side, and the insurance company agreed to it – they really didn't have to – even though the information we had said he wasn't a candidate for rehabilitation. He was sent for several months to a special rehabilitation hospital, near Princeton, at Lawrenceville. He was there for several months and received various kinds of therapy. We also paid extra for speech therapy.

'The doctors told me, when I had to make the decision about whether or not he was a candidate for rehabilitation, that he had a life expectancy of about ten years. A person in that condition is very, very susceptible to respiratory infection, things like that. He was getting physical therapy and we got him a private room. We also had him evaluated at the Hahnemann University Medical Center in Philadelphia, which is a first- class medical center, by a Dr Bill Oakes. They gave him a CT [brain] scan and I remember the scan showed dilated cerebral ventricles. All the ventricles in the brain were dilated, which they concluded was atrophy of the cortex [the brain's outer layer]. Their conclusion was that he was in a chronic vegetative state.

'I think I was his guardian for about a year and asked to be relieved. Another lawyer took it up. His name was Wayne Bryant. He was his guardian for a year. We had him [Jackie] in a convalescent home in Camden County, and then we placed him in Morris Hal, a rehabilitation hospital. Wayne had him placed in a very fine facility, Medford Leas, a Quaker institution.'

Adourian explained, 'Then I think Harlean made a petition and she was appointed his guardian. I think she might have been [appointed] guardian of his person and her lawyer guardian of his property. Joyce McRae was a third factor who came in. I used her as a para-legal for a period. She occupied a room in our office when we were in Camden [New Jersey]. She made a petition [to the New Jersey court] and wanted the guardianship. She had no [legal] standing.

'McRae was a very persistent individual and very difficult to deal with. But she was very concerned with his well-being. She believed he was not in a vegetative state. She believed he was in a conversion hysteria; for some physiological reason he was withdrawing to escape. The neurological evidence, all the clinical findings, said he was in a chronic vegetative state. That's what I had to go on at the time.

'The rehabilitation didn't do him any good. He did have a swallow response. I would stand there and she [McRae] would say, "He's responding; look at that." She wasn't seeing what I was seeing. We gave her the benefit of the doubt and gave him four months of rehabilitation. He had a flat-out encephalogram; it wasn't registering anything. There was no response. They would try to treat him; would put him up on a chair and the nurses would talk to him. He would look back and forth; his eyes were open during the daytime.

'The brain needs oxygen and sugar. The only thing he had was the NG tube [for the supply of sustenance], no other life supports. They took the NG tube away because he had [developed] a swallow reflex. That's one thing Joyce did; she insisted they feed him with a spoon. She could be a real pest to the nursing homes. Joyce would go in and tell the staff what to do. I tell you, if I were ever in that state, I would want Joyce around; keep everybody doing their thing. Her theory was to treat him as much like a human being as possible; as if he had cognition.

'[The new guardian] Wayne Bryant had to go to court to bar her from visiting him. I think that was done in camera because there were some accusations made against her in an affidavit. Another problem, which is a can of worms, is to what extent he was bilked by his agents and people who took advantage of him. We couldn't get involved in that type of litigation, as it is immensely expensive. You really had to know that trade and where to turn the rocks and look for that stuff. We didn't have any expertise. We had limited funds and felt we'd best use the funds for Jackie's physical well-being, rather than go on a wild goose chase to try to nail anyone.'

Within months of Jackie's collapse, Joyce McRae had moved from her home in Chicago to Cherry Hill along with her nine-year-old daughter. She was prepared to sacrifice much of her life to be by Jackie's bedside and endeavour to help with his rehabilitation. Despite being reviled by the entire Wilson family, McRae's behavior appears totally unselfish at that time. There's not much joy in sitting by the bedside, day in, day out, of someone who cannot talk or respond; all the more so if that person is not related.

The *Village Voice* article continued:

> Through Edward Adourian, who had just been appointed Wilson's legal guardian, McRae arranged for a consultation with Dr James Richardson, a physical therapist and former president of the New Jersey State Physical Therapy Society. Richardson gave Wilson propio-ceptive neuromuscular therapy (PNT) to develop new pathways to the brain and revitalise old ones. He also prescribed a therapy known as 'patterning', often used by the Boy Scouts and community groups to treat brain damaged people. Patterning, which has been successful in many cases similar to Wilson's, simulates the act of crawling by moving the arms and legs until the brain takes over the newly redeveloped coordination function of the muscles. But, possibly because patterning can be performed by anyone who knows how, it is scorned by some members of the medical profession. Dr William J. Erdman of the University of Pennsylvania was called in by INA to evaluate Wilson in June 1976, and he reported to INA that Wilson had no rehabilitation potential and that Richardson's'therapy was useless. On the basis of Erdman's report, INA terminated Richardson's therapy. The only therapy Wilson continued to receive was for a range of motion, which keeps the limbs flexible but does not attempt to restore function.

McRae became Jackie's constant bedside companion and did her utmost to have him achieve some semblance of normality. McRae says: 'I had to go to New Jersey and wound up having to pull faeces out of Jackie's ass, because they didn't know how to do a suppository without hurting him.'

McRae tried all forms of stimuli: 'I used to play all kinds of music to stimulate Jack. I knew Jack would not be at peace until the truth was out about what happened subsequent to his collapse. It didn't matter if he never sang again, as long as he could appreciate the sky or a bird and his songs, and watch his children grow. He understood and comprehended; it was stolen from him. Otherwise I couldn't have taught him to eat again. He must have had a certain amount of control; I even had him standing, but they found out and stopped his therapy. Harlean Harris and Nat Tarnopol participated in having it stopped.'

On one occasion an electric lamp had been set up by nursing staff and focused on Jackie's backside, with the object of drying out his bedsores. It was left unattended. Somehow the lamp tipped over, causing Jackie very severe burns. The staff were alerted to the problem by the smell of burning flesh. Relatives of Jackie's blamed McRae even though she wasn't present. They accused her of paying a staff member to do it, to prove Jackie was not being properly taken care of. McRae replies indignantly: 'He was burnt on the ass with a lamp. I was in Chicago. What idiot blames me? That was done at a nursing facility, on a night shift which was understaffed. They allowed him to get bed sores. They treated the bed sores by leaving Jackie – who could not ring a bell or call out, who had muscle spasms – with a light bulb aimed at his ass to try to dry out the bed sores he never should have had. How the fuck did I do that?'

As time went on and it became clear to almost everyone that Jackie was never going to regain much facility for living a normal life, the focus turned more and more to who should be the rightful heirs to his estate. Since attorney Bryant had taken over, McRae's involvement rapidly began to irritate him, as it did with the staff of the facilities Jackie was moved to. The *Village Voice* article best explains it:

> It's possible that Bryant thought from the beginning that it would be unethical for him to allow McRae to be involved with Wilson as she had been under Adourian's guardianship. According to McRae, Bryant even threatened to have her arrested when she tried to accompany Wilson to a nursing home. McRae continued to visit Wilson regularly, but since she was not Wilson's legal guardian, doctors and nurses were less willing to tolerate her criticisms. When contacted, Bryant declined to comment.

McRae deserves credit for taking the role she did. The Wilson relatives suspect her motives were more to do with gaining control of Jackie's estate, but this doesn't stand up to fair scrutiny. Jackie's daughter, Denise, observed, 'She was a guest in Mama's house and her and Mama got along great.' Freda quickly countered, 'He sure didn't bring her to our house. She did ask me to come out to New Jersey. I knew the lady is not quite right. If anything [had] happened she'd say "it's all your fault".'

McRae truthfully admired Freda and believed that, with her nursing background, she could have been helpful. Freda chose to stay at home. Freda's mother also grew fond of McRae and entrusted her with loads of family photographs that she feared would otherwise be lost. 'I love Freda,' McRae explained, 'I begged Freda to come over to take care of Jack. Her mother took me as her child. Mama Liza, she knew what I was doing for Jack.'

There was another incident which Harlean suspects McRae had involvement with. It involved one of the nursing staff, who was on her way to the court to make the damaging accusations against McRae concerning her alleged abuse of Jackie in the nursing home. The staff member was apparently forced off the road by another vehicle. Says Harlean, 'Was she [McRae] behind the kidnapping incident? Both incidents occurred around the same time, within a year of him being in Medford Leas. One of the girls who worked at Medford Leas was forced off the road by black men. It was black men who were driving the cars as they came in to testify against her [McRae]. I received so many phone calls from former friends of my husband in the industry . . . and several threatening things were said in regard to the girl [McRae]. Jackie was loved by millions of people and I got that type of talk from people who were in his fan club. They are not Mafia people. They know Joyce is not what she claims to be.'

The first-court appointed guardian, Ted Adourian, tried to get the best advice and treatment that funds would allow. The *Village Voice* article explains:

> Between 30 March 30 and 6 May 1977, Jackie was tested at Hahnemann Hospital in Philadelphia to find out whether surgery might help his condition, and to again evaluate his chances for rehabilitation. The hospital performed a brain scan on Wilson, and concluded that surgery would not be of value. Dr Wilbur W. Oakes's discharge summary said that Wilson's potential for rehabilitation was limited, but it did recommend that Wilson be given 'the opportunity to avail himself of some rehab program on a continuing basis . . . We made every effort to do more than just a

passive range of motion here.' The summary said, 'We had him on the tilt table and (gave him) physiotherapy trying to get him to stand. It was difficult to have him standing at this time but perhaps a more aggressive physical therapy approach with some braces might be able to accomplish this goal.

Dr Oake's recommendation was never followed. In February 1977, Adourian asked the court to relieve him as guardian because the case was taking too much of his time. At the same time, McRae filed an application for guardianship, asking that she be allowed to care for Jackie at her home. But on 1 April 1 1977, a month before Wilson was discharged from Hahnemann, Judge DiMartino turned down her application on the grounds that she was not a lawyer, and that a lawyer, as an officer of the court, could be held more directly accountable for carrying out the court's wishes. The judge named Wayne R. Bryant, a Camden, New Jersey lawyer, as Wilson's new legal guardian.

Joyce McRae attempted to have herself appointed Jackie's legal guardian, despite being no relation. It was a futile attempt. In April 1978 the *Philadelphia Tribune*, in an article written by Jovida Joylette, announced: 'JACKIE WILSON'S WIFE NAMED HIS GUARDIAN.' The story read as follows:

After numerous guardianship hearings and legal entanglements it appears that the fate and future of rock and roll singer Jackie Wilson has finally been determined. On Friday, 14 April, Camden County Judge Mary Ellen Talbot awarded guardianship of singer Jackie to Harlean Harris Wilson of New York. Judge Talbot's decision to award guardianship to Mrs Wilson has thwarted any chances Joyce McRae, an avowed friend of the singer, may have had in her own attempts to receive guardianship for Jackie Wilson.

Wilson's problems began two and a half years ago when he suffered an apparent heart attack while performing on the stage of the Latin Casino in Cherry Hill, North Jersey. Since then Wilson has remained in a comatose state, residing in various medical institutions and for the past months in a nursing home in South Jersey. Ordinarily, guardianship would have been awarded to next of kin. However, during the first guardianship hearing more than a year ago, there was no ruling as to the legal status of the two women.

The *Village Voice* article further stated:

> Relationships between McRae and Bryant quickly deteriorated. Since INA was only paying for half of the $90-a-day room and board fee at Medford Leas, the other half came from Wilson's estate. When the estate was down to $10,000, Bryant discontinued Wilson's speech therapy. According to McRae, he took this action before he saw an encouraging therapist's report on Jackie's chances of recovering his receptive and expressive language skills.
>
> Infuriated, McRae said that she would pay for continued therapy. 'This has been a consistent pattern in Jackie's health care,' she says, 'and I don't know how to explain it. But as soon as Jackie makes any kind of progress, something always seems to happen to cut off his therapy and allow him to regress.'
>
> After a few more clashes between Bryant and McRae, and after several articles airing McRae's criticisms appeared in Philadelphia and South Jersey newspapers, Bryant banned her from visiting Wilson at Medford Leas and again cancelled the speech therapy. Bryant took this action despite the testimony of several doctors and nurses that McRae's presence had a calming effect on Wilson, and that he had developed a definite emotional attachment to her. McRae quickly obtained a court order that allowed her to visit Wilson for two hours a day, but she wasn't able to get the speech therapy reinstated until three months after it was cancelled.
>
> Bryant's actions prompted McRae to file a suit in Camden County Court asking that he be removed as guardian for allegedly failing to carry out the court's directive to 'do all things reasonable, necessary, and proper to attempt the rehabilitation of Jackie Wilson to whatever degree or extent possible.' She contended that Jackie had regressed badly since Bryant took over as guardian. In addition, McRae again asked the court to name her Wilson's guardian, so that she could care for him in her home. But as the court hearing dragged on and her legal expenses multiplied, McRae ran out of money. Unable to defend herself against charges of interference from Bryant and the doctors at Medford Leas, she had to accept defeat and returned home to Chicago.

The battle for guardianship raged on. Initially Lynn was declared legal heir by the State Court Of Georgia, while Harlean later won the same judgement in the Camden Court, New Jersey. The Camden County Surrogate Court obviously faced a difficult decision.

The facts were Harlean had married Jackie in a civil ceremony on 20 May 1967, while Lynn claimed to have been married to Jackie on 27 March 1971 by the little known Universal Life Church at Modesto, California. Despite Lynn having spent five years living with Jackie, he hadn't arranged a legal divorce with Harlean. On the other hand, Harlean and Jackie, in 1969, after only 18 months of marriage, had both signed a legal separation agreement and Harlean, through the courts, had him arrested on every occasion he set foot in New York state. To all intents and purposes they were divorced. Lynn has had more than her share of heartache since Jackie's collapse. The reality was that she had four children to raise, with no income. She claims, 'I don't want a confrontation with Harlean, 'cause I've beaten her in court already. She doesn't have any right to inherit because of the separation agreement they signed. That's already been decided in the Georgia Court. What is a guardian? She was not a guardian. She did not take care of him. I tried to get him moved to Atlanta, where I could have been with him more often. I'd just had a baby [Li-nie]. I couldn't fight Harlean any more. I didn't work for an attorney like her – and my money ran out.'

On Jackie's well-being, Lynn says, 'I don't know how aware Jackie was, because I couldn't go back up there; I couldn't face it. I had nothing else to fight with and by this time I had started drinking. I went on with my life, but it was always there. I would call [the nursing homes] and say I was a fan, just to check on him.

'I got out of it with Joyce McRae, because of all the bad press she was getting. I didn't know who to believe. The pictures she took of Jackie and released to *Jet* [magazine]. I knew why she did it, but he would not have wanted it. I got upset with Joyce; she was going about it the wrong way. I had to step out of it, because I was close to having a nervous breakdown. I could not deal with it and raise my kids. I had to step away from it, no matter how much it hurt me. I've had to live with that all these years. I had to step back, I had to raise the kids. Because that was his future. That's what he would have wanted me to do.'

Referring to the period of April 1978, the *Village Voice* article continued:

> Bryant resigned his guardianship in April. On Bryant's recommendation, Judge Ellen Talbot named Harlean Wilson, Jackie's estranged second wife as his guardian, and her lawyer, John T. Mulkerin, Jackie's legal representative. Mulkerin and Mrs Wilson are

now faced with the same obstacle that made their predecessors' jobs so difficult: a shortage of funds. 'We would never attempt massive rehabilitation even if the chances for success were only nominal,' says Mulkerin. 'But one of the things that has to be assessed is what monies are available at the present time to accomplish that. If we had a million dollars, there's nothing we wouldn't do.'

In the meantime Joyce McRae kept knocking on doors and accepting contributions. Clearly, funds to rehabilitate and to simply take care of Jackie were not going to be sufficient. Medical care would be required for him for many years, as long as he remained alive. McRae used videos and photos she'd taken of Jackie to elicit sympathy and funds, but the Wilson family were angry about it, while a court also forbade her from doing so.

A benefit concert was arranged him at the Latin Casino, where Jackie had been stricken, on 3 October 1976, just a year after the tragedy. The Spinners, a Detroit vocal group, who were huge at the time, were the prime movers. They hosted the concert, paid for all expenses and contributed an additional $5,000. The show lasted three-and-a-quarter hours and featured Al Green, Harold Melvin And The Blue Notes, BT Express, Stephanie Mills, Sister Sledge, Don Cornelius and comic Irwin C. Watson. The ticket prices ranged from $30 to $100 for ringside seats. Al Green donated $10,000, while the Latin Casino and Gladys Knight And The Pips gave $2,500 each. Dick Clark also attended and showed a film clip from one of Jackie's TV performances. An amazing $60,000 was collected and donated.

Adourian explained: 'We had extra money, because the Spinners group held a benefit for him. We had to do something to prevent the IRS getting money from the benefit. We got some money there and we were able to supplement some of the things that the insurance company wouldn't pay for. The insurance company gave him only a minimum.'

Jackie's wife Lynn reported that the black comedian Ben Vereen was behind the concert. The plan was to set up a trust fund for Jackie, whose medical bills were said to be now costing $3,000 a month, while Jackie had a tax lien of approximately $500,000 against him. The trust would supposedly keep the benefits out of the hands of the tax man (IRS). 'I heard that Michael Jackson sent $10,000,' said Lynn. 'Richard Pryor sent me $1,200 for the kids. James Brown sent a $1,000 cheque, but it bounced. I had to threaten to call *Jet* magazine before he would pick up the cheque. He was broke.' Lynn further recalled: 'Stevie Wonder sent $5,000 to help me pay for going back and forth. Stevie sent the money to the kids. All the other money went to the guardians, Ted Adourian and Wayne Bryant.' Lynn is grateful for the concert, saying, 'The only ones that followed through were The Spinners. I got the message that Elvis called and he sent a telegram – so far as [Elvis sending] money, I never heard. Red Foxx, a black comedian, also sent a telegram. It was worded, 'Get up nigger, we need and love you.' It was exactly the way thousands of Jackie's friends and fans felt. Remarkably, Lynn came to New Jersey for the benefit concert, but didn't take the children in to see Jackie. She said simply, 'I wasn't going to beg Harlean.'

Quite a few visited Jackie while he convalesced. McRae recalls, 'The Jacksons . . . Michael Jackson came. T-Man [Theron Hill] went to see Jackie.' In July 1977 his mentor, Billy Ward, visited and claimed that, although Jackie didn't speak, he was certain, perhaps by the way Jackie gripped his arm, that he had been recognised. There was love between the two men. Ward knew Jackie's character flaws, but said simply, 'Jackie didn't have the advantages I had as a human being.'

Jackie's half sister Joyce Ann Lee visited him in July 1976 and so did his daughter Jacqueline (Denise), announcing to the press that Jackie's prognosis was not good. Other visitors, according to MacRae, were singers: 'Al Green, Phillipe Wynn [lead singer of The Spinners] and Bobby Smith came late at night. Lou Rawls came; I quietly snuck him in. Harlean showed up when she thought it was appropriate. Months and months went by and you wouldn't see her.' Nat Tarnopol apparently never visited or had concern for Jackie's condition.

McRae says: 'Denise came, Tony came. Sandy was too sick to come. They spent time with him. He and Sandy were close because she had that kind of personality. Denise is an interesting situation; she had a real father fixation and her perception of her dad was not totally normal. She loved her daddy, there's no doubt about it – but she was kind of messed up.'

Freda had considerable nursing experience. Her mother suggested that she ought to be at his bedside and begged her to help with his rehabilitation. In a decision that she eternally regrets, she never did visit Jackie, possibly because she was fighting her own battle with alcohol at the time. Most likely in atonement, Freda, for many years up until her death in July 1999, took care of a severely brain damaged man in her own home. Regretfully, she didn't make the attempt with Jackie. Freda explained, 'I didn't go and see Jack, but my mother went up there. She said he didn't look like he was going to come out of it, but they were surprised that he came out of the coma. Jack was a very strong person; he used to will himself to do things.'

But it wasn't as though nobody was trying to help Jackie. Of the many facilities he was moved to, he spent the longest period in Medford Leas Retirement Center at Mt Holly, New Jersey, where he was confined from May 1977. In 1976 Jackie was also admitted to St Francis Medical Center in Trenton, New Jersey, with a possible case of pneumonia. His temperature was 103. As one newspaper reporter commented, 'There is life. There is death. There is something in between. Jackie Wilson had inhabited that chasm.'

· In January 1976, not long after Jackie's collapse, the *Detroit Free Press* wrote an article entitled 'THE LAST SONG FOR DETROIT'S FIRST BLACK ROCK STAR, JACKIE WILSON' (11 January, 1976). Joyce Ann and Denise were interviewed and made interesting comments: 'We'd [the children] see more of him on TV than in the house,' said Denise. 'When we first realised he was a star I was eight years old. He had a record out called 'The Greatest Hurt'. My teachers and friends kept telling me it was No One.' Denise asked her father if it were so, and was amazed at his response. 'He was really hurt. My father sat me down and said: "Don't you ever forget. Your father is a star and always will be so."

'My father loves excitement,' Denise continued. 'As long as my father had his jewellery, fantastic clothes, a big car, and women . . . he liked the idea of being able to throw his weight around. When he was in that position, he could go out and say: "I ain't going to sing" and the people would tear the theater up.' Denise finished by saying, 'I guess other people must dream of what an entertainer's private life is like, but God, all the glory ends when you walk off that stage.'

Joyce McRae had been barred by the court from even visiting Jackie since 14 April 1976. Besides, she'd exhausted all her legal options, and her money. Tony Wilson, Jackie's son with Freda, also sought to become Jackie's legal guardian, but Harlean won in the end. With genuine concern for Jackie, Dick Clark and his wife, Kari, visited Jackie in the nursing home. Said Clark: 'I used to visit him on occasions at the rest home and they told me that if I sat and talked to him he could hear me. So I used to sit for a half-hour or an hour and regale him with stories of the old days. I would study his eyes to see if there was any flicker, but there never was.' Clark liked and respected Jackie. He'd helped Jackie gain nationwide exposure early in his solo career and visited him when he was shot in 1961. When Jackie had the heart attack he was there right along with Jackie, after he was rushed to Cherry Hill Medical Center. But in his view Jackie had no prospect of life other than as a vegetable.

Jackie's second daughter with Freda, Sandra, was better known as Sandy. She loved her father, but Freda wouldn't take her to visit. Sandy had three children, but was estranged from Reginald. On Sunday, 23 October 1977, at 24 years of age, Sandy died in her sleep. Her body was found by her eight-year-old son, Reggie Jnr. Although Sandy suffered throughout her life from chronic eye problems, losing the sight of one eye due to glaucoma, she was otherwise in good health. It was just over two years since her father's collapse. Happily, Jackie was unaware that he had now lost his mother and daughter. Sandra was buried at the Lincoln Memorial Park Cemetery, where her brother Jackie Jnr and Jackie's father were interned.

'Sandy was worried about her daddy,' says Freda. 'A year after he had his heart attack she said, "I've got to see my daddy pretty soon."I guess she knew something, but she had glaucoma in one eye and they kept telling me they wanted to take that one eye out and put another one in. They said that's how bad it had got; and she didn't want that done, she was worried about it. She wasn't supposed to drink then.' Sandy, a troubled woman, had addiction problems, too.

From 1978 to 1984, Jackie ceased to be news. He remained at Meadford Leas with very few visitors bothering to pay their respects. Not that it was an easy matter now to gain entry, as Harlean had to approve every request personally.

On 25 June 1975, the Detroit News, under the headline: 'payola probe indicts 19, 6 record firms,' reported:

Nat Tarnopol, president and controlling stockholder of Brunswick Record Corp. and sole stockholder of Dakar Records Inc., both centered in New York and Chicago, was indicted of charges of conspiracy, mail fraud, wire fraud and evasion of more than $103,000 in personal income taxes and more than $184,000 in corporate income taxes. Six of Tarnopol's employees were also indicted and all were accused of selling records to distributors by illegal and surreptitious means.'

IN MARCH 1976, following the 1975 indictments, Nat Tarnopol faced serious charges in the New Jersey court. If there was one person in a position to give testimony against Tarnopol, assuming that he would, it was Jackie. Fredric Danner's well-researched book on the American music industry, *Hit Men*, best explains the case against Tarnopol:

> The seven senior executives of Brunswick Records, including Nat Tarnopol, were indicted for taking $343,000 in kickbacks from retailers, to whom they allegedly sold records below wholesale price; and for using part of the funds to pay off radio stations. Tarnopol was also indicted for conspiring to cheat the IRS. and for wire fraud.

Also caught up in this net were Carl Davis, who, although Brunswick's vice-president, had nothing to do with the day-to-day running of the company, and Melvin Moore, formerly of Decca, then Brunswick's promotions director.'
Hit Men continues:

> The Newark grand jury was hearing testimony about R&B label Brunswick Records and its president, Nat Tarnopol . . . Nat Tarnopol was acquitted of thirty-eight counts of mail and wire fraud, but found guilty of one count of conspiracy, in a 1976 jury trial. He was sentenced to three years in jail. Then his conviction, too, was overturned on a legal technicality. Though he was tried again in 1978, the proceeding ended in a mistrial, and the government ultimately dropped the case.
> The loss was a sad blow because Tarnopol was a notorious abuser of artists, on a par with Morris Levy. He had taken ruthless advantage of Jackie Wilson by designing contracts that left the singer perpetually in debt to Brunswick, even as his records made hundreds of thousands for the label . . . Even the appellate judge who overturned Tarnopol's conviction took pains to note in his decision that 'there was evidence for which a jury could find that artists were defrauded of royalties.'

Robert Pruter's 'must-read' book, *Chicago Soul*, explains about the Brunswick fraud in more detail:

> In March 1976 . . . Nat Tarnopol and three other Brunswick officers were convicted of various fraud charges and one conspiracy

242

charge. The government found that the defendants sold nearly 500,000 singles and albums at a discount for $300,000 cash and $50,000 in merchandise. Such transactions, according to the government, defrauded the company's artists and writers of rightful royalties and the government of tax monies.

Pruter continues:

> Despite the seeming dishonesty of such practices, the defence contended that selling records at a discount was a common means of doing business and a necessity for an independent company competing against the majors in the 1970s. Furthermore, Nat Tarnopol and the other defendants were not intentionally trying to defraud anybody. In an elaboration to me, Tarnopol asserted that selling records wholesale at discount was a means to get the volume to put a record up the charts, which in the end helps an act rather than hurts it. He suggested all companies at one time or another did this, and said that compared to others, 'Brunswick was a baby'.
>
> <A> Tarnopol appealed his conviction and in December 1977 the conviction was overturned. In June 1978, following a retrial, a judge dismissed the charges and declared a mistrial after the case fell apart. Undoubtedly contributing to the weakness of the government's case was the prosecution's failure to bring any witnesses to the stand to testify that they had been defrauded.

'[Carl] Davis said he was mystified by the events: "Nat was a very good executive and that's one of the reasons why I was confused, that he would do something like that. I really liked him and I considered him a good friend of mine, but then after the trial started, I realised that he wasn't as good a friend as I thought . . . During and after the trial Davis and all the key creative persons abandoned the company, and all the important artists left as well."

Carl Davis explained it was revealed in the court that Sims had assisted Tarnopol in defrauding the artists. 'Then, after that, Nat started stealing money from the records,' recalled Davis. 'He'd take a guy like Sims, load up a U-hire truck and sell records all over the country for cash. Nat bought an El Dorado [Cadillac] with records. Then he had a thing with Cardinal Red-something, an import-export company and, my God, they exchanged a lot of records for money.'

After the court ruling freeing the Brunswick artists they went over with Carl Davis. The artists felt more loyalty to Davis and generally pursued their careers through him. Brunswick was effectively finished as a recording company while its top artist, Jackie, lay in a nursing home with the grimmest prognosis. Davis explained: 'It was enough that the judge at the trial gave every artist on the label their release, because Brunswick was selling their records and not paying them by not putting it on the books. Then [the court declared] you are all released from this company. That was too late for Jackie.'

However, to this day Brunswick still owns the masters for all the numerous artists who recorded with it over the previous 18 to 19 years.

'Tarnopol tried to get me killed,' says Davis, 'because I said I was leaving. Nat Tarnopol said, "Well, Carl is getting ready to leave the label. They [Tarnopol and mobsters] had three or four different meetings; they had me one time up in his office and they had the little guy who represented the godfather and some big 6' 6", 300-pound goon who made the suggestion. We were on the 27th floor. [They said] "Let's throw this cock-sucker out of the fucking window." The only thing that protected me was they knew I was with Tommy [Vastola]. And the little guy – he was a little tiny guy – told this big guy, "Why don't you sit your ass down." He said, "Carl, you make sure you tell Tommy, you tell him that I was the one that took up for you and didn't let anybody bother you. I was just trying to find out what the truth is to this, and what's going on."'

Another meeting was set up. Davis explained: 'So Tommy said, "You go to the meeting. You don't have to worry about nothing; just tell them the truth." It wasn't that I'd done anything wrong, it was that they had a funny thing among themselves; "If I bring you into this business and you do something and I don't like it, I can have you killed." That's just the way it is. But Tarnopol didn't bring me into Brunswick, Tommy brought me in, and that's a whole different story.'

Without saying so directly, Davis is claiming that Vastola controlled Brunswick. Why else would Vastola arrange for Gene Chandler to sign to it? Also, Vastola was the person who brought Davis to Brunswick. As to Jackie's situation, Davis said simply, 'Jackie couldn't get off the Brunswick label It was proven that Nat didn't bring me in, but it took three weeks to clear that up. There was one meeting at the office and two meetings in Jersey, at the restaurant and at the airport. There was some guy that had made a threat to Tommy. Tommy wanted to kill him and they said, "No, Corky, leave him alone."' Almost certainly, the person who had made the threat to Vastola was Tarnopol. Luckily for him, he too had his 'protectors'.

'I left Brunswick with a hat and a coat and didn't take even a pencil,' said Davis, in a sad ending to a once-wonderful association.

Lynn Crochet is bitter to this day concerning what happened to the man she loved: 'Nat stripped Jackie of the company. Jackie owned the company; he had contracts and all. When Nat lost the case and was convicted, all of that was in the court records.' Lynn, who liked and respected Johnny Roberts, admits: 'JR may have been part of the records being sold out of the back door.'

Tommy Vastola had a particular fondness for the music business, no doubt due to his long and deep friendship with Morris Levy, his childhood friend. In the mid-1960s, Vastola was arrested by the FBI on charges of record piracy. This concerned the not uncommon, but highly illegal, practice of copying hot selling records and passing them off as the genuine article. This was known in industry parlance as 'bootlegging', a term no doubt derived from the prohibition era.

Hit Men devotes most of its pages to the activities of Tommy Vastola and Morris Levy. In September 1986, the FBI made some important arrests. *Hit Men* reports:

> A force of 60 FBI agents had fanned out across Metropolitan New
> York and New Jersey and had rounded up and arrested 17 men
> allegedly connected with Gaetano Vastola's illegal business empire,
> including Sonny Brocco, Lew Saka, Dominick Canterino and Nicky
> Masaro. Vastola and Rudy Farone were charged in the indictment
> but managed to elude arrest, authorities believed, because they were
> tipped off to the government's planned move.

The cause of the FBI interest in Vastola, in the first instanc, was because Vastola had lost his temper and severely assaulting a major records wholesaler, John LaMonte. The assault, which involved one punch, fractured bones in LaMonte's head and nearly caused him to lose the sight of one eye, permanently. More seriously for Vastola and the others, it caused LaMonte to cooperate with the FBI and led to the racketeering charges against Vastola and his colleagues.

Hit Men further states:

> The Vastola Organisation, headed by Gaetano [Tommy] Vastola, had

'carried out a pattern of racketeering activity'. [The US attorney for the District of New Jersey] Greelish said, 'involving heroin and cocaine trafficking, loan-sharking, use of threats and violence in the collection of debts and takeover of businesses indebted to the Organisation . . . If convicted on all counts, Vastola faced 286 years in prison.

August Sims, Jackie's road manager from 1963 to 1972, worked for Vastola through Johnny Roberts. He described a particular event indicative of Vastola's power: 'I remember in Lake Tahoe, Tommy Vastola came in. I gave him $5,000 [from Jackie's earnings]. Then he said, "Come with me, I got to get money from Vic Damone." Poor son-of-a-bitch, I felt sorry for him. But he [Vastola] had his hands on him, too. Vic had to give up $100,000; he was making that kind of money. He worked the big room. See, in the big room you make $200,000 to $300,000. The Mob would tell them [what they were to be paid]. 'We want $200,000 to 300,000 for this act,' they'd say, and they would give it. The casino paid the act anyway. They didn't have to worry about no money.' This first-hand account implies that the payments were good business for the casino, and very good business for the Mob, who took the cream off the top of the artists earnings, tax free.

As a direct result of the assault, in October 1991 Tommy Vastola was sentenced to a hefty 17 years after being found guilty of racketeering, extortion and 18 other charges, including the assault. Ironically, his conviction had nothing to do with Brunswick Records or Jackie. Vastola is, by most accounts, a very polite and likeable character, but Davis told of another serious incident: 'The Chi-Lites were owed $90,000 [by Brunswick]. Tommy [Vastola] put us on the *Flip Wilson Show*. 'Oh Girl' [written by Eugene Record] became a big hit. The Chi-Lites wanted some money. Nat said "No." We had a meeting with Johnny Roberts, Nat Tarnopol and Eugene Record. Gene said, 'Where's that $90,000 [for session work]?' When he said that, Johnny Roberts reached over and grabbed him by the mouth. Gene was crying. Johnny said, "I'm going to get my pistol." Nat was right behind him. I sat there with Eugene and told him he had to be careful. Tommy [Vastola] walked in and said, "What's this nonsense?" He ran them out. In the trial it sounded like I set it up. Before Eugene left town, they [the Chi-Lites] got a $60,000 check.'

It was probably just as well for Tarnopol that Jackie was lying in bed semi-comatose, because he could presumably have given damaging testimony had he chosen to do so. Johnny Roberts, surprisingly, was not called on to testify. Nobody would have known more than he.

In the years following Tarnopol's trial, life became very hard for him. His son Paul says that his health suffered greatly from the stress of it all. Tarnopol had no finances of his own, though he did own the master recordings, which he licensed out. Paul, too, believes his father was unfairly singled out. 'Every ten years, payola would become an issue. My dad and [syndicated DJ] Alan Freed were good friends; I am sure favours were exchanged.'

Medford Leas Nursing Home decided to move Jackie to Burlington County Memorial Hospital on 8 January 1984, apparently because 'he was having trouble taking nourishment'. The great man's will to live had gone. At 11 a.m.on 21 January 1984, his heart finally beat no more. Jackie was five months short of his 50th birthday. At 11:20 a.m. he was pronounced dead by Dr James Atkinson MD.

THE CAUSE OF HIS DEATH was listed as 'aspiration pneumonia'. No autopsy was performed, but a hospital spokeswoman said, 'Wilson's family [ie Harlean] asked that no information about the circumstances of his death be released.' It had been eight-and-a-quarter agonising years since he'd suffered the heart attack at the Latin Casino, Cherry Hill.

Jackie climbed from humble origins to become a world-recognised recording artist and a dynamic performer. His collapse cut short a career that still had a long way to go. His old friend Roquel 'Billy' Davis was deeply saddened on hearing the news. He states: 'Jackie, of course, burned it at both ends; thought it was going to last forever. Everything he did was to the extreme. I was hoping and praying when "Higher and Higher" became a big hit that was going to do it for him. Then nothing happened after that. But the one thing his life story can't take away from him is his talent.'

Launa Toledo, Harlean's friend, says: 'He'd been living healthy for the last six years of his life [prior to the collapse]. When he was drinking he was fine. When he quit drinking, it killed him. Harlean called me, crying, within 30 minutes of his dying,' recalled Toledo. 'In fact, they'd been trying to call her. She was on her way there [to the hospital]. Lynn's kids learnt about the death on the TV. They thought he was dead – she'd told them he'd died. She wasn't going up there [to New Jersey] any more.'

The New Jersey undertaker, who shipped the body back to Detroit, found Jackie's legs so constricted through years of inactivity that he had to break them to get him into the coffin. At the Russell Street Baptist Church, in Detroit, an impressive funeral was conducted. Jackie had been baptized and sung there with his gospel group as a child. Harlean, being legally declared his wife, arranged proceedings. Many of the women in his life attended, along with all his fans and relatives from Michigan and Columbus, Mississippi.

Even at such a solemn occasion, Lynn Crochet was shunned by the rest of the family. Dressed in white, she sat alone with her children and Sabrina, Jackie's daughter with Molly. 'I showed up at the funeral,' says Lynn. 'I got the message not to show; just to send my children. I told them, you'd better meet me at the city limits with an injunction to keep out of Detroit. Me and the children went; I sat at the back and watched the circus, because that's what it was. When I got there and saw the casket open, and where they had him, I went berserk. I called Joyce Ann and said, "What are you doing to your brother? You don't have him down there in a place like that, and you shouldn't have the coffin open." He wouldn't have wanted people to see him like that. He was a very vain man. He didn't look good in the casket; not to me he didn't. The clothes didn't fit him and it was not something that he would have worn. I just went whacko. As soon as I called Joyce . . . it was a big production and the casket was closed.'

The open coffin was probably Freda's decision. Freda explains, 'He wouldn't have wanted to look like he did. He was vain; he liked to look pretty all the time. If he'd seen some of those pictures . . . He wanted people to remember him, in my opinion, like when he did "Lonely Teardrops" – Mr Excitement! That was his exit. Mrs Williams, who fixed his body when he came back from the nursing home; she did a good job. It was the same funeral home, Mason and Williams, that handled his [step]father, Johnny Lee and my kids [Jackie Jnr and Sandra]. It wasn't decided to have a closed or open casket, but when Harlean, Jacqui [Freda's sister] and I went over to view the body, the people were lined up to see him . . . he'd come back home. I said, "We have to leave it open." Jackie looked so young and his skin so pretty.'

Mrs Williams, who had prepared Jackie for burial, confirmed that. She said, 'Freda personally asked Harlean to let the people [fans] view Jackie before his body left for the cemetery; to say goodbye. It was very cold out there and they had been waiting. They were the ones who truly loved him and she knew that. We didn't straighten his hair like he did it. He'd been sick for so long. '

On 28 January, 1984, the Reverend Anthony C. Campbell performed the eulogy to a packed congregation of around 1,500. Campbell said, 'It's a glorious day to send Jackie home. We cannot gloss it over; we're here to say goodbye.' He commented that there were 'four escape routes from the ghetto; crime, politics, sport and entertainment'. It may have escaped his notice that the first and the last professions are common to all four.

Amongst the notables in attendance were The Detroit Spinners group, who had been responsible for the benefit concert in 1976. Uzziel Lee, who formerly owned Lee's Club Sensation where Jackie had sung as a 15-year-old, was there. Said Lee of Jackie's chosen career, 'That was all he wanted to do; that was his heart.'

Masses of floral tributes adorned the back of the church, including an arrangement of white carnations in the shape of a record, from 'James Brown and Friends'. There was an arrangement from Dick Clark, Detroit's Mayor Young, and Phelps Lounge where Jackie's career had commenced. Lead singer of the Four Tops, Levi Stubbs, addressed the congregation: 'Jackie Wilson was loved. People wouldn't be here for any other reason. Jackie was street people in that he never became bigger than street people.'

Johnny Collins, Jackie's brother-in-law, is just as bitter about Harlean's involvement. Collins said: 'Harlean came to the funeral in a mink coat which was horrendous, awful – torn to threads. I wouldn't have shoved my dog in it. Her tears were real; tears of guilt, that's the reality. When you play with the devil and he burns you, don't be surprised. It's just his nature. She loved him, but she couldn't own him. She's partly responsible for all the shit that ever happened to him. I can't come to any other conclusion but that.'

'Everyone in the neighborhood cried when we heard what happened to him,' says Loretta DeLoach, who'd known Jackie from childhood. 'Tears were just streaming from everyone's eyes. It was beautiful but sad, of course. There is beauty sometimes in death. When you see the love, everything that was there, all through those years; to me that's beautiful. All the singers came from all over and honoured him.'

Harlean chose the pallbearers. The Four Tops were selected along with Jackie's oldest friend, a greying Johnny Jones (JJ), and his former road manager, August Sims. McRae said bitterly, 'Harlean ran everything, so it's no surprise that Sims was there. The only person who wasn't there was Nat, and Sims was there in his place. It was disrespectful for Sims to be a pall bearer.'

Jackie's body was then taken to Westlawn Cemetery at Wayne, just outside Detroit, where he was finally laid to rest. His mother is buried at the same cemetery. After the funeral, close friends and family went to the home that Jackie had purchased for his mother on Strathmoor Avenue. His sister Joyce Ann lived there with her family. Lynn Crochet, whom Jackie accepted as his wife up until the time of his collapse, wasn't invited.

After Jackie's burial, few at the ceremony would have dreamt that his burial site would remain entirely unmarked, save for a gravesite number; B261. Not even a simple headstone. Responsibility for this gross omission is Harlean's. It was her funeral arrangement. Harlean claims she couldn't afford a headstone, despite apparently collecting $45,000 life insurance after Jackie died. But Freda blames Joyce Ann, Jackie's half-sister, whose envy seems to have carried even beyond his death. 'Joyce had all that money,' says Freda, 'I couldn't see why she didn't put a headstone out there. Harlean wouldn't care. Even the people [Jackie's relatives] in Pontiac wanted to put a stone out there, but Joyce didn't want to give her money.'

Despite not having a large part of Jackie's life in terms of the total time they spent together, nevertheless Lynn Ciccone has never stopped loving him. Lynn travelled from her home in Springfield, Illinois in 1986 with a view to saying a final goodbye. Arriving at the Westlawn Cemetery she had difficulty locating the grave site. Says Lynn Ciccone: 'I was horrified when I went to Detroit and I said, "This man has no monument." Al Dobbins, the caretaker at cemetery, put up the wooden cross.' The cross had 'Jackie Wilson' written on it with a felt-tipped pen. Lynn, devastated at the lack of a proper headstone, contacted Joyce McRae. Says McRae, 'She contacted me and sent me pictures of the unmarked grave. I hit the roof. I hadn't gone to the funeral because I felt there'd already be too much controversy . . . and it wouldn't bring Jack back. So I got in touch with Dave Marsh [a writer with *Rolling Stone* magazine] who was one of the founding members of the Rhythm and Blues Foundation. Dave is from Dearborn, Michigan.

'Dave said, "I can get a fabulous headstone for wholesale price of $2,000. Why don't we get Le Baron Taylor?" He was a vice-president at CBS; does special projects on black music. Le Baron contacted Jack the Rapper [Jack Gibson an influential black DJ] thinking he could help. Next thing Dave contacted me and said, "What the fuck is going on? Have you seen Jack the Rapper?"' McRae contacted Jack Gibson and was taken aback by his response. She continued: 'He told me, "It had all started from us [meaning himself]," and he said, "We don't want any white-honky, mother-fucking money." At that point Jack and Harlean got together and raised over $20,000.' Money poured in from sympathetic fans, even from overseas, due to Gibson's radio broadcast requests.

With the approximately $18,000 in donations from loyal fans, it was now possible to erect a magnificent tomb and to move both Jackie and his mother into the common gravesite. Jackie's body had to be exhumed and moved a short distance to his final resting place. The body of his mother likewise was moved to rest by his side.

On what would have been Jackie's 53rd birthday, 9 June 1987, around 150 people attended a dedication ceremony at Westlawn Cemetery where Jackie and Eliza Mae Lee were interned together in the magnificent $18,000 marble and granite tomb. The original plan had been to inscribe the headstone with the epitaph 'YOUR LOVE KEEPS LIFTING ME HIGHER AND HIGHER', however this was changed to a fitting 'NO MORE LONELY TEARDROPS'. Says Gibson, 'The family [Harlean] allowed me to write the epitaph. I can go to my maker knowing that I did something for somebody. That was the motivation I had. We [Jackie and I] had so much fun together.' Above his dates of birth and death was inscribed 'MR EXCITEMENT – JACKIE'. To the right-hand side of the tomb is inscribed simply 'ELIZA', with her dates of birth and death.

In attendance were Jack Gibson, Harlean and her son John (Petey), now 24, and other family members including Jackie's sister, Joyce Ann. Three years earlier she wasn't prepared to contribute for a simple headstone. August Sims again travelled from New York to pay his respects. At the moving ceremony, two women sang and Jack Gibson spoke. He said, 'Thank you for touching The Rapper's life. And thank you for the many entertainers that adopted your style. You're truly a legend we will not forget. Here, your final resting place with your mother, will be a shining beacon for all to see long after we are all gone.'

The person who was indeed responsible for instigating the movement to have the tomb erected, Lynn Ciccone, sadly remained in the background with her and Jackie's 24-year-old daughter, Gina.

Absent was Jackie's first wife Freda, the person who had sacrificed more than anyone to ensure the man she loved would become a star – as she knew he surely would. Lynn Crochet, the last woman he had lived with and the mother of two of his children, also chose not to attend. She had done what nobody else was able to do; help Jackie overcome his addictions. She says, 'I sent Thor to the memorial; I stayed out of it. I wanted him remembered as a family man, not with the two wives. Me and Harlean would have got into it, because I felt she killed him.'

In the evening, Detroit's Latin Quarter Club hosted a celebration, which heaveyweight boxing campion Muhammad Ali attended. Entertainment was provided by The Dramatics and Floaters groups and others, none of whom were well-known outside of Detroit. Motown vice-president, Esther Gordy Edwards, showed up for this affair.

More money had been collected than was necessary, so a granite bench was later installed in front of the tomb. On Jackie's birthday, 9 June 1991, Jack 'The Rapper' Gibson went back to the cemetery, this time to dedicate a stone 'meditation bench' which had been placed in front of the tomb. In bold letters it proclaims 'JACKIE – THE COMPLETE ENTERTAINER'. On this occasion, Motown singer Marv Johnson attended. So, too, did the well-known black DJ, 'The Queen', Martha Jean.

Jackie may have been only 49 when he died, and 41 when he collapsed, but he'd lived those years to the fullest and achieved much. There were disappointments in his life, but the great triumphs and the fruits of his life will forever be available for music lovers to listen to and be thrilled by. At last this troubled man found the peace that had for so long eluded him. Next to him lay the woman who had loved him more than life itself – his mother.

17. POSTSCRIPT

THE ROCK 'N' ROLL HALL OF FAME was established in 1986. In that year the inductions included Chuck Berry, James Brown, Ray Charles, Sam Cooke, Fats Domino, The Everly Brothers, Buddy Holly, Jerry Lee Lewis, Elvis Presley and Little Richard. The next year, it was Jackie's turn, and he was in good company; Aretha Franklin, Marvin Gaye, Bill Haley, BB King, Clyde

McPhatter, Roy Orbison, Smokey Robinson, Big Joe Turner, T-Bone Walker and Hank Williams were all inducted. Jackie had been rightly honored as one of the giants of contemporary music. However, the acrimony that had become so pronounced since his collapse in 1975, still managed to carry over to this occasion 12 years later. 'Harlean excluded Sabrina [Jackie's daughter to Molly Byndon],' claimed Joyce McRae. 'I wound up getting Sabrina, and Li-nie, who I helped pay for, to fly to New York, when Jackie was getting inducted into the Rock 'n' Roll Hall Of Fame. It was $300 a person at that time. I got someone to pay the $600. I paid for Li-nie's dress, I paid for part of the plane ticket and we all piled in a room together, within walking distance of the Waldorf Astoria [venue of the induction].' Harlean seemingly wanted to bask in the glory of the occasion without Jackie's children.

Nat Tarnopol died of a heart attack in Las Vegas on Christmas Day 1987. He had moved to Las Vegas in 1985 where protection was provided by friends there. He no longer felt secure in New York, but would sometimes slip into the city. 'He'd come back from time to time,' explains Melvin Moore, a former promotions man with Brunswick. Moore left after Jackie's collapse: 'He'd kinda sneak in 'cause he had problems with these people. My friend [almost certainly Sims] is a real big guy, so when Nat would come into town he'd call him to watch him.'

Says son Paul, 'Nat was a workaholic. He'd often be up all night and be at the office before everyone. He had a massive heart attack in 1982. After the trial in the 1970s, my father was all alone. He had no friends, no money. When he was flying high it was different. He was sad in his heart. After dad died, Johnny Roberts called and said, "It's your Uncle Johnny." They think you're brain dead.' Paul didn't consider Roberts an uncle and certainly not a friend of the family: 'My father had a couple of million dollars in assets. We had a nice big house in Purchase, Westchester County [in 1963]. He was young and not particularly careful with money. We lost most of everything including the house."

Launa Toledo, through Jackie, had long known Johnny Roberts. The word was out that Roberts had died, but a phone call was to dispel this rumour. 'New Year's Eve I got a call from JR,' says Launa, 'who I thought was dead. "Happy New Year, Baby." I went "Ugh?" Someone's playing a joke. "Who is this?" "Come on baby, you know who this is." My mother was sitting here at the bar. I guess my face drained. She said, "What's the matter?" It's scary. I said, "But you're dead!" He said, "That's the first I knew about it." I said, "I know people who attended your funeral." He said, "I called to give you my new phone number."' There was another reason Roberts had called. It was to give her the 'good news'; Nat Tarnopol had died in Las Vegas five days earlier. Says Launa: 'Nat Tarnopol was the biggest crook that lived... Johnny and Nat Tarnopol were getting ready to be called up before the grand jury. The only one who could put JR away was Nat Tarnopol. When he died, all of a sudden JR is alive again. So I want to know *who's* [actually] in that grave?'

'When Nat died on Christmas Day, you could hear the whole world rejoicing his death,' says Hank Ballard, 'I doubt that even his family would have attended his funeral. I believe in fair play; I don't believe in someone gaining by stepping on someone else.'

Another record promotions man, Larry Maxwell, also knew Tarnopol and met him in a restaurant only a month before he died. He says: 'Nat became greedy, that's why he died of a heart attack. Nat [effectively] killed himself. He turned out not being a nice guy. Everyone knows that Nat did bad things.'

Many recalled August Sims was 'Tarnopol's man.' Certainly they worked together for many years and were respectful of one another, although initially being employed by Johnny Roberts. Says Sims: 'Jackie had his faults, too, but, goddamn, this Nat man wouldn't help bury the man... and he made millions from him. See, like I say, fate has a way of making up for when you do people wrong... you know how Jews is. They hurt each other, and they hurt Jackie.'

In his book *Chicago Soul*, Robert Pruter says: 'Tarnopol continued the Brunswick operation while attempting to sort out his legal difficulties, but obviously he did not have much of a company to work with. The Chicago office mysteriously was kept open, but the staff's principal function seemed to be to turn the lights on in the morning and turn them off at night. After 1981, Brunswick was moribund as an active label, and existed only to license old masters to other firms for reissue purposes.' Paul Tarnopol, as the present owner of Brunswick Records, holds the masters to all the 341 songs recorded by Jackie, and so far released, during his 18 years on the label. However, additionally there are 40 songs that were not released on the Brunswick label. Happily quite a few of these can now be heard on current Jackie Wilson CD releases on various labels under license.

Carl Davis left Brunswick in 1979 after being found not guilty of fraud. He later opened a bar, the Palace Bar in Chicago, although it didn't do well. He then joined the Sheriff's Department.

The Internal Revenue Service (IRS) had a lien against future earnings by Jackie's estate with a view to recouping outstanding taxes of $243,331.37 covering the years 1963 to 1973. Specifically the lien detailed; $66,000 for the year 1963, $8,247 for 1964, $27,226 for 1966, $44,495 for 1967, $27,737 for 1970, $10,565 for 1971, $22,875 for 1972 and $18,048 for 1973. The total amounted to $192,172.52 plus interest and penalties of $42,258.58. A settlement was reached with the IRS and the debt was settled.

JACKIE WILSON

The hand of fate once again reached out on the night of 22 August, 1988 and struck another of Jackie's children down. This time it was thirty-seven-year-old Jacqueline (Denise), the eldest of his children. Denise had just walked out from a party store on the busy Woodward Avenue in Highland Park and, without a word being spoken, she was shot to death. Freda lived just over the road at the time in what was described as 'a flop-house'; she is said to have cried for days. Incredibly, by 1988, three of Jackie's four children with Freda were dead.

It was claimed that Denise was an accidental victim of a drug dispute. The Detroit News quoted Highland Park Detective Hubert Yopp as saying: 'She happened to be in the wrong place at the wrong time. The man [claimed to be a known drug user] had taken off with drugs and money. They [other men who were chasing him] caught up with him [at the store]. The dealer fired six shots at him as he fled. The shots were fired just as Jacqueline Wilson was leaving the store… She was hit once in the back.'

There was a sequel to the story, and justice of a sort. The *Detroit Free Press* reported that a twenty-eight-year-old man, Gary Johnson, was charged with Denise's murder. Johnson was released on a bond of $50,000 and the following July was himself gunned down as he was about to enter a home. Freda believes that his death was a reprisal because of who Denise's father was.

For many years Johnny Roberts had resided in Palm Springs, California. The New York Mob had banished him to the west coast for some major infringement said to involve large sums of money. Says Carl Davis: 'I think what happened with him is he got himself in some kind of trouble. He couldn't go back to New York. I think what they probably did was, somebody probably called out to California and said, "We'd got to get rid of Johnny, so we want to send him to your area. We want to let you know he's coming. He still has our protection."' Someone who knew him at this time says, 'I know Johnny Roberts, he has a face like an ice cube-cold as ice. A person not to be messed with.' After a long debilitating illness Roberts died on 14 December, 1994. This time he really was dead. He left a Korean-born wife and two children.

Tommy Vastola went to New Jersey jail in October 1991 to serve a 17-year sentence which had been handed to him by the Federal Court. He appealed his conviction as far as the Supreme Court. His attorney and daughter, Joy, employed all of her efforts to have his convictions overturned. By 1999 Vastola was a free man again.

In 1987 New York producer Dick Jacobs, who had been involved with most of Jackie's major hits, died. Years before he had been viciously knifed when he answered a knock at the door. Domestic problems had led to his being set up and his assailant had nearly succeeded in killing him. After his recovery he married for a third time.

Singer, LaVern Baker who'd recorded duets with Jackie in the early 1960s died on 11 March, 1997, at age 67. Jackie and LaVern had also shared the same first manager, Al Green. Jackie's first wife, Freda Wilson, who was a huge help with this book passed away on 25 July, 1999. Billy Ward, of Billy Ward and the Dominoes fame, who was very much Jackie's mentor died on 16 February, 2002, after a long illness. Ward was 80 years old. Roquel Billy Davis, co-writer of most of Jackie's major hits passed away, at the age of 67, on 2 September, 2004. Davis believed Jackie to be the greatest singer of them all and he was involved with many. Davis, also, was a great help in the making of this book. In March 2005, August Sims, who was both mob enforcer and Jackie's road manager in the last years of Jackie's career, died in his Bronx home at the age of 81.

In his radio interview Noman N. Nite asked Jackie about his audiences. Jackie replied: 'Some people want to cry, some come to laugh, some to knock-down, drag-out, some come to plain listen; study. And it's a beautiful feeling; a beautiful sight to see.'

Hopefully this book has helped reveal a highly talented and dedicated artist who was totally unique. Trying to explain with words the magnificence of his honey-rich, emotion-racked voice is like trying to describe a Rembrandt painting to a blind person who has never had the power of sight. Jackie, known as 'Mr Excitement', was destroyed by the career he had chosen. He would have called it *kismet* – fate or destiny. However he had thrilled and brought happiness to millions. Surely that is what he most wanted from his life, and the rest of us should be grateful for that experience, because that's what it is: an experience.

Many fine books, magazines and newspapers have been consulted in my research for this book. Some I have quoted from directly and these are fully credited throughout. Others provide general background. To all I am indebted.

JACKIE WILSON

BOOKS

Clarke, Donald ed., *The Penguin Encyclopaedia Of Popular Music*
Dannen, Fredric, *Hit Men* (Vintage Books)
Fox, Ted, *Showtime At The Apollo* (DaCapo Press)
Gargan, William and Sharma, Sue, *Find That Tune* (Neal-Schuman)
George, Nelson, *Death Of Rhythm And Blues* (Pantheon Books)
Gordy, Berry, *To Be Loved* (Warner Books)
Groia, Philip, *They All Sang On The Corner* (Phillie Dee)
Guralnick, Peter, *Last Train To Memphis: The Rise Of Elvis Presley*
Jackson, John A., *The Big Beat* (Schirmer Books)
Knoedelseder, William *Stiffed* (Harper Perennial)
Miller, Jim, *The Rolling Stone History Of Rock 'N' Roll*
Morrell, Gerald, *Book Of Golden Discs*
Pruter, Robert ed., *The Blackwell Guide To Soul Recordings*
Pruter, Robert *Chicago Soul* (University Press)
Warner, Alan, *Who Sang What In Rock 'N' Roll* (Blandford)
Wells, Mary, *Dreamgirl*
Whitburn, Joel, *The Billboard Book Of US Top 40 Hits 1955 To Present*
Williams, Otis, *Temptations* (GP Putman's Sons)

PERIODICALS

Big Town Review
Detroit Free Press
Detroit News
Downbeat
Goldmine Record Collector
Hustler
Jet Magazine
Melody Maker
Michigan Chronicle
Musician Magazine
New York Sunday Times
Philadelphia Inquirer
Philadelphia Tribune
Rolling Stone
Sepia Magazine
Variety
Village Voice

JACKIE WILSON USA SINGLE RELEASES

(All on the Brunswick label)

Date Chart Position R&B Pop

'Reet Petite' 8/'57 No 62

'By The Light Of The Silvery Moon' UK No 6 (1986 re-issue UK No 1)

'To Be Loved' 2/'58 No 7 No 22

'Come Back To Me' UK No 23

'I'm Wandering' 5/'58

'As Long As I live'

'We Have Love' 8/'58 No 93

'Singing A Song'

'Lonely Teardrops' 10/'58 No 1 No 7

'In The Blue Of The Evening'

'That's Why (I Love You So)' 3/'59 No 2 No 13

'Love is All'

'I'll Be Satisfied' 6/'59 No 6 No 20

'Ask'

'You Better Know It' 8/'59 No 1 No 37

'Never Go Away'

'Talk That Talk' 10/'59 No 3 No 34

'Only You, Only Me'

'Night' 3/60 No 3 No 4

'Doggin' Around' No 1 No 15

'(You Were Made For) All My Love' 6/'60 No 12 (UK No 33

'A Woman, A Lover, A Friend' No 1 No 15

'Alone At Last' 9/'60 No 20 No 8 (UK No 50)

JACKIE WILSON

'Am I The Man' No 10 No 32
'My Empty Arms' 12/'60 No 25 No 9
'The Tear Of The Year' No 10 No 44
'Please Tell Me Why' 2/'61 No 11 No 20
'Your One And Only Love' No 40
'I'm Coming On Back To You' 5/'61 No 9 No 19
'Lonely Life' No 80
'You Don't Know What It Means' 7/'61 No 19 No 79
'Years From Now' No 25 No 37
'My Heart Belongs To Only You' 10/'61 No 65
'The Way I Am' No 58
'The Greatest Hurt' 12/'61 No 34
There'll Be No Next Time No 75
'I Found Love' 3/'62 No 93
'There's Nothing Like Love'
(both of the above with Linda Hopkins)
'Hearts' 4/62 No 58
'Sing'
'I Just Can't Help It' 6/62 No 17 No 70
'My Tale Of Woe'
'Forever And A Day' 9/62 No 82
'Baby, That's All'
'What Good Am I Without You' 12/62
'A Girl Named Tamiko'
'Baby Workout' 2/'63 No 1 No 5
'I'm Going Crazy'
'Shake A Hand' 5/'63 No 21 No 42
'Say I Do'
(both with Linda Hopkins)
'Shake! Shake! Shake!' 6/'63 No 21 No 33
'He's A Fool'
'Baby Get It (And Don't Quit It)' 9/'63 No 61
'The New Breed'
'Silent Night' 11/'63
'O Holy Night' (Cantique de Noel)
'Haunted House' 2/'64
'I'm Travelin' On'
'The Kickapoo' 3/'64
'Call Her Up'

'Big Boss Line' 5/'64 No94
'Be My Girl'
'Squeeze Her – Tease Her' 8/'64 No89
'Give Me Back My Heart'
'She's All Right' 9/'64 No 102
'Watch Out'
'Danny Boy' 2/65 No25 No94
'Soul Time'
'When The Saints Go Marching In' 4/'65
'Yes Indeed'
(both with Linda Hopkins)
'No Pity (In The Naked City)' 6/'65 No 25 No 59
'I'm So Lonely'
'I Believe I'll Love You' 10/'65 No 96
'Lonely Teardrops' (slow version)
'Think Twice' 12/65 No 37 No 93
'Please Don't Hurt Me' (I've Never been In Love Before)'
(both with LaVern Baker)
'I've Got To Get Back (Country Boy)' 1/66
'3 Days, I Hour, 30 Minutes'
'Soul Galore' 3/66
'Brand New Thing'
'Be My Love' 5/66
'I Believe'
'Whispers (Gettin'Louder)' 9/66 No 5 No 11
'The Fairest Of Them All'
'I Don't Want To Lose You' 1/'67 No 11 No 84
'Just Be Sincere' No 43 No 91
'I've Lost You' 4/67 No 35 No 82
'Those Heartaches'
'(Your Love Keeps Lifting Me) Higher And Higher' 7/'67 No 1 No 6
(UK No11)
(1975 re-issue UK No25)
(1987 re-issue UK No 15)
'I'm The One To Do It'
'Since You Showed Me How To Be Happy' 11/'67 No 22 No 32
'The Who Who Song'
'For Your Precious Love' 1/'68 No 49
'Uptight (Everything's Alright)'

(Both of the above with Count Basie)
'Chain Gang' 4/'68 No 37 No 84
'Funky Broadway' 4/'68 No 37 No 84
(Both of the above with Count Basie)
'I Get The Sweetest Feeling' 6/'68 No 12 No 34
(1972 UK No 9)
(1987 re-issue UK No 3)
'Nothing But Blue Skies'
'For Once In My Life' 10/'68 No 70
'You Brought About A Change In Me'
'I Still Love You' 2/'69 No 39
'Hum De Dum De Do'
'Helpless' 8/'69 No 21
'Do It The Right Wa'
'Do Your Thing' 11/69
'With These Hands'
'Let This Be A Letter (To My Baby)' 4/'70 No 91
'Didn't I (I Can Feel The Vibrations)'
'This Love Is Real' 11/'70 No 9 No 56
'Love Uprising'
'This Guy's In Love With You' 4/'71
'Say You Will'
'Love is Funny That Way' 10/'71 No 18 No 95
'Try It Again'
'You Got Me Walking' '1/72 No 22 No 93
'The Fountain'
'The Girl Turned Me On' 4/'72
'Forever And A Day'
'You Left The Fire Burning' 7/72
'What A Lovely Way'
'Beautiful Day' 1/'73
'What'cha Gonna Do About Love'
'Because Of You' 4/'73
'Go Away'
'Sing A Little Song' 7/'73 No 95
'No More Goodbyes'
'Shake A Leg' 11/'73
'It's All Over'
'Don't Burn No Bridges' 10/'75 No 91

JACKIE WILSON

'Don't Burn No Bridges' (instrumental, with the Chi-Lites)
'Nobody But You' 1977
'I've Learned About Life'
'Silent One' (this single was first released in 1994 on the Rhino CD boxed set)

JACKIE WILSON USA ALBUM RELEASES
(All on the Brunswick label)
Chart Position Date R&B Pop
1) *HE'S SO FINE* 3/1958

'Etcetera'
'To Be Loved'
'Come Back To Me'
'If I Can't Have You'
'As Long As I Live'
'Reet Petite'
'It's Too Bad We Had To Say Goodbye'
'Why Can't You Be Mine'
'I'm Wandering'
'Right Now'
'Danny Boy'
'It's So Fine'

2) *LONELY TEARDROPS* 2/1959

'Lonely Teardrops'
'Each Time (I Love You More)'
'That's Why (I Love You So)'
'In The Blue Of Evening'
'The Joke'
'Someone To Need Me (As I Need You)'
'You Better Know It'
'By The Light Of The Silvery Moon'
'Singing A Song'
'Love Is All'
'We Have Love'
'Hush-A-Bye'

JACKIE WILSON

3) *SO MUCH* 11/1959

'So Much'
'I Know I'll Always Be In Love With You'
'Happiness'
'Only You, Only Me'
'The Magic Of Love'
'Wishing Well'
'Talk That Talk'
'Ask'
'I'll Be Satisfied'
'It's All A Part Of Love'
'Never Go Away'
'Thrill Of Love'

4) *JACKIE SINGS THE BLUES* 4/1960
'Please Tell Me Why'
'Doggin' Around'
'New Girl In Town'
'Nothin' But The Blues'
'Passin' Through'
'Excuse Me For Lovin''
'She Done Me Wrong'
'Sazzle Dazzle'
'Please Stick Around'
'Come On And Love Me Baby'
'Comin' To Your House'
'It's Been A Long Time'

5) *MY GOLDEN FAVORITES* 8/1960
'Reet Petite (The Finest Girl You Ever Want To Meet)'
'To Be Loved'
'I'll Be Satisfied'
'Only You, Only Me'
'Talk That Talk'
'Ask'
'That's Why (I Love You So)'
'It's All A Part Of Love'
'Lonely Teardrops'

'I'm Wandering'
'You Better Know It'
'We Have Love'

6) A *WOMAN, A LOVER, A FRIEND* 11/1960
'A Woman, A Lover, A Friend'
'Your One And Only Love'
'You Cried'
'The River'
'When You Add Religion To Love'
'One Kiss'
'Night'
'(You Were Made For) All My Love'
'Am I The Man'
'Behind The Smile Is A Tear'
'We Kissed'
'(So Many) Cute Little Girls'

7) *YOU AIN'T HEARD NOTHIN' YET* 2/1961
'Toot, Toot. Tootsie Goodbye'
'Sonny Boy'
'California Here I Come'
'Keep Smiling At Trouble (Trouble's A Bubble)'
'You Made Me Love You (I Didn't Want To Do It)'
'My Yiddishe Momme'
'Swanee'
'April Showers'
'Anniversary Song'
'Rock-A-Bye Your Baby With A Dixie Melody'
'For Me And My Girl'
'In Our House'

8) *BY SPECIAL REQUEST* 9/1961

'Cry'
'My Heart Belongs To Only You'
'tormy Weather (Keeps Rainin'All The Time)'
'Tenderly'
'Lonely Life'

JACKIE WILSON

'The Way I Am'
'Try A Little Tenderness'
'Mood Indigo'
'You Belong To My Heart'
'Indian Love Call'
'One More Time'
'I'm Comin'On Back To You'

9) *BODY AND SOUL* 4/1962
'Body And Soul'
'I Don't Know You Anymore'
'I Got It Bad (And That Ain't Good)'
'The Greatest Hurt'
'I'll Always Be In Love With You'
'Crazy She Calls Me'
'The Tear Of The Year'
'Blue Moon'
'I'll Be Around'
'There'll Be No Next'
'We'll Be Together Again'

10) *JACKIE WILSON AT THE COPA* 8/1962 No 137
'Tonight'
Medley; 'Body And Soul' / 'I Apologize'
'Love For Sale'
'And This Is My Beloved'
'The Way I Am'
'I Love Them All'-Part 1
  1) 'What I Say'
  2) 'Night'
  3) 'That's Why'
   -Part 2
  1) 'Danny Boy'
  2) 'Doggin' Around'
  3) 'To Be Loved'
  4) 'Lonely Teardrops'
'St. James Infirmary'
'A Perfect Day'

11) *JACKIE WILSON SINGS THE WORLD'S GREATEST MELODIES* 1/1963
'Forever And A Day'
'Take My Heart'
'Pianissimo'
'My Eager Heart'
'Each Night I Dream Of You'
'Night'
'My Empty Arms'
'(You Were Made For) All My Love'
'A Heart Of Love'
'Alone At Last'
'You Thing Of Beauty'

12) *BABY WORKOUT* 4/1963 No 36
'Shake! Shake! Shake!'
'The Kickapoo'
'Yeah! Yeah! Yeah!'
'You Only Live Once'
'Say You Will'
'Baby Workout'
'It's All My Fault'
'Love Train'
'Now That I Want Her'
'(I Feel Like I'm In) Paradise'
'(So Many) Cute Little Girls'
'What Good Am I Without You'

13) *SHAKE A HAND* (with Linda Hopkins) 7/1963
'Swing Low Sweet Chariot'
'Nobody Knows The Trouble I've Seen'
'Yes Indeed'
'Joshua Fit The Battle Of Jericho'
'Old Time Religion'
'Shake A Hand'
'He's Got The Whole World In His Hands'
'When The Saints Go Marching In'
'Do Lord'
'Every Time I Hear The Spirit'
'Dry Bones'

'Down By The Riverside'

14) *MERRY CHRISTMAS FROM JACKIE WILSON* 10/1963
'Silent Night'
'White Christmas'
'O Holy Night (Cantique de Noel)'
'The First Noel'
'Deck The Hall'
'Silver Bells'
'Joy To The World'
'It Came Upon The Midnight Clear'
'Adeste Fideles (O Come All Ye Faithful)'
'I'll Be Home For Christmas'
'O Little Town Of Bethlehem'
'God Rest Ye Merry, Gentlemen'

15) *MY GOLDEN FAVORITES: VOLUME 2* 11/1963
'Baby Workout'
'Doggin' Around'
'Baby Get It (And Don't Quit It)'
'The Tear Of The Year'
'Shake! Shake! Shake!'
'My Heart Belongs To Only You'
'Night'
'Am I The Man'
'Alone At Last'
'The Way I Am'
'Please Tell Me Why'
'(You Were Made For) All My Love'

16) *SOMETHIN' ELSE!!* 6/1964
'Big Boss Line'
'Groovin''
'Deep Down Love'
'Take One Step (I'll Take Two)'
'Love (Is Where You Find It)'
'Give Me Back My Heart'
'Squeeze Her – Tease Her (But Love Her)'
'Be My Girl'

'Baby (I Just Can't Help It)'
'Rebecca'
'My Best Friend's Girl'
'Twisting And Shoutin'(Doing The Monkey)'

17) *SOUL TIME* 4/1965
'No Pity (In The Naked City)'
'Danny Boy'
'An Ocean I'll Cry'
'Soul Time'
'Teardrop Avenue'
'She'll Be There'
'Star Dust'
'A Kiss, A Thrill And Goodbye'
'Mama Of My Song'
'She's All Right'
'Better Play It Safe'
'No Time Out'

18) *SPOTLIGHT ON JACKIE* 9/1965
'Over The Rainbow'
'Pledging My Love'
'Georgia On My Mind'
'You'll Never Walk Alone'
'Rags To Riches'
'You Don't Know Me'
'What Kind Of Fool Am I'
'I Wanna Be Around'
'Until The Real Thing Comes Along'
'I Apologize'
'Lonely Teardrops' (slow version)
'We Have Love'

19) *SOUL GALORE* 2/1966
'Brand New Thing – Part 1'
'3 Days 1 Hour 30 Minutes'
'I've Got To Get Back (Country Boy)'
'So You Say You Wanna Dance (Workout No 2)'
'Stop Lying'

'Let Me Build'
'Brand New Thing – Part 2'
'Soul Galore'
'What's Done In The Dark'
'I Got My Mind Made Up'
'Everything's Going To Be Fine'
'Your loss, My Gain'

20) *WHISPERS* 12/1966 No 15 No 108
'I Don't Want To Lose You'
'My Heart Is Calling'
'Who Am I'
'Whispers'
'The Fairest Of Them All'
'(Too Much) Sweet Loving'
'I Can Do Better'
'Just Be Sincere'
'Only Your Love Can Save Me'
'To Make A Big Man Cry'
'I've Got To Talk To You'
'Tears Will Tell It All'

21) *HIGHER AND HIGHER* 10/1967 No 28 No 163
'(Your Love Keeps Lifting Me) Higher And Higher'
'I Don't Need You Around'
'I've Lost You'
'Those Heartaches'
'Soulville'
'Open The Door To Your Heart'
'I'm The One To Do It'
'You Can Count On Me'
'I Need Your Loving'
'Somebody Up There Likes You'
'When Will Our Day Come'

22) *MANUFACTURERS OF SOUL* (with Count Basie) 3/1968 No 18 No 195
No195
'Funky Broadway'
'For Your Precious Love

'In The Midnight Hour'
'Ode To Billy Joe'
'Chain Gang'
'I Was Made To Love Her'
'Uptight (Everything's Alright)'
'I Never Loved A Woman (The Way I Love You)'
'Respect'
'Even When You Cry'
'My Girl'

23) *I GET THE SWEETEST FEELING* 10/1968
'You Keep Me Hanging On'
'Once In A Lifetime'
'Who Can I Turn To (When Nobody Needs Me)'
'People'
'Don't Go To Strangers'
'I Get The Sweetest Feeling'
'You Brought About A Change In Me'
'Nothing But Blue Skies'
'A Woman Needs To Be Loved'
'Growin' Tall'
'Since You Showed Me How To Be Happy'

24) *DO YOUR THING* 10/1969
'To Change My Love'
'This Guy's In Love With You'
'Why Don't You Do Your Thing'
'This Bitter Earth'
'Helpless'
'Light My Fire'
'That Lucky Old Sun (Just Rolls Around Heaven All Day)'
'With These Hands'
'Hold On, I'm Comin''
'Eleanor Rigby'

25) *IT'S ALL A PART OF LOVE* 2/1970
'It's All A Part Of Love'
'Only You, Only Me'
'Night'

JACKIE WILSON

'For Once In My Life'
'People'
'We Have Love'
'Who Can You Turn To (When Nobody Needs Me)'
'Don't Go To Strangers'
'This Guy's In Love With You'
'(You Were Made For) All My Love'
'Alone At Last'

26) *THIS LOVE IS REAL* 3/1970
'This Love Is Real'
'Don't Leave Me'
'Where There Is Love'
'Let This Be A Letter (To My Baby)'
'Love Uprising'
'Think About The Good Times'
'Didn't I'
'Love Changed Her Face'
'Working On My Woman's Heart'
'Say You Will'

27) *YOU GOT ME WALKING* 11/1971
'You Got Me Walking'
'What A Lovely Way'
'You Left The Fire Burning'
'My Way'
'Try It Again'
'Forever And A Day'
'The Girl Turned Me On'
'Hard To Get A Thing Called Love'
'Love Is Funny That Way'
'The Fountain'

28) *BEAUTIFUL DAY* 3/1973
'Beautiful Day'
'Because Of You'
'Go Away'
'Pretty Little Angel Eyes'
'Let's Love Again'

'It's All Over'
'I Get Lonely Sometimes'
'This Love Is Mine'
'Don't You Know I Love You'
'What'cha Going To Do About Me'

29) *NOBODY BUT YOU* 1976
'Where Is Love'
'You're The Song'
'Nobody But You'
'Just Call My Name'
'Just As Soon As The Feeling's Over'
'Don't Burn No Bridges'
'You'll Be Good For Me'
'It Only Happens When I Look At You'
'Satisfy My Soul'
'I've Learned About Life'